American Selections

FROM THE SAMUEL P. HARN MUSEUM OF ART

Dulce María Román   Kerry Oliver-Smith   Thomas W. Southall

Samuel P. Harn Museum of Art
University of Florida, Gainesville

American Selections from the Samuel P. Harn Museum of Art

Samuel P. Harn Museum of Art
University of Florida, Gainesville

This publication is made possible by a generous
grant from The Henry Luce Foundation, Inc.
Additional support is provided by the National
Endowment for the Arts, the University of
Florida Office of Graduate Research and
Dr. Madelyn M. Lockhart.

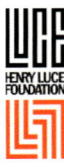 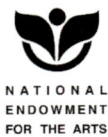

Library of Congress Cataloging-in-Publication Data

Samuel P. Harn Museum of Art.
   American Selections from the Samuel P. Harn
Museum of Art / Dulce María Román, Kerry
Oliver-Smith, Thomas W. Southall.
      p. cm.
   Includes index.
   ISBN 978-0-9762552-8-4
   1. Art, American--Catalogs.
   2. Art--Florida--Gainesville--Catalogs.
   3. Samuel P. Harn Museum of Art--Catalogs.
   I. Román, Dulce María. II. Oliver-Smith, Kerry.
   III. Southall, Thomas W., 1951- IV. Title.

N6505.S36 2009
709.73'07475979--dc22

                              2009034128

Editing: Lauren Nagel Richardson, Esq.
Design: Suissa Design, Hollywood, Florida
Photography: Randy Batista Photography, unless
noted otherwise

Cover:
Top left: (detail) Raphael Soyer, *In Washington
Square*, c. 1935. See page 58
Top right: (detail) Maggie Taylor, *Girl with a bee
dress*, 2004. See page 182
Bottom: (detail) Kehinde Wiley, *Dogon Couple*,
2008. See page 186

Published by the Samuel P. Harn Museum of Art
University of Florida
SW 34th Street and Hull Road
Gainesville, Florida 32611-2700
www.harn.ufl.edu

Contents

FOREWORD AND
ACKNOWLEDGEMENTS

Rebecca M. Nagy, PhD
Director

The Samuel P. Harn Museum of Art at the University of Florida will celebrate its twentieth anniversary on September 22, 2010. The opening in 1990 of a 64,470-square-foot museum at UF's Cultural Plaza was the culmination of two decades of dedicated work and planning on the part of university and community leaders. The museum was made possible by a generous founding donation from Dr. David A. and Mrs. Mary Ann Harn Cofrin. They elected to name the museum for her father, Samuel P. Harn, a beloved Gainesville businessman and civic leader. Since that momentous day in 1990, the museum, designed by Kha Le-Huu and Partners of Orlando, has expanded dramatically with the addition of the 18,000-square-foot Mary Ann Harn Cofrin Pavilion, made possible by a gift from Dr. and Mrs. Cofrin and designed by the same architect as the original building. The Pavilion includes expansive exhibition galleries, multipurpose classrooms, a café and a garden for outdoor sculpture. On April 9, 2009, a groundbreaking ceremony was held for a 26,000-square-foot wing for the exhibition, study and conservation of Asian art, once again designed by Kha Le-Huu and Partners and very generously supported by a donation from Dr. and Mrs. Cofrin. The Asian wing is scheduled for completion in late 2010 and will include an Asian garden designed by landscape architect Hoichi Kurisu.

Just as the museum facility has grown dramatically since 1990, so, too, have the collections grown in depth, breadth and importance. The museum opened with a collection of almost 3,000 objects either donated or purchased by the University of Florida over the preceding decades, primarily through the efforts of faculty in the College of Fine Arts. Today the collections include around 7,000 objects with concentrations in five major areas: African art, Asian art, photography, modern art of Europe and the Americas, and international contemporary art. The museum also houses collections of works on paper, Ancient American art and Oceanic art. The museum's holdings of American art are particularly strong and include works from the modern, contemporary, photography and works on paper collections. Of 2,490 American works of art in the collection, 88 have been selected for inclusion in this publication by Dulce Román, curator of modern art, Kerry Oliver-Smith, curator of contemporary art, and Thomas Southall, curator of photography.

One of the core collections when the Harn Museum of Art opened its doors in 1990 was American painting of the first half of the 20th century, with many donations from William H. and Eloise R. Chandler. As the Chandlers continued to enrich the holdings of the new museum during the early years of its existence, their marvelous example served to inspire other

donors to contribute to the growth of the collection. The modern collection
has been enriched by many generous donors, with particularly notable
contributions from Dr. and Mrs. David Cofrin, Ruth Pruitt Phillips, Stephen
and Carol Shey and Mickey and Donna Singer. The contemporary collection
has grown with the support of Dr. and Mrs. David Cofrin, Dr. Robert and
Mrs. Nancy Magoon, Norman and Irma Braman, Martin Z. Margulies, and
many other wonderful donors. The photography collection has also had
many generous benefactors, especially Dr. Melvin and Mrs. Lorna Rubin,
Martin Z. Margulies, and the Andy Warhol Foundation for the Visual Arts. In
addition, many outstanding gifts have been given by former faculty and
students of UF's highly ranked undergraduate and graduate programs in
photography. The names of these wonderful supporters of the Harn, along
with many others, are included on the next page and throughout this
publication with the individual works of art they donated. In addition,
donors who established endowments to support the acquisition of works
of art are recognized on the next page and in the credit lines of objects
purchased using these funds.

This beautiful publication celebrating American art in the Harn Museum's
collection has been made possible through generous funding from the
Henry Luce Foundation, the National Endowment for the Arts, the Graduate
Research Office of the University of Florida and Dr. Madelyn Lockhart. We
are extremely grateful for their support, which enables the museum to
share its American art collection with a national and international audience.
I also wish to thank Dulce Román, curator of modern art and chair of the
curatorial department, for her excellent work as project manager for the
book and for her insightful entries on works from the modern collection.
Thanks are also due to Kerry Oliver-Smith, curator of contemporary art,
and Thomas Southall, curator of photography, for their hard work and
informative entries on selections from their collections as well. The beautiful
photographs for the book were taken by Randy Batista. The curators and
photographer were assisted at every step along the way by Registrar Laura
Nemmers and her talented staff. For the elegant design of the publication
I wish to thank Joel Suissa of Suissa Design. For her thoughtful and careful
editing of the text I am grateful to Lauren Richardson.

We dedicate this book to all of the generous people who donated works of
art or funds for acquisitions to build the museum's outstanding holdings
of American art and hope that this publication will enlighten, inspire, educate
and enrich the lives of many people.

Art Donors and Acquisition Endowments

Donors of American Art

The Harn Museum of Art is pleased to acknowledge the following donors who have given works of art and supported acquisition funds for the American art collection. The museum would also like to acknowledge other generous donors who wish to remain anonymous. Every effort has been made to ensure the accuracy of this summary.

2004 Photo Forum Acquisition Fund
Ben and JoAnne Adams
Clinton Adams in honor of Kenneth Kerslake
Clinton and Mary Adams
Warren and Jan Adelson
Friends of Virginia Carter Ahrens
American Federation of Arts through a grant from
   the Edward John Noble Foundation, New York
Andy Warhol Foundation for the Visual Arts
Richard Anuszkiewicz
John Taylor Arms
Atlantic Center for the Arts from the
   Hester Merwin Ayers Collection
Charlotte T. Bannister in memory of
   Dean Turpin C. Bannister
Doris Bardon
Efrain Barradas
Kathryn L. Barrett
Sadie Bartling
John Wm. Beck and Municipal Bond Partners,
   Joseph Wittenstein, Managing Partner
Chris and Sue Beechler
Jo Berg in memory of Martha Gruber Simoes
Ruth Bernhard Trust
Howard Wayne Bishop
Budd and Julia Bishop
Rodney Layton Bishop
Kim Williams Boyd
Exilda Dumas Brady in memory of her mother,
   Margaret L. Dumas
Norman and Irma Braman
David Burchfield
Beth Callahan
Mrs. Kenneth Callahan
Dr. and Mrs. Corbin S. Carnell in memory of
   E. Muriel Adams
Leonard Carter

Eloise Ricks Chandler
Eloise R. Chandler in memory of
   William H. Chandler
Margaret S. Chandler in memory of
   William H. Chandler
William H. and Eloise R. Chandler
Keith Chinn and W. Deane Lee
Jill Ciment
Dr. and Mrs. David A. Cofrin
Edith Dee Cofrin
Mary Ann P. Cofrin
Members of the Cofrin family
Sharon Cohen
Van Deren Coke
Darin Cook
Louise H. Courtelis
Lorna and Roy Craven
Doris Davis
R. Hunt Davis, Sr.
Mrs. Snead Young Davis in memory of
   Alice Young Lindsey
DC Moore Gallery in honor of
   Stephen and Carol Shey
Daniel DelRowe
Dorothy C. Duryea and F. Charles Duryea, Jr.
Steve Elbert
Dallas Ernst
Barbara Off Evans
Helen Sawyer Farnsworth
Diane Farris
Robert and Nancy Fichter in honor of my
   University of Florida teachers: Ken Kerslake,
   Jerry Uelsmann and Jack Nichelson
Alleen K. and Carl Feiss
Florida State Museum transfer
Florida's Art in State Buildings program
Mrs. Ella Stone Francis

Frederick Weisman Company
FRW Associates, Inc.
Becky Gaver
Family of Charles H. and Marion S. Gilliland
   in honor of Budd Harris Bishop
Elaine Glass in memory of Joseph Glass,
   University of Florida College of Law,
   Class of 1955
Rusty, Maggie and Brian Green
Eugene E. Grissom
Nancy and Eugene E. Grissom
James W. Hall
David R. Hancock
James P. Harrington
John A. and Clarice T. Harrison
Richard H. and Jane Gale Heirs
Barbara Hirschl
Hogtown Graphics
Hollis Holbrook
Mrs. Vivian Nickels Holbrook
Estate of Vivian N. Holbrook
Caroline P. Ireland
Caroline P. and Charles W. Ireland Foundation
Larry and Marita Jacobs
Everette James, Jr.
Sue Jester
Ann Jonas
Alan and Linde Katritzky
J. Eugene Kelley in memory of
   Anna Bernice Kelley
Michael Kemp
Michael A. Kenny
Sarah A. and Kenneth A. Kerslake
Nancy Wallace Kirk in honor of
   Rebecca and Paul Nagy
Mr. and Mrs. Milan Kolarik
Casey and Joe Konopka in memory of Philip Desind

Lachaise Foundation in honor of
Budd Harris Bishop
Lannan Foundation
Jane and R. Paul Larkin
Roslyn Levy
Len and Veda Lewis
Dr. and Mrs. Robert C. Magoon
in honor of Sam and Bessie Proctor
Friends of Wallace Eugene Manis
Martin Z. Margulies
Martin Z. Margulies Foundation, Inc.
Ann and Robert Marston
Mary Ryan Gallery to honor Dr. and Mrs. Cofrin
Mr. and Mrs. Robert Barbeau Mautz
Robert Barbeau Mautz in memory of
Esther Guthery Mautz
David Jameson McCreery Estate
Eric McCready in honor of Julia and Budd Bishop
Patricia P. Medina
John and Linda Mendell
Melissa Meyer in memory of Dr. Paul Meyer
Aaron J. Miller
Elayne and Marvin Mordes
Charles Morris
Museum Visitors Donation Box
National Endowment for the Arts
Aphrodite Désirée Navab
Bea Nettles
Jack Nichelson in memory of Roy C. Craven Jr.
Miss Lucy Nulton
Stephen C. O'Connell
Charles Turner O'Neal
Reese and Marilyn Arnold Palley
William E., Tim Ann and Nevil Parker
Caroline J. Rister Penn
Mr. and Mrs. Michael R. Perez
Carole M. Pesner, Kraushaar Galleries, New York
in honor of Budd Bishop
Eric Lang Peterson
Kenneth and Vivian Pfeiffer
Ruth Pruitt Phillips
Estate of Ruth Pruitt Phillips
Elinor Poindexter

Fred Pomerantz in memoriam of
Helene Pomerantz
Mrs. Mary May Purser
Stuart Purser
Mary and Stuart Purser
Dr. Robert S. Purser
Mr. William Ray
Moe Rhine
Caroline Julier Richardson
Friends of James G. Richardson
Andrea Robbins and Max Becher
Celeste Roberge
Dr. H.J. Roberts
Hyman J. Roberts, M.D. and
the Honorable Carol A. Roberts
Mr. and Mrs. Doyle Rogers
Mr. and Mrs. Lewis H. Rogers
Michael and Jean Rose
Richard Ross
Melvin and Lorna Rubin
Andrée Ruellan
Helen Sawyer, daughter of Wells M. Sawyer
William N. Schaaf
Eugene Ivan Schuster
Stephen and Diana Sessums,
Oscar and Anna Alvarez, and Dr. Jon Mundorff
S.F.I.
Dr. and Mrs. Daniel E. Sharkey
Merle C. Shera
Stephen and Carol Shey
Roy and Sophia Sieber
Raphael D. Silver and Joan Micklin Silver
Michael A. Singer
Michael A. and Donna Singer
Brook Smith
Thomas W. Southall
Southern Graphic Arts Circle
Robert Staub
Mr. and Mrs. William Stephens
Mr. Theodore W. Strauel
Evon Streetman
Mrs. Dorothy Strong
Carol Summers

Toshiko Takaezu in memory of Caroline J. Rister
John Taylor
Maggie Taylor
Maggie Taylor and Jerry Uelsmann
Anne Wall Thomas in memory of Howard Thomas
Margaret Tolbert
Transfer from the Florida Museum of Natural
History, gift of Mrs. William Loring Spencer
Transfer from University Archives
Jerry Uelsmann
Dorothy and William Unger
University Gallery
University Gallery transfer,
Student Purchase Award
University Gallery transfer,
Olive Briggs Scarrett Memorial Purchase Award
University of Florida Department of Art and
the Printmaking Program's International
Visiting Artist Print Program
University of Florida President's
Special Purchase Fund
University of Florida Presidential
Student Purchase Award
University Women's Club
Sergio Vega
Todd Walker
Estate of Todd Walker
Hiram and Avonell Williams
Hiram and Avonell Williams, by exchange with
the Columbus Museum, Columbus, Georgia,
in memory of Lamar Baker
Dr. and Mrs. Ralph C. Williams Jr.
Mr. and Mrs. William Wright
Amy Yasuna Denny, Edward C. Yasuna and
Martin S. Yasuna
Museum Purchase Fund Collection,
established by Gloria Vanderbilt under the
auspices of The American Federation of Arts
Leonard Velick
Virginia M. Zabriskie
Zabriskie Gallery, New York
Joseph Zimmerman

ENDOWMENTS SUPPORTING THE ACQUISITION OF AMERICAN ART

In addition to those who made gifts of works of art and supported acquisition funds, the museum gratefully acknowledges individuals who established endowments that have supported the acquisition of American art.

The Caroline Julier and James G. Richardson
Acquisition Fund
The Melvin and Lorna Rubin Fund
The David A. Cofrin Acquisition Endowment
The Phil and Barbara Emmer Art Acquisition
Endowment
The Ruth Pruitt Phillips Endowment
The Gladys Harn Harris Art Acquisition
Endowment
The Fogler Family Endowment

American Selections

FROM THE SAMUEL P. HARN MUSEUM OF ART

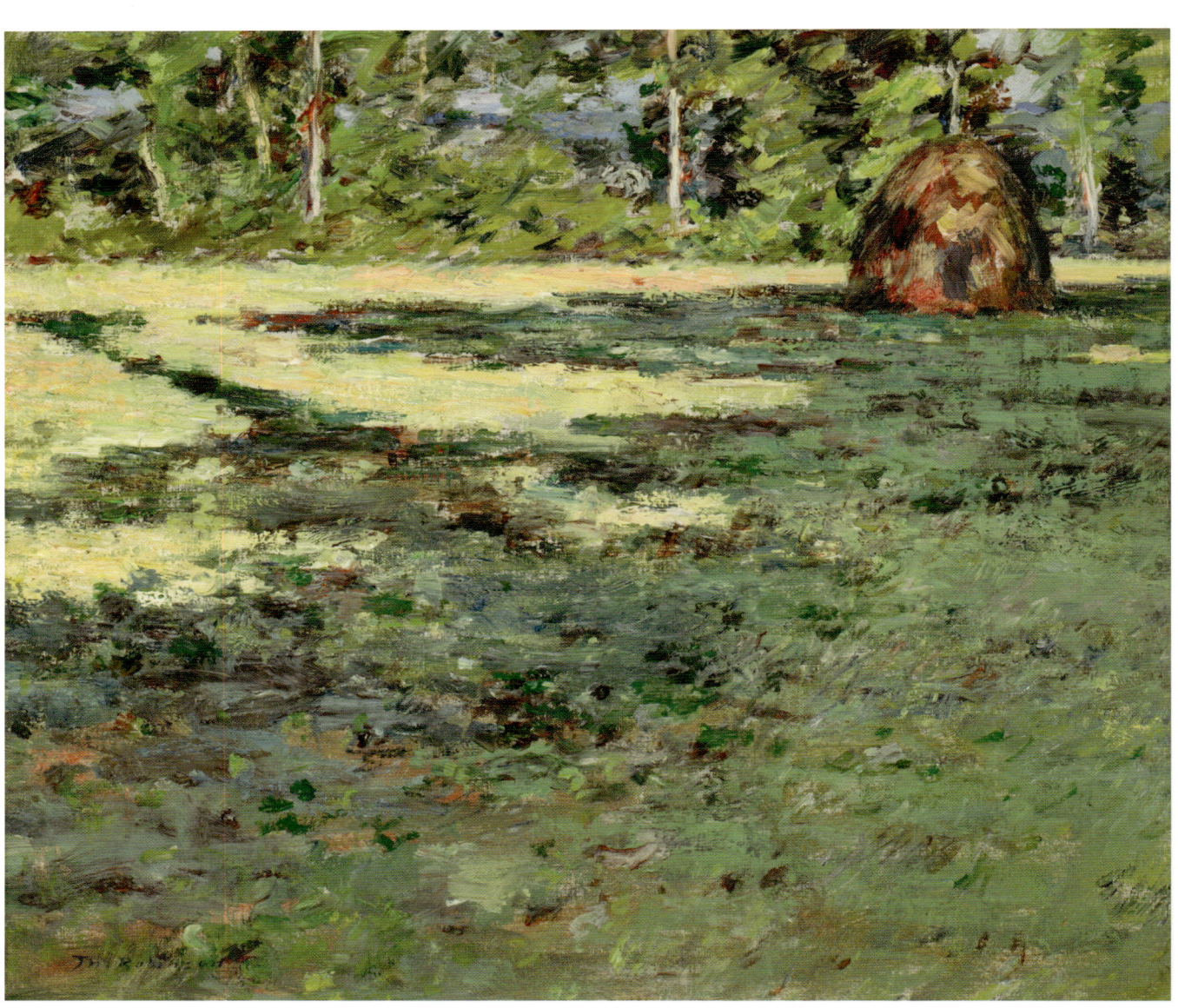

Theodore Robinson
American, 1852-1896

Afternoon Shadows
1891, oil on canvas
19 x 22 ½ in. (48.3 x 57.2 cm)
Museum purchase, funds provided by
Michael A. and Donna Singer
2007.7

Theodore Robinson, one of the first American artists to embrace the innovations of the French Impressionist movement, enjoyed a close personal friendship with Claude Monet, the father of French Impressionism. Between 1887 and 1892, Robinson spent half of each year in Giverny, France, where his mature artistic style—characterized by a powerful sense of design, atmospheric effects, and lively surface texture—evolved under the direct influence of Monet.

An academically trained figure painter, Robinson studied at the Art Institute of Chicago and the National Academy of Design in New York City between 1870 and 1874. Following this early period of study, Robinson continued his studies in Paris between 1876 and 1879 at the École des Beaux-Arts and the Académie Julian. Between 1887 and 1892, Robinson made six extended visits to Giverny, where he formed a friendship with Monet. Robinson's diary includes numerous accounts of lively exchanges between the two about art and artists. This friendship enhanced Robinson's knowledge of Impressionist techniques.

Painted at Giverny in the summer of 1891, *Afternoon Shadows* depicts a single stack of grain in a meadow of vivid greens and yellows bordered by a line of trees along the horizon. The deep shadows in the foreground recede toward the sunlit boundary of the field, suggesting midday. *Afternoon Shadows* forms a pair with another work of identical composition in the collection of the Museum of Art, Rhode Island School of Design. Painted at different times of day, both versions explore changing color and light in the landscape and owe their inspiration to Monet's haystack series of the mid-1880s and 1890-1891. The varied and expressive brush technique of *Afternoon Shadows* provides a lively surface texture, while the abrupt cropping of the vista along the high horizon line enhances the spontaneity of the composition. The high-keyed palette of greens and yellows with touches of blue and red conveys the effects of afternoon sunlight and shadow on this pastoral vista.

DR

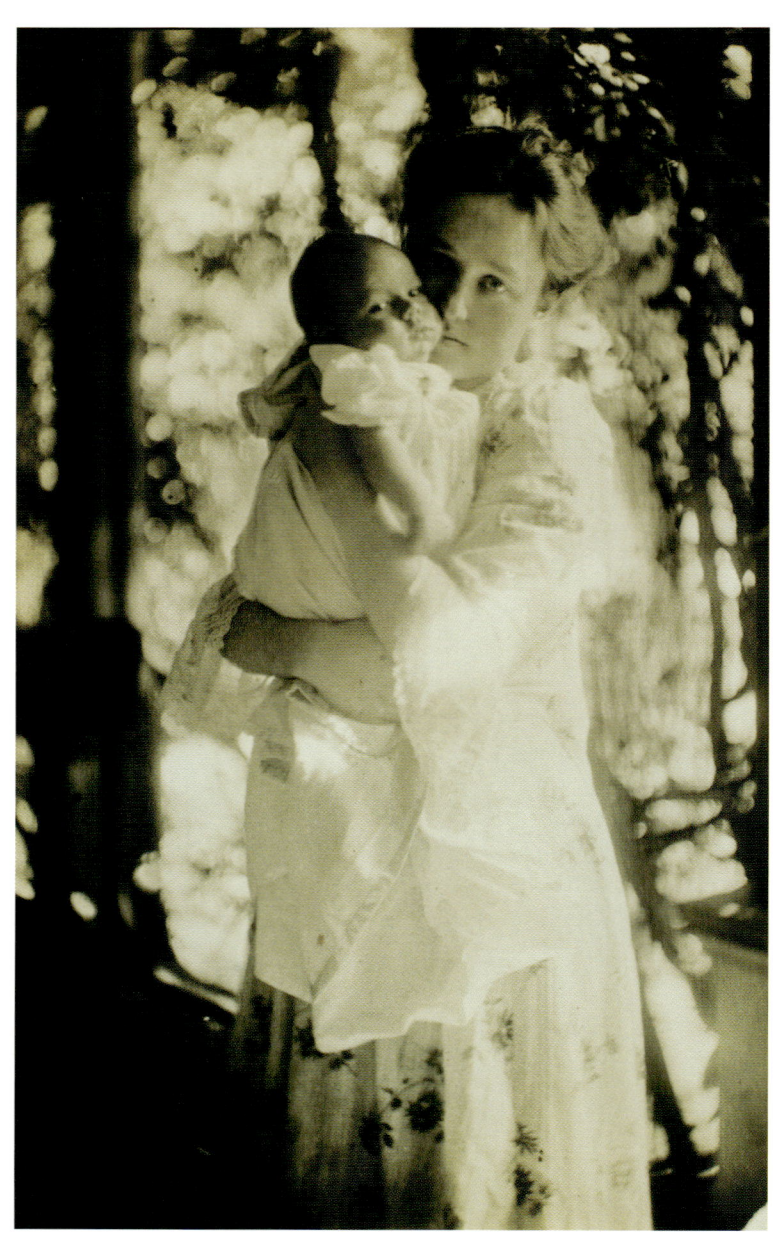

GERTRUDE KÄSEBIER
American, 1852-1934

GERTRUDE O'MALLEY AND HER SON CHARLES ON THE PORCH
1900, platinum print
image and sheet: 8 ⅛ x 5 in. (20.6 x 12.7 cm)
Museum purchase with funds provided by the
David A. Cofrin Acquisition Endowment
2007.23

Gertrude Käsebier's soft-focused photographs of mothers with their children, society belles and Native Americans earned her both commercial and professional success. She belonged to a group known as the Pictorialists who thought of photography as an artistic expression equivalent to painting and printmaking and sought to elevate the medium from documentation to a respected art form. Her portrait photographs often employed relaxed poses in natural light and emphasized the play of light and dark. Active mostly in New York City, Käsebier met and worked with many famous photographers of the time including Alfred Stieglitz, Edward Steichen, Clarence H. White and Alvin Langdon Coburn.

Käsebier was born in Iowa and spent her early childhood in Colorado Territory before moving with her family in 1864 to Brooklyn, New York. On her 22nd birthday in 1874, she married Eduard Käsebier, a shellac importer from Germany with whom she had three children. Käsebier began photographing her family in the late 1880s, just as cameras were becoming more portable and the ranks of amateur photographers were growing. In 1889 she enrolled in drawing and painting classes at Pratt Institute in New York City but soon shifted her interests to portrait photography. Recognizing her talent, Stieglitz invited her to join his Photo-Secessionist group and reproduced a number of her photographs in the first issue of *Camera Work*, his journal of art and photography, in 1903.

Gertrude O'Malley and her Son Charles on the Porch is one of many photographs depicting Käsebier's family in private moments. This close-up of unusual intimacy captures the intense gaze of Käsebier's first grandson, Charles, who was born in 1900. Created when she was at the peak of her career as a professional portrait photographer, this photograph remains a universal image of maternal nurturing and devotion. Käsebier continued to be productive until about 1915, but by the time of her death in 1935, her soft-focused photographs were considered passé by the next generation who favored a more sharply-focused aesthetic.

DR

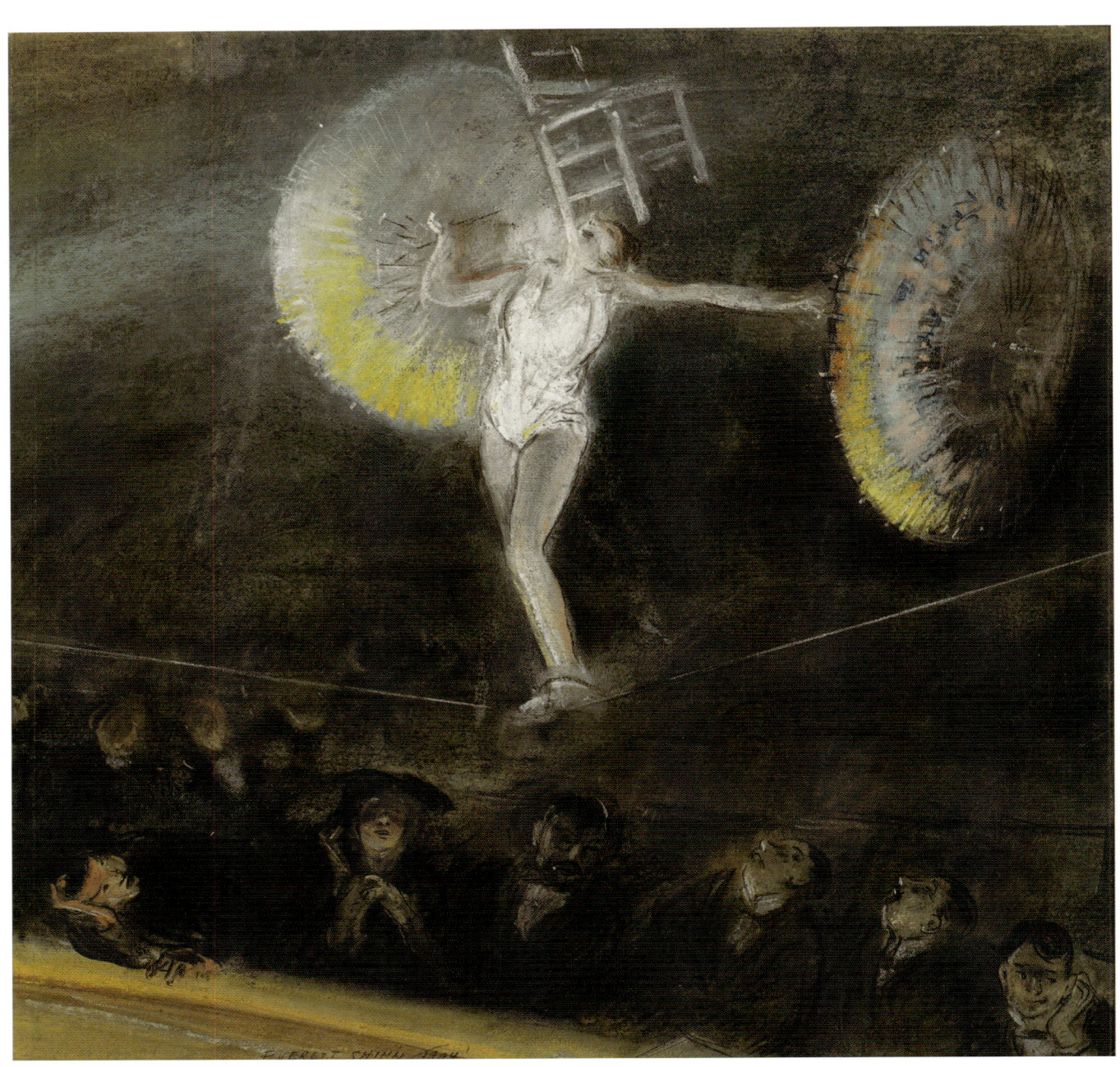

EVERETT SHINN
American, 1876-1953

THE TIGHTROPE WALKER
1904, pastel on board
11 ³/₈ x 11 in. (28.9 x 27.9 cm)
Bequest of Ruth Pruitt Phillips
2005.23.4

Everett Shinn was associated with an innovative group of New York artists known as the Ashcan School who promoted depictions of city life painted in an Urban Realist manner. Born in New Jersey, he left his hometown of Woodstown in 1888 at the age of fifteen to study industrial design at the Spring Garden School in Philadelphia. In 1893 Shinn began working at the *Philadelphia Press* as an artist-reporter and also enrolled at the Pennsylvania Academy of the Fine Arts, where he met fellow artists Robert Henri, John Sloan, William Glackens and George Luks. Following Henri's example, Shinn focused on urban subjects such as life in the slums and café society.

In 1897 Shinn moved to New York City, where he worked as an illustrator for several newspapers and magazines before departing for Europe in 1901. Inspired by the theater scenes of French painter Édouard Manet, Shinn developed a fascination with vaudeville, theater and circus performers whom he depicted in drawings, pastels and paintings throughout his career. Several paintings of such themes were included in a group exhibition at Macbeth Galleries in New York City in 1908. Frustrated that paintings inspired by daily life were routinely rejected for exhibition at the National Academy of Design, Henri organized this exhibition of his work and that of Shinn, Luks, Glackens, Sloan, Maurice Prendergast, Ernest Lawson and Arthur Davies, who became known as The Eight, and later as the Ashcan School.

The Tightrope Walker is a masterful work in pastel that deals with the joyful aspects of leisure and entertainment. *The Tightrope Walker* demonstrates Shinn's personal response to the experience of live theater which gave him the perfect motif in which to blend realism with colorful spectacle. Favoring views of performers from unusual vantage points, Shinn often portrayed his subjects from the back or from the side wings or the orchestra pit. In this dramatic composition, the viewer shares the same viewpoint as the tightrope walker high above the audience, thus heightening the spontaneous excitement of the performance. Shinn's passion for performance led him, beginning in 1913, to devote less time to his art and to pursue work as a playwright, set designer and film director.

DR

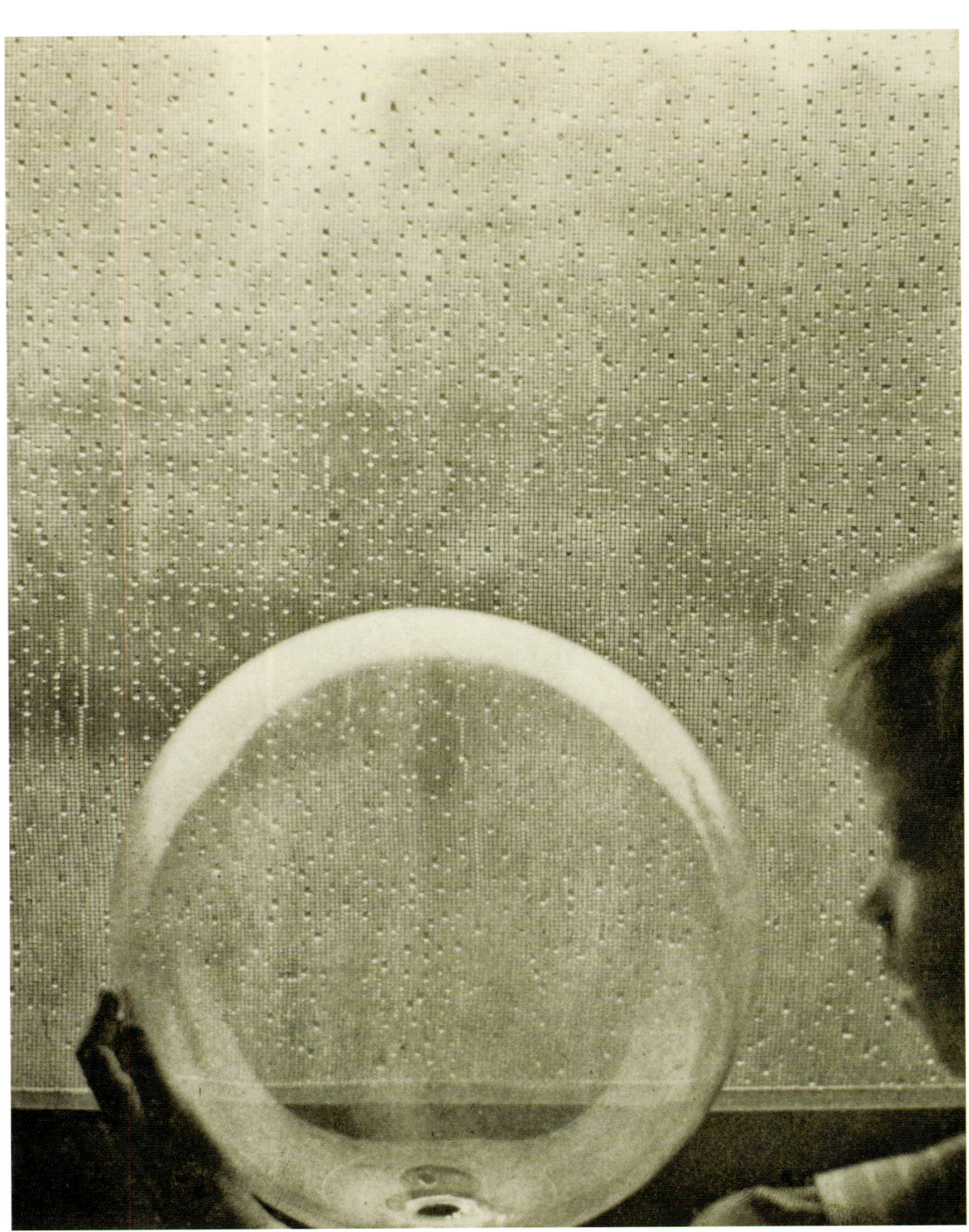

Clarence Hudson White
American, 1871-1925

Drops of Rain
1908, photogravure, *Camera Work*, No. 23
image and sheet: 7 $\frac{1}{16}$ x 6 $\frac{1}{8}$ in. (18 x 15.5 cm)
Gift of Ben and JoAnne Adams
2006.41.2

Clarence White helped shape the style and direction of 20th-century photography through his own photographic work as well as his activities as a teacher and mentor at his Clarence White School of Photography founded in New York in 1914. He was a close associate of Alfred Stieglitz, Edward Steichen and other photographers in the Photo-Secession movement who were united by the common goal of elevating the status of photography. Among his influences were the paintings of James McNeill Whistler and John Singer Sargent as well as the flattened planes and patterns of Japanese woodblock prints.

White was born in the small town of West Carlisle, Ohio, and at the age of sixteen, moved to Newark, Ohio, where his father was a traveling sales-man for a grocery firm. Following his high school graduation, White went to work as a bookkeeper while exploring interests in music, painting, architecture and finally photography, which eventually became a serious pursuit. Despite his lack of formal training in art or photography, he achieved international renown by the turn of the century for his genre scenes, rural landscapes and family portraits. In 1902 White became a founding member of Stieglitz's Photo-Secession group, and in 1906 he moved to New York City, the recognized center of American photography. His work regularly appeared in *Camera Work*, Stieglitz's journal of art and photography, giving him wide exposure in the United States and abroad.

White's early work emulated the soft focus and atmospheric quality of romantic 19th-century French Barbizon paintings. These early works demonstrated his fascination with light and his attention to the delicate play of light and dark. For *Drops of Rain*, White placed his subject before a brightly lit window, taking full advantage of the reflection and refraction of light through a glass globe. In 1910 White and others left Stieglitz's circle and eventually formed a new organization, the Pictorial Photographers of America, in 1916. Under White's lead, the group valued composition over expression and favored a more modernist aesthetic of sharply focused images with optical clarity and precision.

DR

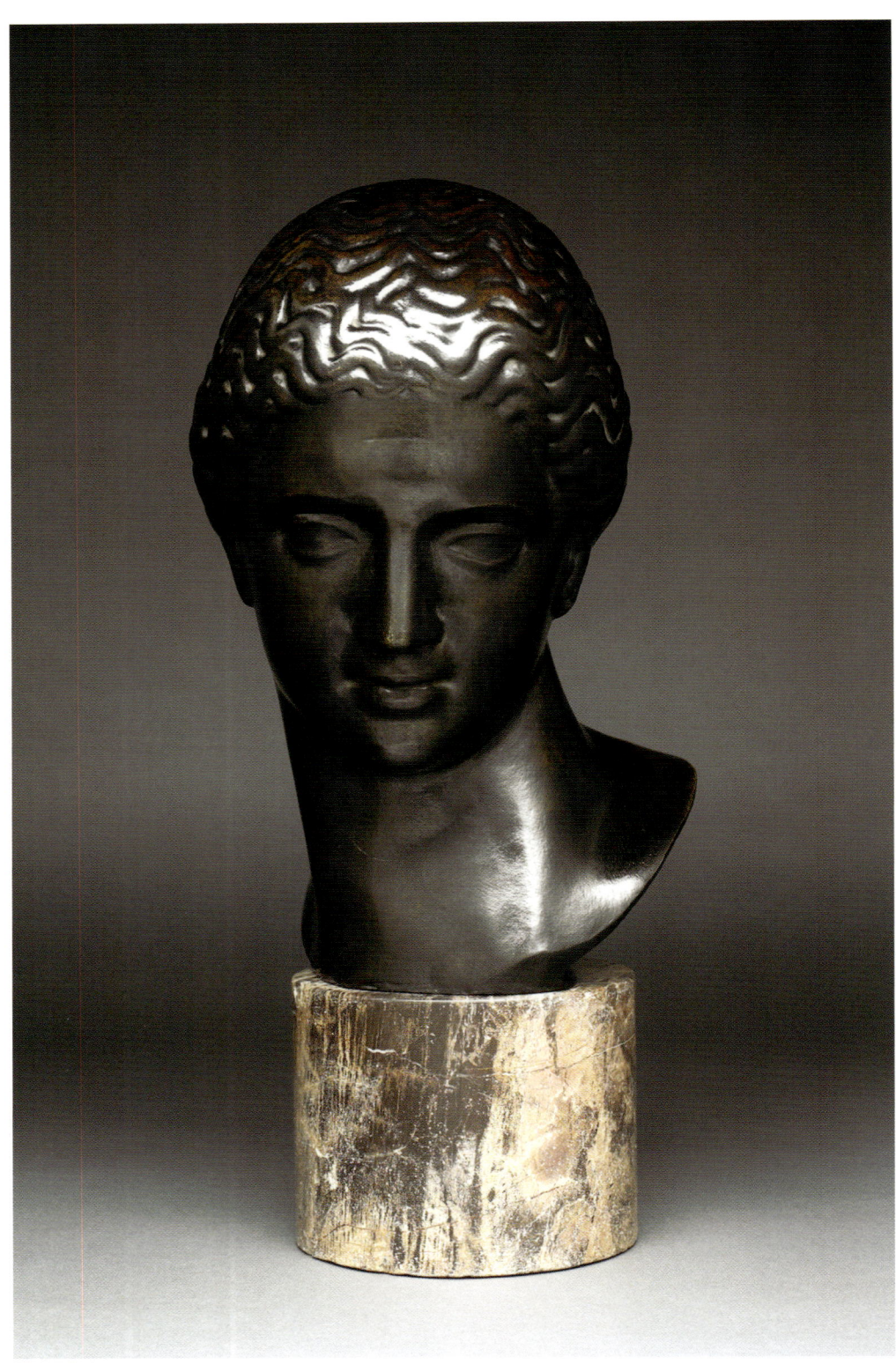

ELIE NADELMAN
American, born Poland, 1882-1946

CLASSICAL FEMALE HEAD
c. 1910, bronze with rich dark brown
patina on veined brown stone base
20 x 9 x 11 in. (50.8 x 22.9 x 27.9 cm)
Museum purchase, Caroline Julier and
James G. Richardson Acquisition Fund,
Dr. and Mrs. David A. Cofrin and
Ruth Pruitt Phillips
1994.10

Elie Nadelman was born to a prosperous Jewish family in Warsaw, Poland. Following studies at Warsaw's School of Drawing and a brief period living in Munich, Nadelman moved to Paris in 1905. In Paris he became a regular at Leo and Gertrude Stein's vanguard art soirees and began exhibiting in galleries and the Paris salons, gaining critical acclaim for his classically inspired, idealized figures. At the onset of the First World War, Nadelman immigrated to the United States, becoming a citizen in 1927. Nadelman quickly settled in New York City with the help of his fellow expatriate, Polish cosmetics magnate Helena Rubinstein, who kept him busy making sleek marble heads and busts for her beauty salons.

Working in a variety of media—bronze, plaster, terracotta, marble, papier-mâché and wood—Nadelman sought to convey in his work what he called "significant form" and favored curvilinear gestures as the basis of his harmonious sculptures. His many influences included ancient Greek sculpture, Art Deco, Renaissance bronzes, and European and American folk art. *Classical Female Head*, a lyrically stylized portrait in bronze, exemplifies the geometric elegance and radically simplified forms of Nadelman's sculptures during this period. Its subject matter relates to a series of plaster and bronze classical female heads and full-length standing nudes featured in Nadelman's first solo exhibition in 1909 at the Galerie Druet in Paris.

Beginning around 1917, Nadelman's preferred themes shifted away from classical subject matter toward images based on folk art and American popular culture. Beginning in the 1930s, Nadelman's art underwent another dramatic change as he abandoned the smooth surfaces and idealized, geometric forms of his earlier work in favor of small plaster figures with a rough, unfinished look. These late works combine Nadelman's new preference for a smaller scale with his earlier interests in classical motifs and everyday art.

DR

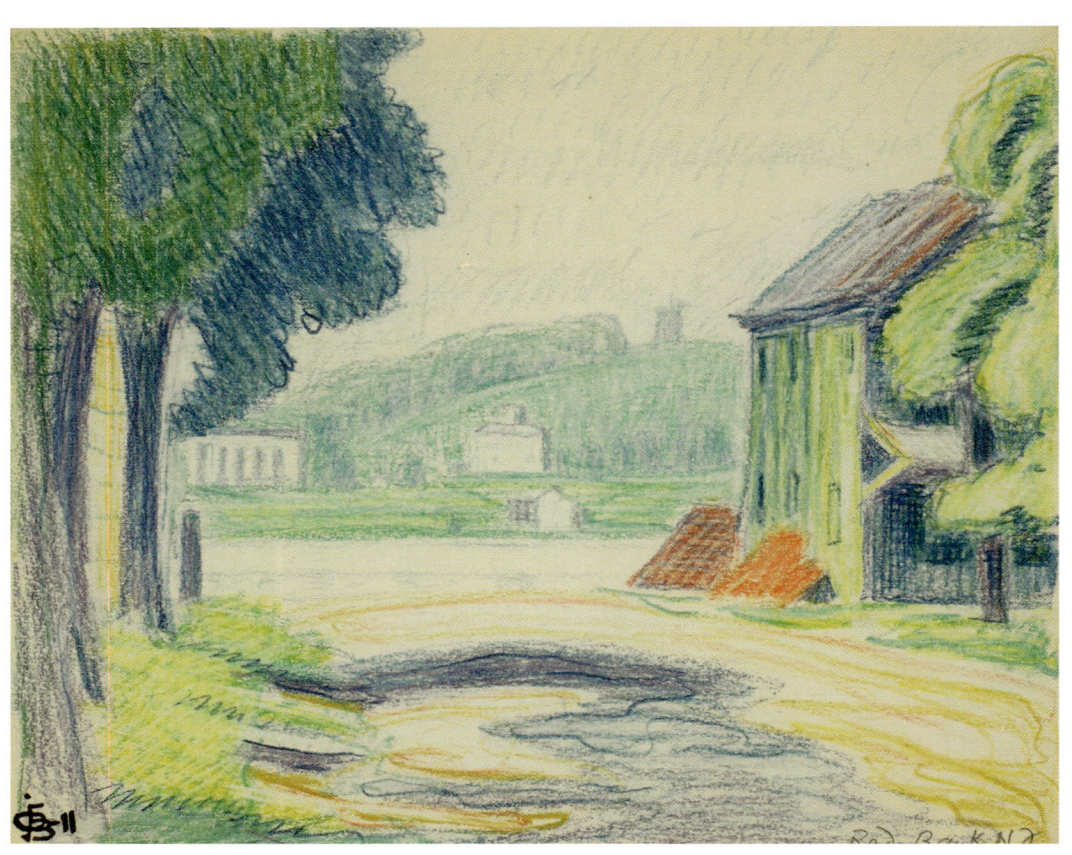

OSCAR FLORIANUS BLUEMNER
American, born Germany, 1867-1938

A VIEW OF RED BANK, NEW JERSEY
1911, crayon on paper
5 ½ x 7 in. (14 x 17.8 cm)
Funds provided by friends of the
Harn Museum of Art
2006.19.2

Oscar Bluemner is best known for his boldly simplified geometric compositions and provocative use of color. Born in Germany, Bluemner began studies in architecture at the Königliche Technische Hochschule in Charlottenburg at the age of twenty. He left Germany for the United States in 1892 and for the next twenty years worked on a variety of architectural projects in Chicago and the New York City area. Following a breach of contract suit involving his 1904 design for the Bronx County courthouse—a majestic Beaux-Arts structure—Bluemner decided to abandon architecture and take up painting around 1911. The artist was already in his forties when he decided to reinvent himself as a painter under the influence of Alfred Stieglitz, the photographer and art dealer who played a central role in the emergence of early modernist style.

While living in New York and various New Jersey towns between 1900 and 1926, Bluemner concentrated on representing local small-town streets, factories and landscapes, incorporating expressive, abstract forms with interlocking grids of pattern and color. A View of Red Bank, New Jersey dates to Bluemner's early period of artistic exploration with the media of drawing and watercolor. Although still earning his living as an architect between 1907 and 1911, Bluemner began taking lengthy sketching trips across rural Long Island and New Jersey, executing numerous small landscape drawings and watercolors in which he sought to capture each scene's mood through color.

Bluemner's early onsite sketches formed the basis for his first series of oil paintings executed between June 1911 and February 1912. The few surviving paintings from this series reveal his unique use of arbitrary color and staccato strokes of highly saturated color. After completion of this series, Bluemner traveled in Europe for a period of seven months and familiarized himself with the latest currents in avant-garde painting. He returned to New York in October 1912, convinced that his work included too much detail. Consequently, he sought to create compositions with large, simple motifs broadly defined by color.

DR

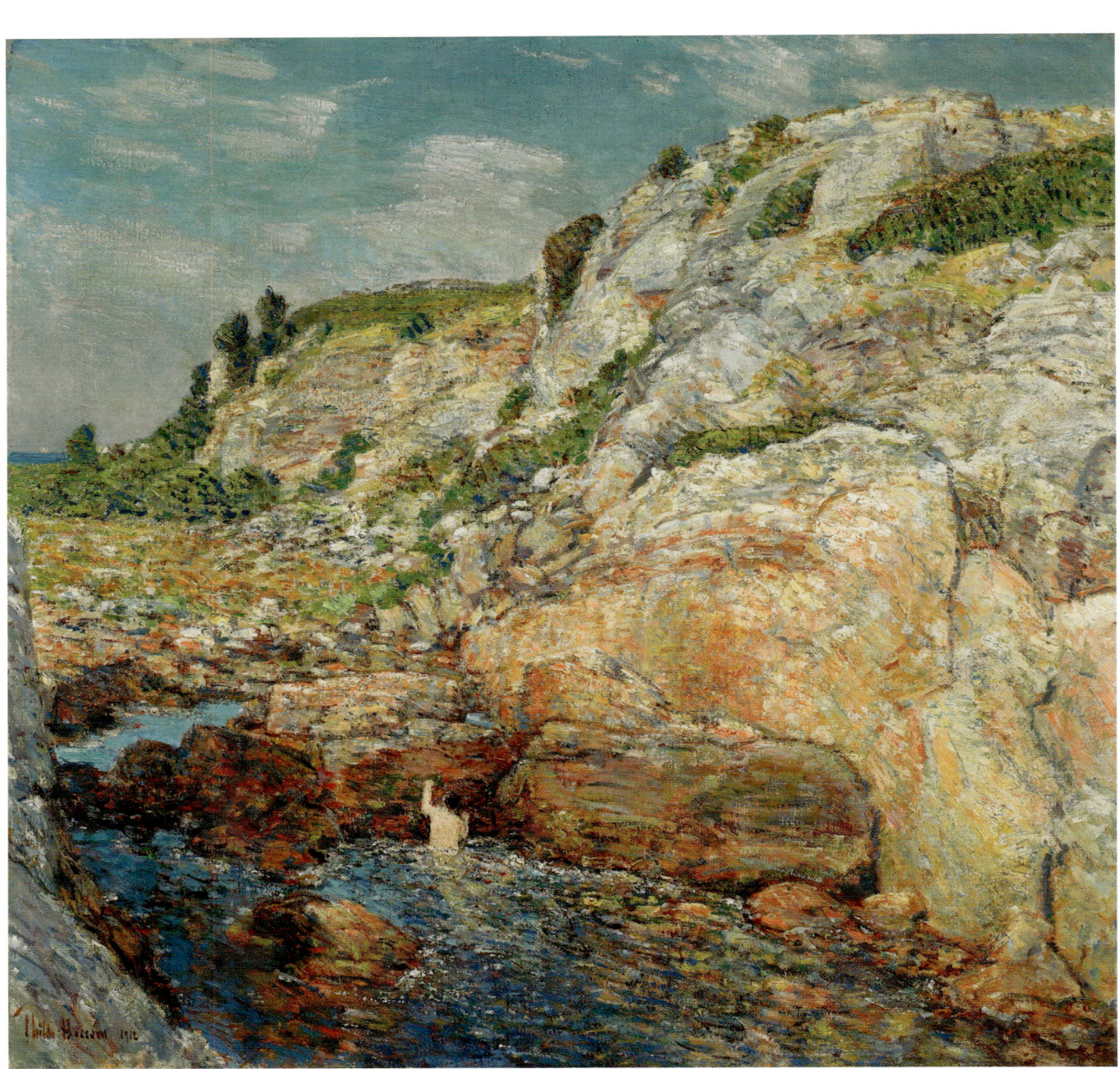

CHILDE HASSAM
American, 1859-1935

NORTHEAST GORGE AT APPLEDORE
1912, oil on canvas
24 ½ x 26 ½ in. (62.2 x 67.3 cm)
Museum purchase by exchange, gift of Louise
H. Courtelis with additional funds provided by
Michael A. Singer
2004.22

Considered America's preeminent Impressionist painter, Childe Hassam adopted the French style of Impressionism for his vivid paintings of distinctly American subjects. Born in Dorchester, Massachusetts, Hassam was the son of a hardware merchant and a distant relative of Boston landscape painter, William Morris Hunt. Following a brief period of art classes at the Boston Art Club and travel in Europe in 1883, Hassam made plans to study at the Académie Julian in Paris where he enrolled from 1886 to 1889. While in Paris in the 1880s, Hassam developed an interest in Impressionism and began to loosen his brushwork and lighten his palette to record brilliant sunlight. Hassam returned to the United States in 1889 and settled in New York City, America's artistic and cultural center at the time.

Beginning in 1890, Hassam made extended summer visits to New England, where he joined enclaves of artists in towns such as Cos Cob, Old Lyme and Gloucester. Hassam's paintings of picturesque New England villages and harbors, churches, gardens and rugged coastlines were popular among collectors who found in them the essence of American culture and values. Hassam produced some of his most celebrated paintings in these scenic locales—works that underscored the pleasant aspects of daily life and alluded to his own New England heritage.

Northeast Gorge at Appledore illustrates Hassam's fascination with Appledore's rocky ledges and breathtaking views of chasms, roughly piled gorges and square stone quarries. Hassam made his first visit to this remote island off the coast of Maine and New Hampshire in the summer of 1890. Here the poet Celia Thaxter established an informal salon, where distinguished writers, musicians and noteworthy artists gathered. Thaxter's sprawling garden and the rambling, rocky coastline of Appledore inspired a series of paintings considered to be some of Hassam's foremost achievements in Impressionism. At Appledore, Hassam explored the full range of his palette, his paintings becoming a gorgeous saturation of color and light, resonating with visual energy.

DR

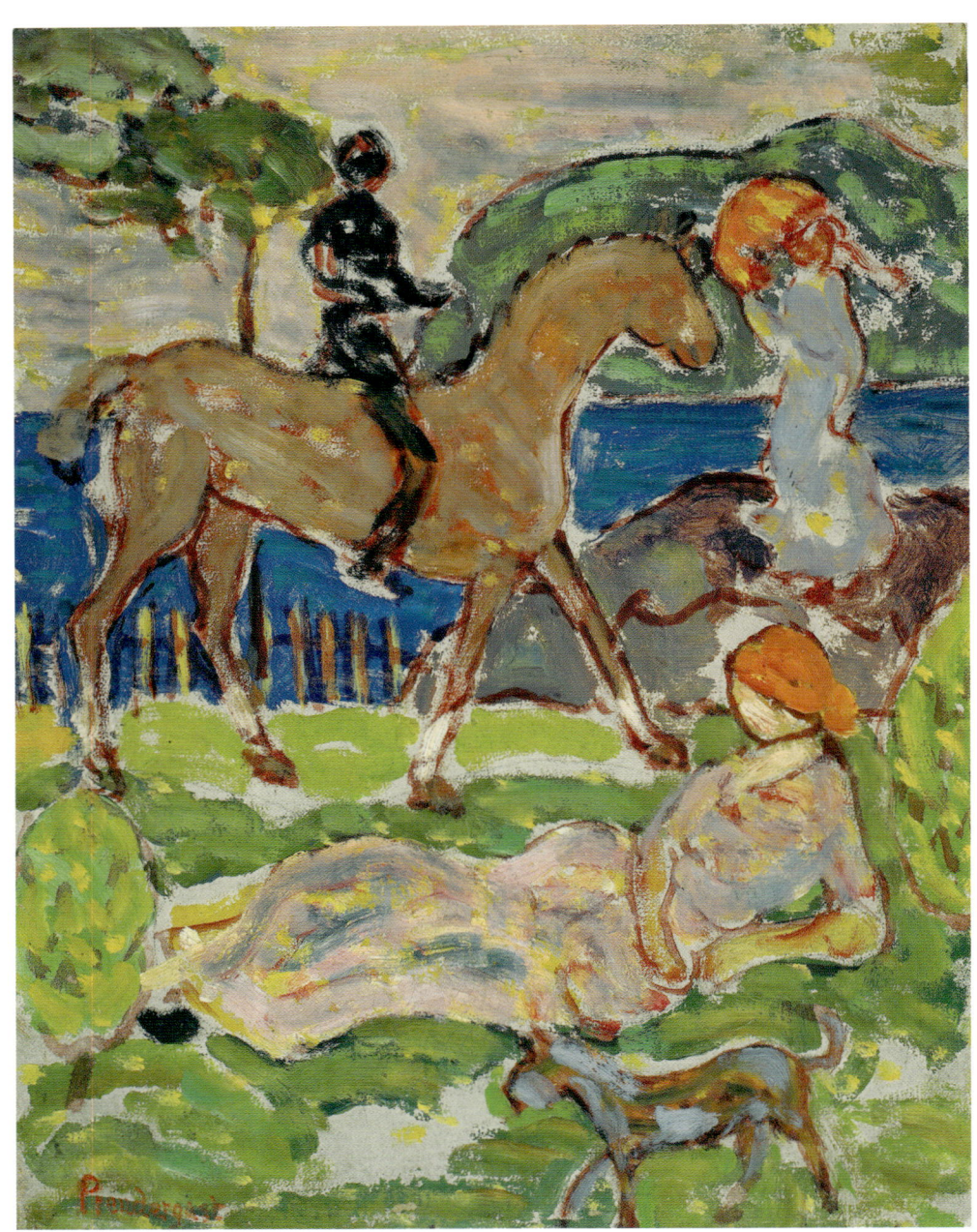

MAURICE BRAZIL PRENDERGAST

American, 1858-1924

IDYLLIC LANDSCAPE

c. 1914, oil on canvas
15 ½ x 12 ½ in. (39.4 x 31.8 cm)
Gift from the Carol and Stephen Shey Collection
2005.46.1

Maurice Prendergast was one of the most innovative American artists of the early 20th century. Influenced by Impressionist and Post-Impressionist painting in France, he developed a highly personal style marked by boldly contrasting bright colors, pattern-like forms and rhythmic compositions. Prendergast was born in St. John's, Newfoundland, where he spent his early youth before moving with his family to Boston in 1868. After completing his studies at Rice Grammar School in 1872, Prendergast went to work wrapping packages at a dry goods store. Within seven years, he had built a career as a commercial artist in Boston, working as a graphic designer of hand-painted signs and advertisements.

Prendergast was 32 when he traveled to Paris in 1891 to continue his art education. Accompanied by his brother Charles who was also an artist, Prendergast lived in Paris for three and a half years, studying at the Atelier Colarossi and the Académie Julian. He soon began executing small sketches on wood panels of elegantly dressed women and playful children at the French seaside resorts of Dieppe and Saint-Malo. Following his return to the United States, Prendergast continued to focus his art on depictions of men, women and children at leisure, strolling in parks, on the beach or traveling the city streets. At the forefront of advances in American art, he participated in the progressive 1908 exhibition of The Eight at Macbeth Galleries, the 1910 Exhibition of Independent Artists and the landmark 1913 Armory Show.

Idyllic Landscape was painted during the last decade of Prendergast's career, when multi-figured park and seashore scenes were among his favorite subjects. A return trip to France in 1907 had exposed Prendergast to works by Paul Cézanne and the Fauve painter Henri Matisse. Integrating these new influences into his work, Prendergast began using startlingly bright colors and staccato brushstrokes. *Idyllic Landscape* depicts a woman, dressed in bright pink, reclining on the grass along a shore with a wandering dog in the foreground and a large horse looming over her in the middle ground. The horizontal bands of saturated color are interrupted with vertical forms and diagonals. Prendergast's interest in the tactile qualities of paint is evident in the thickly applied layers of contrasting colors that create a brightly-hued, tapestry-like effect.

DR

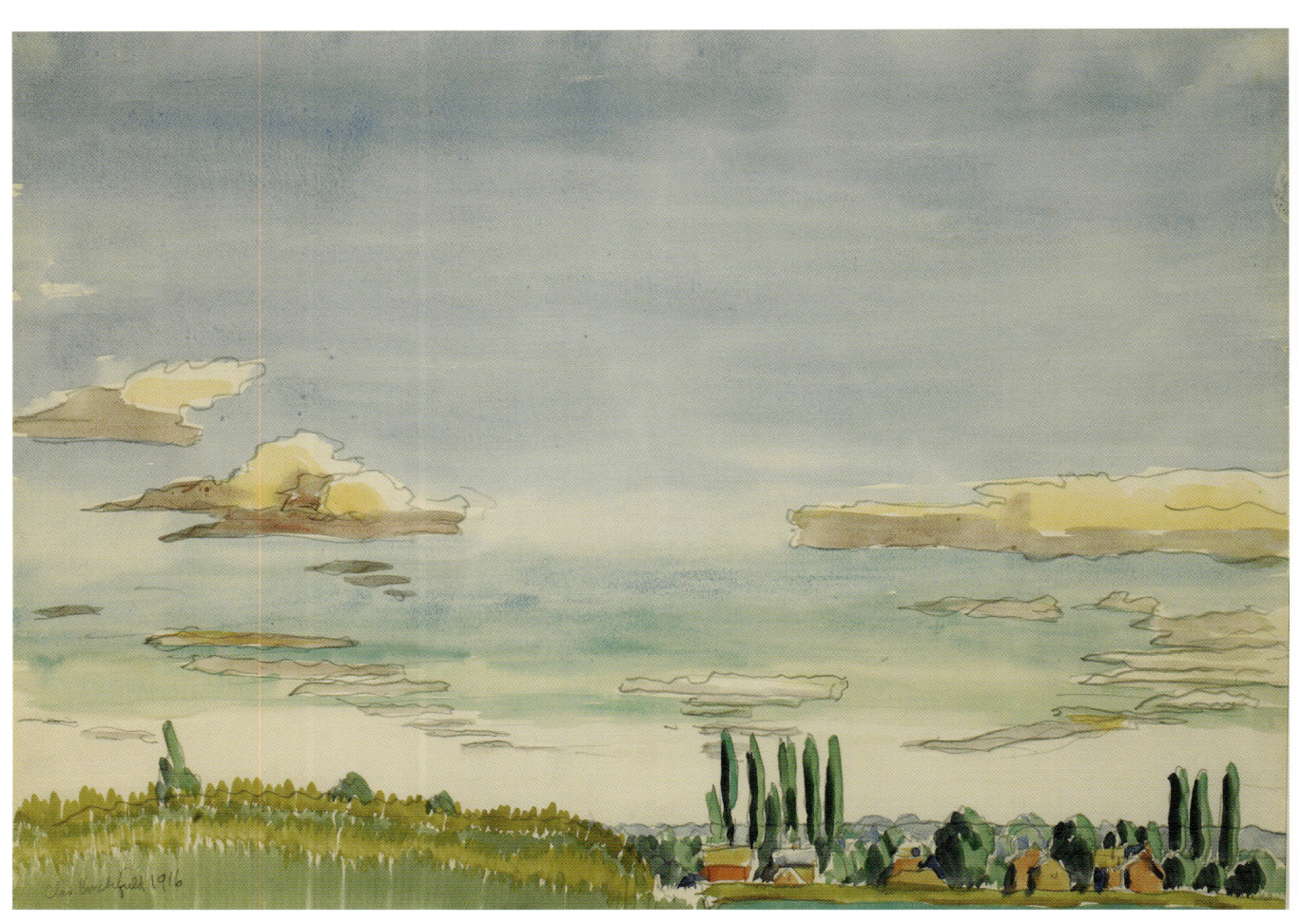

CHARLES EPHRAIM BURCHFIELD
American, 1893-1967

LONG SUMMER EVENING
1916, watercolor and pencil on paper
14 x 20 in. (35.6 x 50.8 cm)
Museum purchase, funds provided by
Dr. and Mrs. David A. Cofrin
Reproduced with permission of the
Charles E. Burchfield Foundation
2006.4

Charles Burchfield is known for his expressive treatment of nature and his ability to find the magical and transcendent in the world around him. Following studies at the Cleveland School (now Institute) of Art from 1912 to 1916, Burchfield returned to his hometown of Salem, Ohio, where he worked at the Mullins metal fabricating plant and painted in his spare time. His early watercolors depicting landscapes near his home reveal the optimism and fresh outlook of a young romantic artist. These were painted in a very personal style marked by fantasy, the use of arbitrary color, and a free distortion of form.

Long Summer Evening, inspired by Burchfield's native Ohio landscape, was painted in 1916, the year he completed his studies in Cleveland. Attempting to convey more than a fleeting visual impression of a familiar scene, Burchfield emphasized the mood of a summer evening through the qualities of light, the verdant landscape in the middle ground, and an expansive sky as the yellows of sunset transform into a blue night sky. The energetic brushwork with its emphasis on pattern and two-dimensional effect is closely linked to his early appreciation of Chinese and Japanese art.

Long Summer Evening exemplifies Burchfield's method of painting immediately following his formal training in which he carefully drew and outlined a composition in pencil before filling in the shapes with color. Drawing continued to form an important component of Burchfield's working method throughout his life. The artist frequently made drawings outdoors and added notations about color, tone, light and mood. He kept these in folders organized by subject, season, weather, and location for easy reference. The large-scale paintings of his later years were based on careful preparatory studies, sometimes incorporating sketches Burchfield had created decades before.

DR

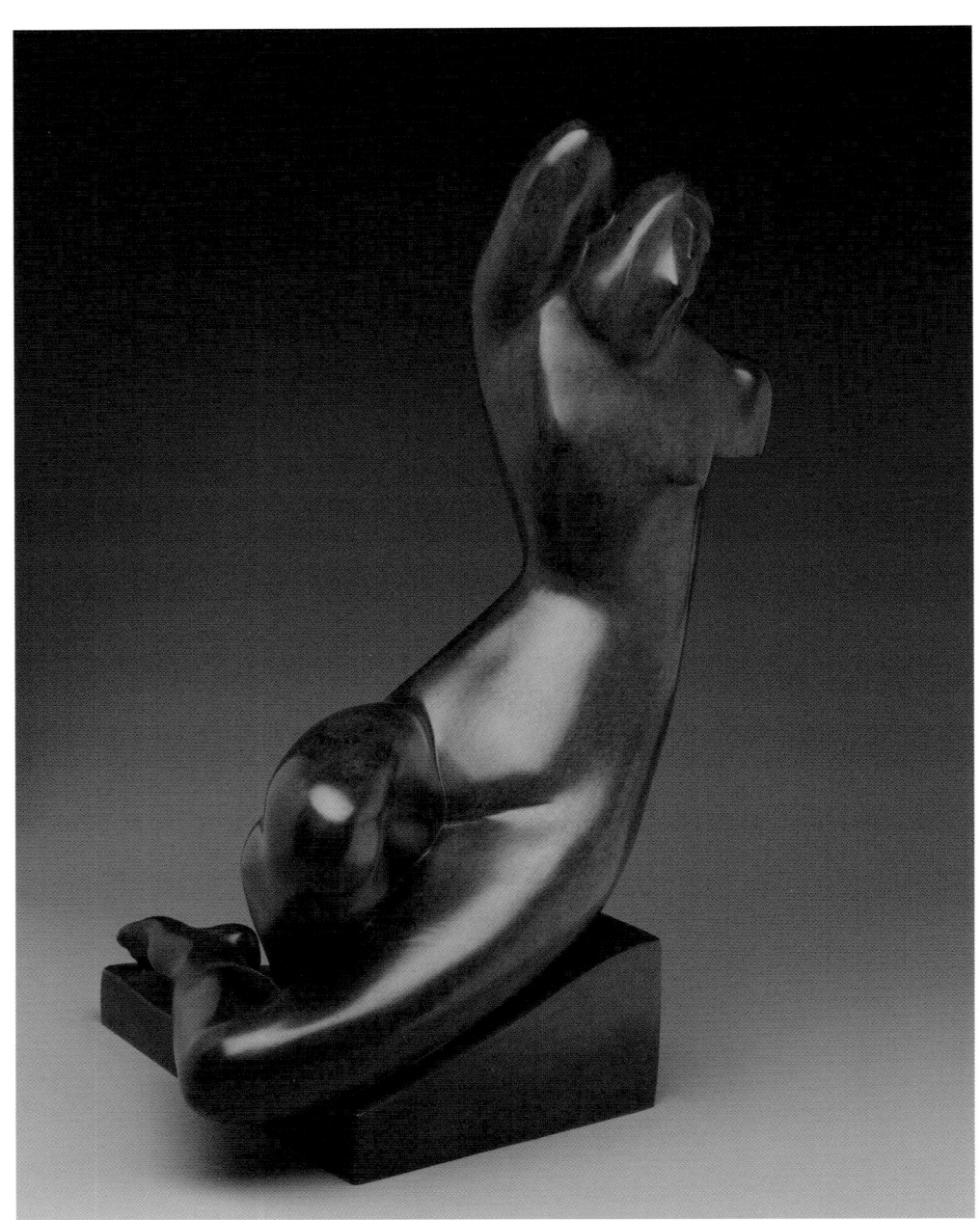

ALEXANDER ARCHIPENKO
American, born Ukraine, 1887-1964

RECLINING
1922, bronze
17 ½ x 11 x 11 ¼ in. (44.5 x 27.9 x 28.6 cm)
Bequest of Ruth Pruitt Phillips
© 2009 Estate of Alexander Archipenko /
Artists Rights Society (ARS), New York
2005.23.5

Widely acknowledged as the first Cubist sculptor, Alexander Archipenko maintained a lifelong fascination with the human figure in the round. Archipenko began studies at the School of Art in Kiev, Russia (now Ukraine) in 1902 but was forced to leave in 1905 after criticizing the academicism of his instructors. Next he lived briefly in Moscow before settling in Paris in 1909, where he enrolled at the École des Beaux-Arts. Yet he left after just two weeks of formal studies, believing that he could teach himself through the direct study of sculpture in the Musée du Louvre.

The decade following Archipenko's arrival in Paris proved to be his most inventive. By 1910, Archipenko began exhibiting with the Cubists at the Salon des Indépendants and Salon d'Automne, earning international renown for his nearly abstract sculptures. His work was represented in many international Cubist exhibitions and also in the landmark Armory Show of 1913 in New York. Following his marriage in 1921 to German sculptor Angelica Bruno-Schmitz, Archipenko moved to Berlin, where he opened an art school. He left Berlin for New York in 1923, becoming a United States citizen in 1929.

As a young artist in Paris, Archipenko began to adapt Cubist techniques to sculpture. Influenced by the Cubist notion of integrating the figure with surrounding space, Archipenko interchanged solids and voids so that protruding elements seemed to recede and internal features to advance. *Reclining* is a beautiful example of his personal approach to the human form as a platform for analyzing volume, space and geometric planes. Through his unique interpretation of the human form, Archipenko sought to challenge traditional concepts of sculpture. With their boldly simplified geometric forms, works such as *Reclining* helped redefine modern sculpture as an intellectual endeavor rather than simply a means for copying observed reality.

DR

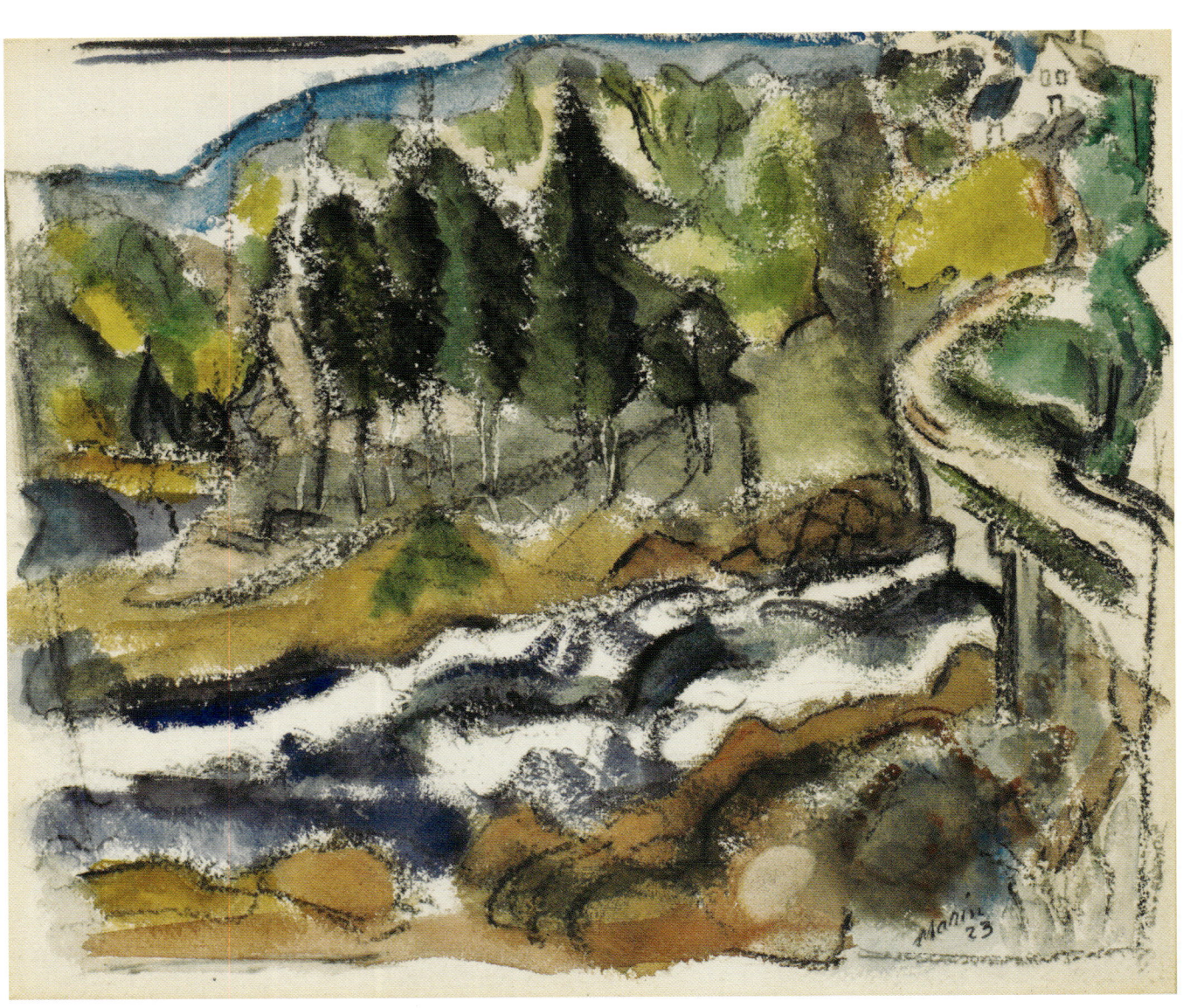

John Marin
American, 1872-1953

Tidal Falls, Deer Isle (Rustling Brook)
1923, watercolor
13 ¼ x 16 ½ in. (33.7 x 41.9 cm)
Gift of William H. and Eloise R. Chandler
© 2009 Estate of John Marin / Artists Rights
Society (ARS), New York
PA-84-159

Recognized as one of the greatest American watercolorists, John Marin studied at the Pennsylvania Academy of the Fine Arts and the Art Students League in New York after first pursuing a career as an architect. Between 1905 and 1909, Marin's formal education was supplemented by a period of travel in Europe, where he absorbed influences from Cubism and Futurism. In 1911 Marin settled in New York City and became a member of the avant-garde circle associated with artist and gallery owner Alfred Stieglitz, exhibiting regularly at Stieglitz's galleries.

During the 1920s, Marin worked almost exclusively in watercolor and developed a broad, fluid style with increasing abstraction. *Tidal Falls, Deer Isle* depicts the quiet community of Deer Isle on the Maine coast, where fishing is the mainstay of the economy. Beginning in 1914, Marin spent nearly every summer on the coast of Maine, and the following year, he purchased a small island at Small Point which he named "Marin Island." The spruce-crowned pink granite ledges of Deer Isle with its quiet woods and vistas of surrounding islands captivated Marin, a frequent visitor to this remote location. Marin's use of tilting perspective and shifting points of view heightens the dynamic interplay of line and color in *Tidal Falls*. These represent a few techniques used by Marin to depict the dynamic tension he saw at work in his subjects.

Beginning in 1922, Marin painted a group of watercolors utilizing an internal framing device derived from Cubism. This device is evident in *Tidal Falls* in the lines forming a 90 degree angle at the bottom right and the horizontal lines at the top of the composition. The vigorous lines of this frame-within-a-frame add a sense of stability to an otherwise dynamic and spontaneous landscape.

DR

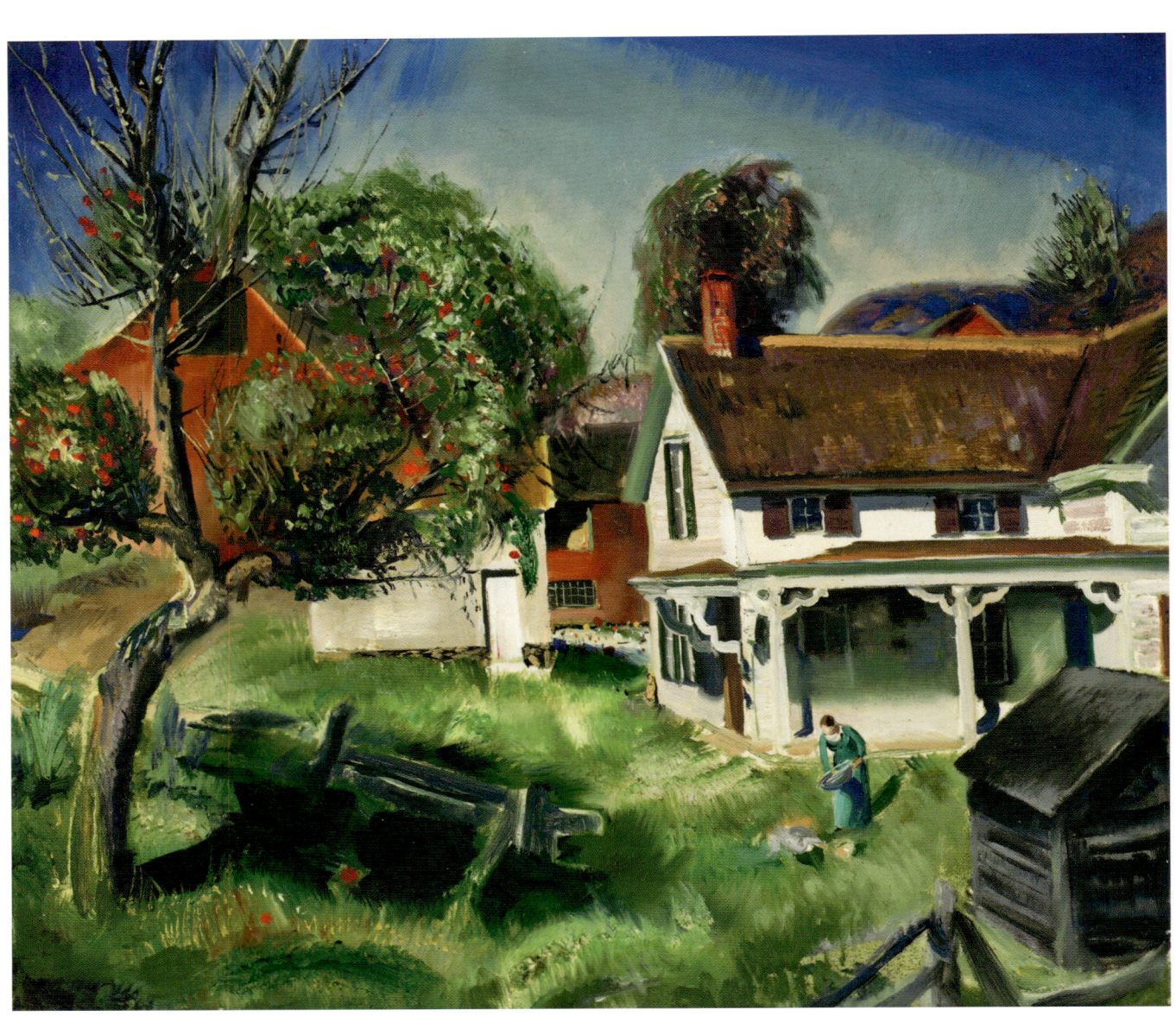

GEORGE WESLEY BELLOWS
American, 1882-1925

JIM TWADELL'S PLACE
1924, oil on canvas
20 x 24 in. (50.8 x 61 cm)
Gift of William H. and Eloise R. Chandler
1992.12

George Bellows was one of the most significant American artists of the first half of the 20th century. Bellows trained at New York's Chase School of Art, a prestigious school run by painter William Merritt Chase. There he met Robert Henri, founder of the Ashcan School, who encouraged his students to paint urban subject matter drawn from New York City's working-class neighborhoods. Among Bellows' favorite subjects were snowy landscapes along the Hudson River, seascapes, dramatic boxing matches, industrial scenes and crowded city views.

Completed while Bellows was working at the artist colony of Woodstock, New York, *Jim Twadell's Place* is a great departure from his widely celebrated scenes of urban life and amateur boxing matches. This bucolic image of rural life depicts the home of Jim Twadell, a horse trainer and drover who transported animals from the country to New York City. Between 1920 and 1924, Bellows executed more than 100 paintings while at Woodstock. During the summers of 1920 and 1921, Bellows and his family rented a hillside home with beautiful mountain views. The following summer, Bellows broke ground on his own house and studio and eventually hung *Jim Twadell's Place* over the mantel of his Woodstock living room.

While at Woodstock, Bellows painted some of the most vibrant and spontaneous works of the last five years of his life. Many of his Woodstock landscapes were painted substantially outdoors while others were painted mainly in the studio with the aid of his sketches. These expressionistic landscapes show a renewed interest in strong color and reveal Bellows' joyous response to nature. During his last summer at Woodstock in 1924, Bellows stayed on into early November before returning to New York, where he continued work on several larger Woodstock compositions in his studio. He died suddenly on January 8, 1925, of peritonitis caused by a ruptured appendix.

DR

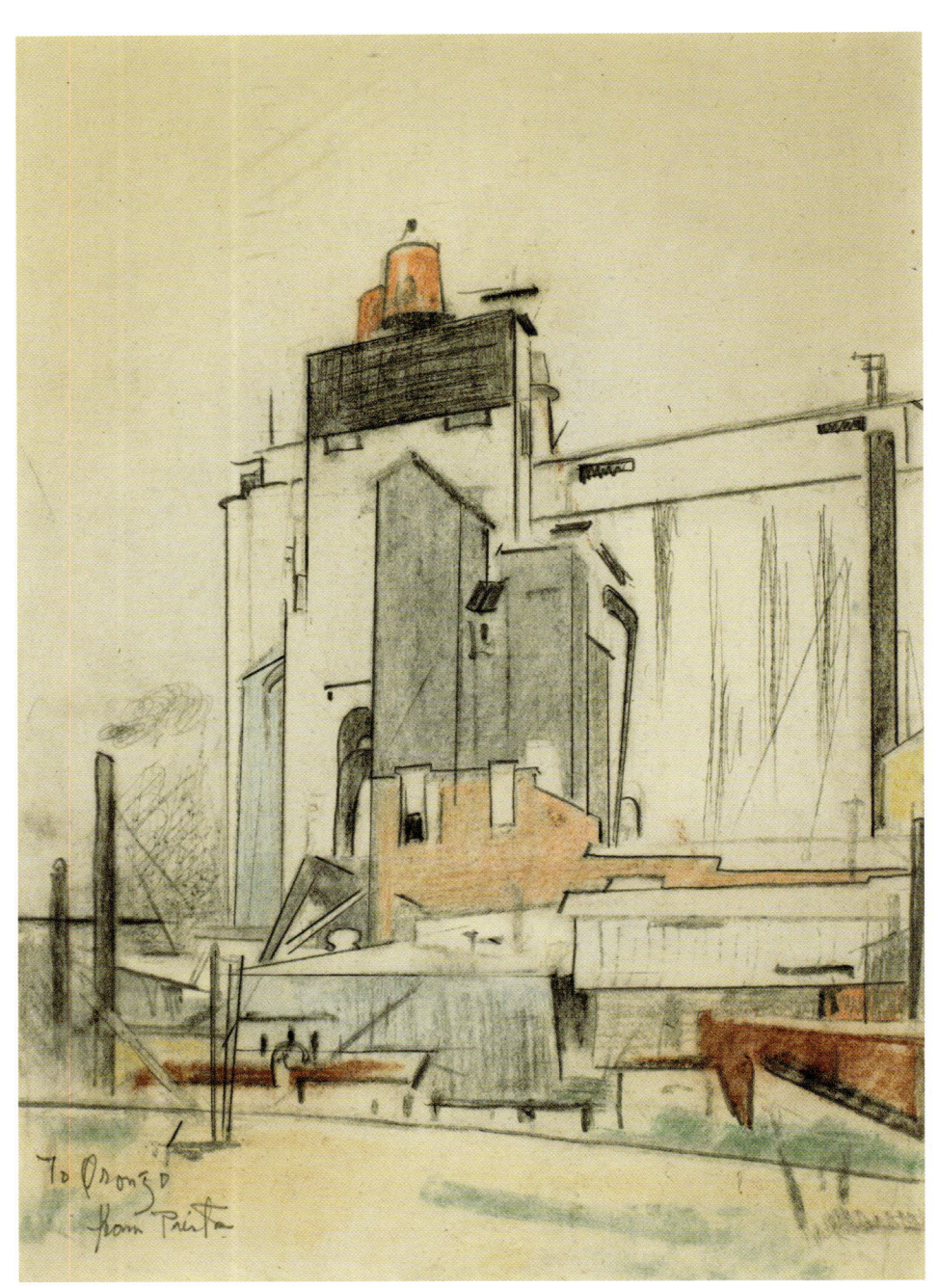

To Orozco
from Prieto

PRESTON DICKINSON
American, 1891-1930

GRAIN ELEVATORS
1924, crayon, chalk and colored pencil on paper
13 ⅛ x 9 ½ in. (33.3 x 24.1 cm)
Museum purchase, funds provided by the
David A. Cofrin Acquisition Endowment
2004.16.1

Preston Dickinson is known for his depictions of architectural subjects, especially industrial scenes, rendered in a precise, sharply defined geometric style. Dickinson attended the Art Students League in New York from 1906 to 1910 before sailing for Europe in 1911. Brief studies at the École des Beaux-Arts and the Académie Julian in Paris were supplemented by extensive travel in Belgium, England and Germany. Dickinson returned to New York in 1914 following the outbreak of World War I and began painting Realist scenes of the Harlem River and its environs in upper Manhattan. By the 1920s, Dickinson's work began to show the clarity, hard lines and geometric reduction associated with the Precisionist movement, combined with elements of analytic Cubism such as tilted perspective and flattened overlapping planes.

Dickinson sketched *Grain Elevators* during a visit to the Peters Mills industrial complex, where he was inspired by the grain elevators and other buildings that towered over the flat, desolate Nebraska plains of Southern Omaha. Dickinson produced at least ten variants of *Grain Elevators*—all considered to be masterpieces of his Precisionist style. In these drawings, Dickinson simplified the pictorial elements to their basic Cubist, geometric forms, enlivening them with bright flat planes of color. The foreshortened vantage point, the emphasis on verticality, and the flatness of form and color all lend to the beautiful complexity of these works.

Dickinson seldom inscribed or dated his works, yet the lower left corner of *Grain Elevators* includes a dedication in pencil, "To Oronzo from Preston." The inscription refers to Oronzo Vito Gasparo (1903-1969), a fellow artist who was best known for his surreal, modernist townscapes. In the summer of 1930, Gasparo accompanied Dickinson to France and Spain, where they hoped to live and support themselves through their art. However, on November 25, 1930, Dickinson died of pneumonia in Northwest Spain at the age of 41.

DR

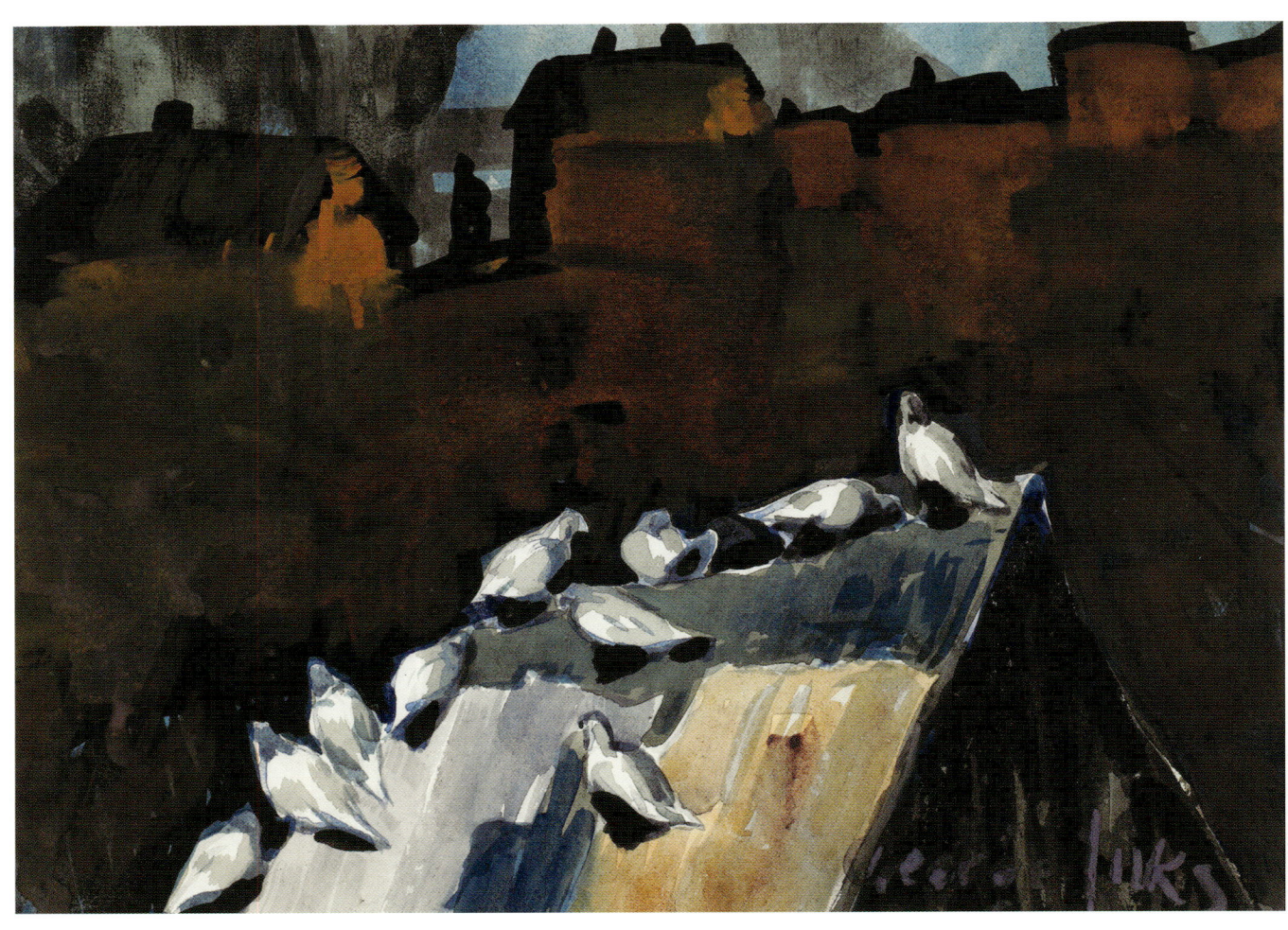

GEORGE BENJAMIN LUKS
American, 1867-1933

DOVE COTE
c. 1925, watercolor on paper
9 ¾ x 13 ⅞ in. (24.8 x 35.2 cm)
Museum purchase, gift of Ruth Pruitt Phillips
1998.17

George Luks, a leading figure in the New York art scene in the early part of the 20th century, is best known as a painter of portraits and genre scenes depicting life in Lower Manhattan. Luks was raised in the coal-mining region of eastern Pennsylvania and moved to Philadelphia in 1883 to study art at the Pennsylvania Academy of the Fine Arts. In 1885, Luks traveled to Europe, living in Düsseldorf, Munich, Paris and London for most of the next decade. Returning to the United States in 1894, he worked as an illustrator for the *Philadelphia Press* and a cartoonist for the *New York World*. By 1902 Luks abandoned his interest in newspaper illustration and dedicated himself to painting scenes of New York's outcasts: street urchins, beggars and laborers.

In 1908 Luks exhibited with fellow artists Robert Henri, Maurice Prendergast, Everett Shinn and four others at New York's Macbeth Gallery. Following the advice of Henri, Luks and this group, later dubbed The Eight, adapted the American genre tradition to realistic portrayals of urban scenes usually painted in a dark palette. Luks and other members of The Eight were eventually absorbed into a larger group of artists known as the Ashcan School, which continued the exploration of modern, urban realities focused on the city's grimier side.

Dove Cote incorporates two of Luks' great interests—pure landscape and the watercolor medium. In addition to portraits and genre scenes, Luks depicted landscapes of the lower Hudson River in winter, waterfront views of New York City's industrial areas, and compositions focused on the city's buildings and squares. In 1910 Luks joined the American Watercolor Society and developed a great interest and talent in the watercolor medium. The close-up view in *Dove Cote* removes the work from any reference to a specific scene and focuses attention on Luks' experimentation with brush stroke, color and form bordering on abstraction.

DR

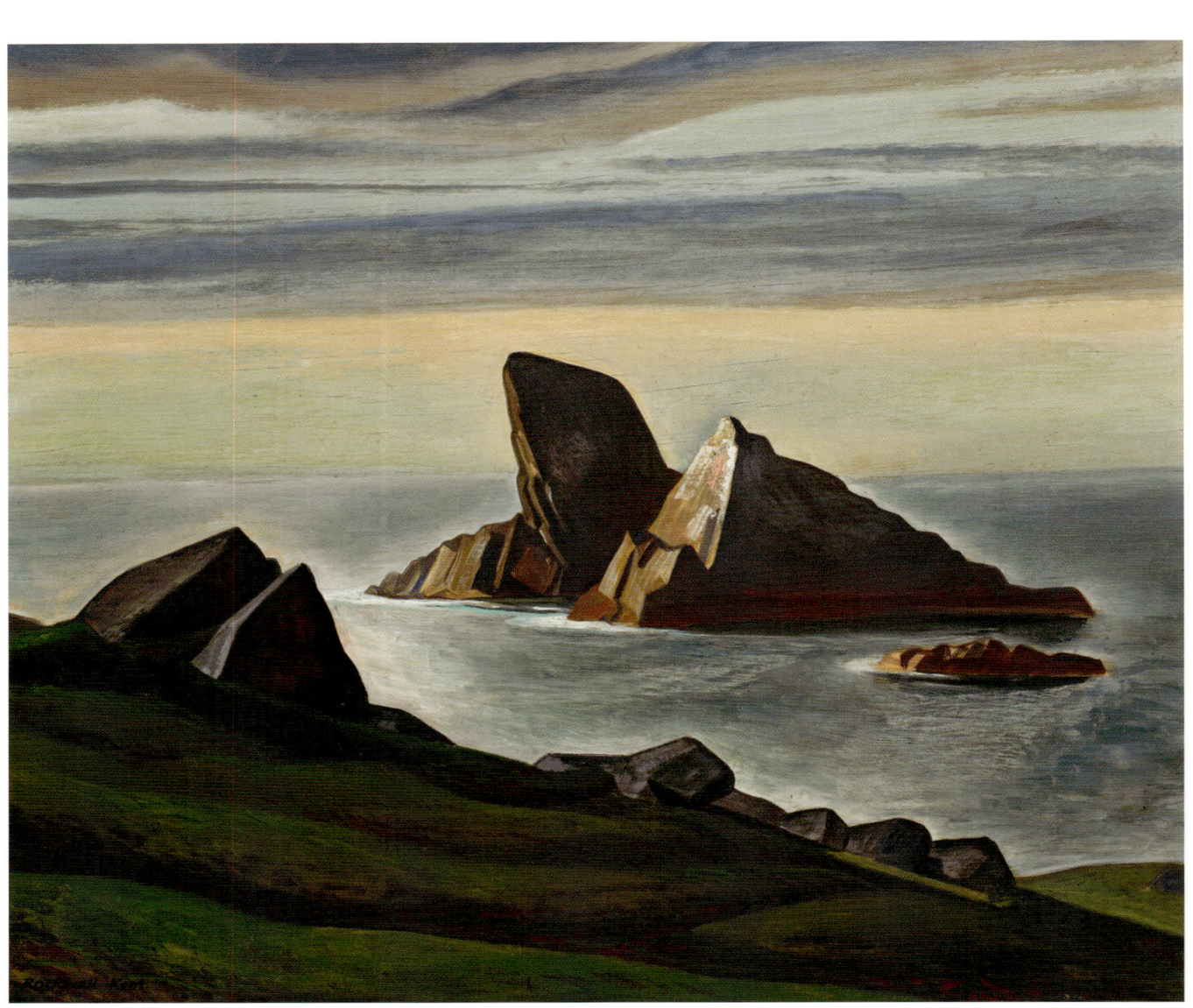

Rockwell Kent
American, 1882-1971

Ireland Reef
1926, oil on panel
24 x 30 in. (61 x 76.2 cm)
Gift from the Carol and Stephen Shey
Collection
Image permission courtesy of the
Plattsburgh State Art Museum,
Plattsburgh College Foundation,
Rockwell Kent Collection. Bequest of
Sally Kent Gorton.
2008.15

During his lifetime, Rockwell Kent was one of the most renowned painters in the United States as well as a famous printmaker and illustrator of classics such as Herman Melville's *Moby Dick* (1930). He was also active as a book designer, graphic artist and architect. Kent's formal art education included studies in plein-air painting at William Merritt Chase's summer art school at Shinnecock Hills near Southampton, Long Island. Although Kent had enrolled at Columbia University's School of Architecture in 1900, he soon decided to pursue painting as his main career and enrolled at the New York School of Art. His teachers included Chase and the Realist painters Robert Henri and Kenneth Hayes Miller. These eclectic influences led Kent to develop a unique style combining naturalism with decorative stylization.

Kent's adventurous spirit led to extensive travel in search of subject matter for his paintings in which he explored the complex relationship between man and nature. His adventures to such remote places as Alaska, Tierra del Fuego and Greenland were the subjects of numerous books authored and illustrated by Kent. Inspired by the writings of Transcendentalists Henry David Thoreau and Ralph Waldo Emerson, Kent found beauty in the austerity and starkness of rugged coastlines and wilderness. Recalling the tradition of 19th-century Romantic painting, his landscape subjects often depict a vast, untamed nature, either completely uninhabited or populated by a lone individual or a few figures.

Ireland Reef demonstrates Kent's taste for precise rendering of forms with strong contrasts of light and dark. It was painted in the summer of 1926 during the artist's four-month sojourn in Ireland, an extended honeymoon following his second marriage. Staying mostly on the isolated northwest coast in County Donegal, he completed 36 paintings as well as additional watercolors and drawings that were exhibited in New York upon his return.

DR

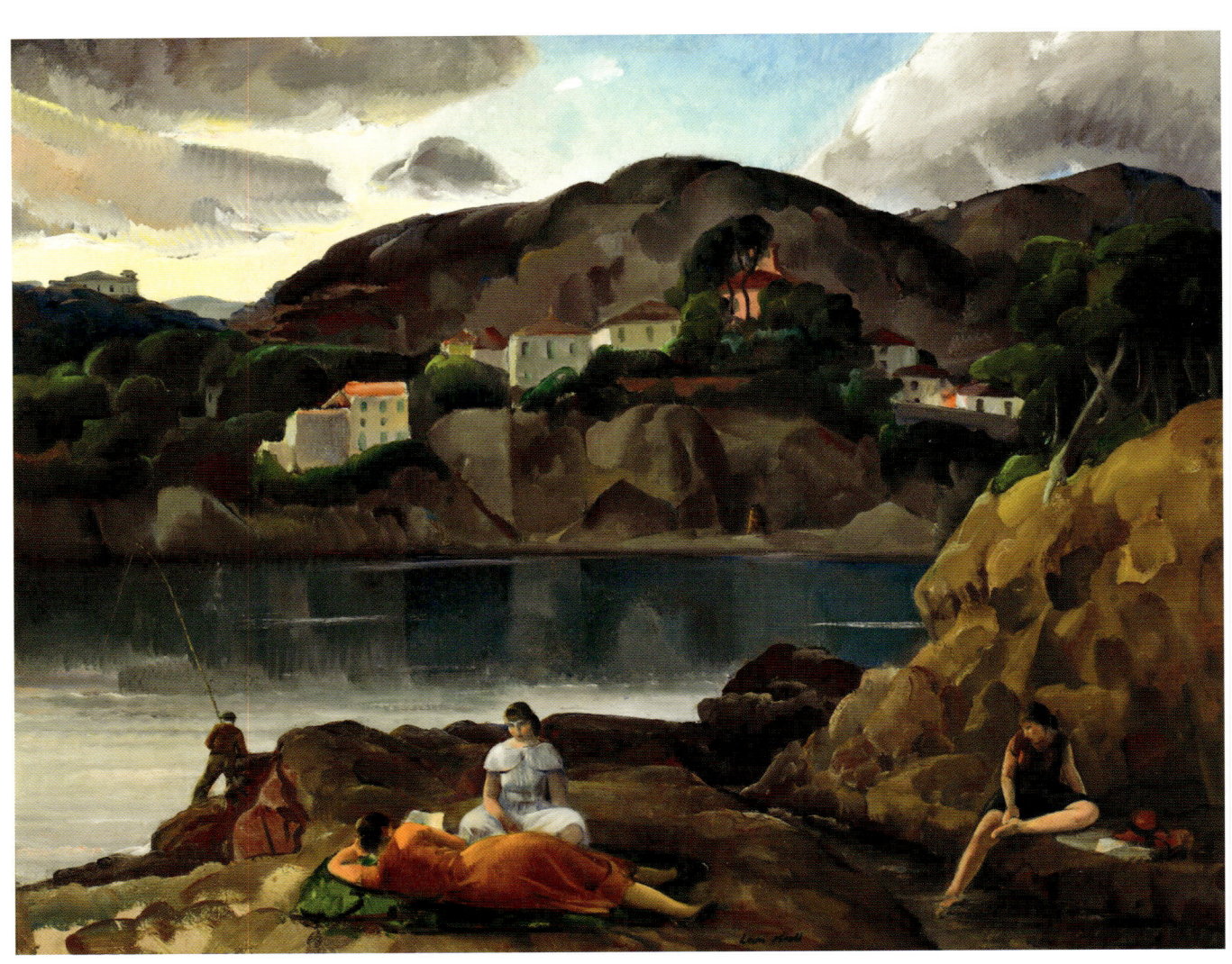

Leon Kroll
American, 1884-1974

St. Jean's Bay
1926, oil on canvas
27 ½ x 35 ½ in. (69.9 x 90.2 cm)
Gift of William H. and Eloise R. Chandler
PA-83-123

Leon Kroll worked as a painter, lithographer, art critic and teacher. Born in New York City, he first studied at the Art Students League under the Impressionist painter John Henry Twachtman and in 1906-1908 enrolled in classes at the National Academy of Design. Kroll traveled to Paris in 1908, studied at the Académie Julian and exhibited in several major Paris exhibitions. While in Paris, Kroll came under the influence of the Impressionists and was especially drawn toward the subtle planes of color in Paul Cézanne's landscapes. Upon his return from Europe in 1910, Kroll exhibited 85 paintings completed in France in a critically and financially successful one-person show.

Settled in New York City, Kroll painted landscapes, cityscapes, and still-life and figural subjects with bold colors and vigorous brushwork. His cityscapes attracted the attention of Realist painter George Bellows who introduced Kroll to Robert Henri and members of his Ashcan School of painters such as John Sloan, Everett Shinn and George Luks, among others. Kroll shared with Bellows, Henri and their closest associates an interest in painting from life and capturing the rhythms of everyday experience. Throughout his career, Kroll maintained a balance between the teachings of the academies, influences from progressive European artists, and the ideas promoted by Henri and the New York Realists.

Painted during Kroll's return trip to France in 1925-1927, *St. Jean's Bay* demonstrates his merging of idealized figures and romanticized landscape with the style of Cézanne. Kroll's statuesque men and women reflect his interest in Classicism and the sculpture of ancient Greece and Rome. Typical of Kroll's style is the fragmentation of forms and the use of hatching and patches of color as a means to define space and create distinctions between natural elements. Although the title of this painting cites a specific locale in France, the landscape represents a composite of views. This process of selection and amalgamation was motivated by Kroll's embrace of traditional modes of landscape painting promoted by the academies that advocated the representation of ideal types based on the best individual features drawn from many disparate sources.

DR

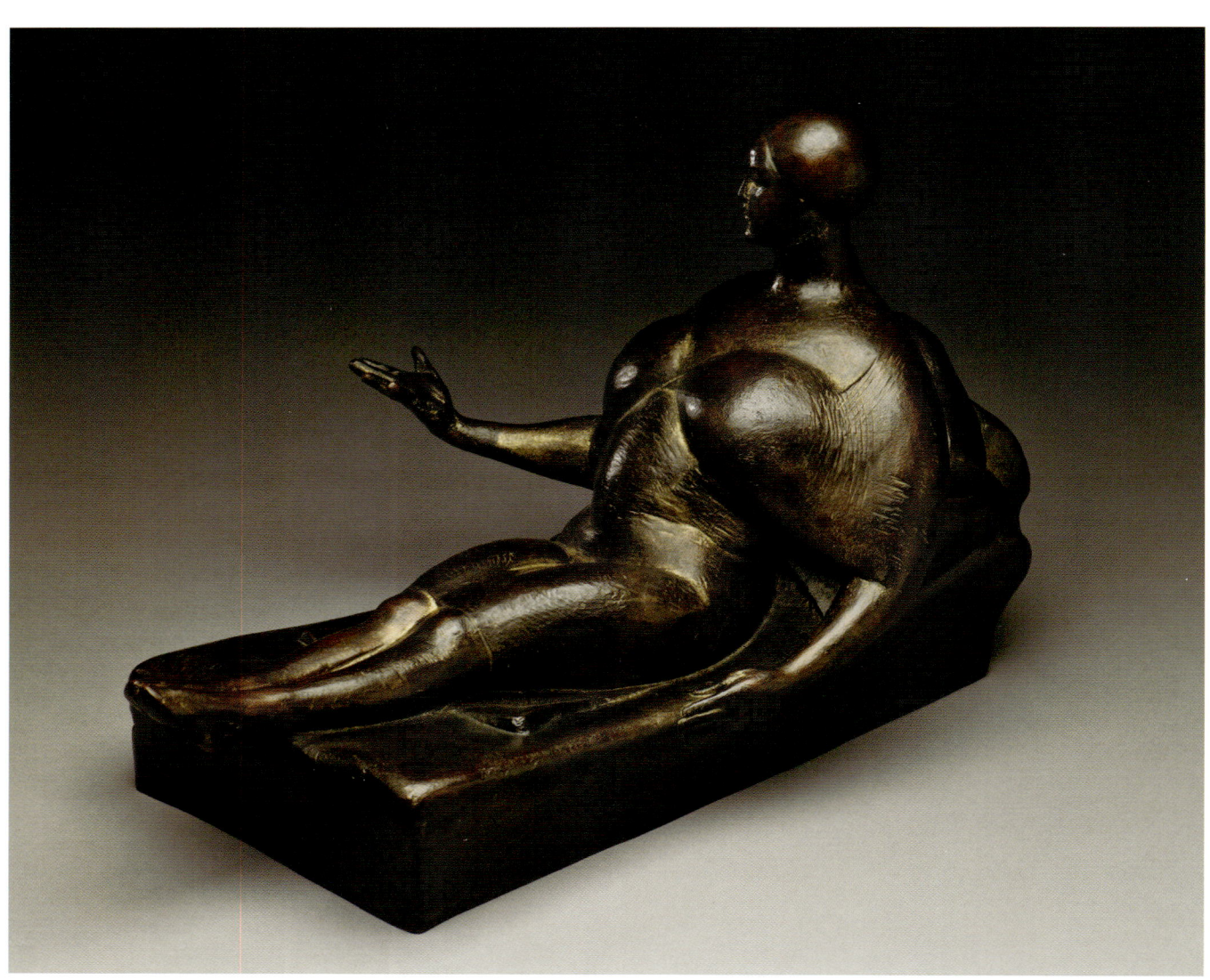

GASTON LACHAISE
American, born France, 1882-1935

WOMAN ON A COUCH
1928 (cast 1999), bronze
9 ⅜ x 16 ¾ x 10 ¾ in. (23.8 x 42.5 x 27.3 cm)
Gift of The Lachaise Foundation
in honor of Budd Harris Bishop
1999.7

Gaston Lachaise is most renowned for his sculptures of women—standing, walking, seated or reclining—who are rendered as goddesses and images of exalted womanhood. Born in Paris, Lachaise was the son of a master cabinet-maker and wood carver. He studied sculpture at both the École Bernard Palissy and the Académie Nationale des Beaux-Arts and exhibited at four annual Paris Salons before immigrating to the United States in 1906. Settled first in Boston and then New York City, Lachaise became a citizen in 1916. The following year he married Isabel Dutaud Nagle, his lifelong inspiration for sculptures of voluptuous women.

In Boston, Lachaise worked for H. H. Kitson, an academic sculptor of military monuments. In 1912 he moved to New York City and worked as an assistant to the sculptor Paul Manship. Lachaise was a prodigious sculptor, creating a body of complex and varied works, including single figures, torsos, portrait busts, bas-relief, fragments and figural groups. His figurative works are characterized by their simplified form and his unique ability to integrate physical description with an idealized approach to the human body.

Lachaise treated the subject of the reclining woman early in his career, and later it became one of his favorite subjects. One of his earliest reclining sculptures is a portrait of his mother seated on a chair (around 1903). In *Woman on a Couch*, Lachaise captured his wife Isabel in a moment of informal repose while reading, her hand and fingers outstretched as though holding an open book. The figure's regal pose conveys a feeling of dignity and grandeur and endows the sculpture with a sense of monumentality despite its modest scale. The inclusion of furniture, in this case a couch, was a common motif in late 19th-century French academic sculpture and was employed occasionally by Lachaise.

DR

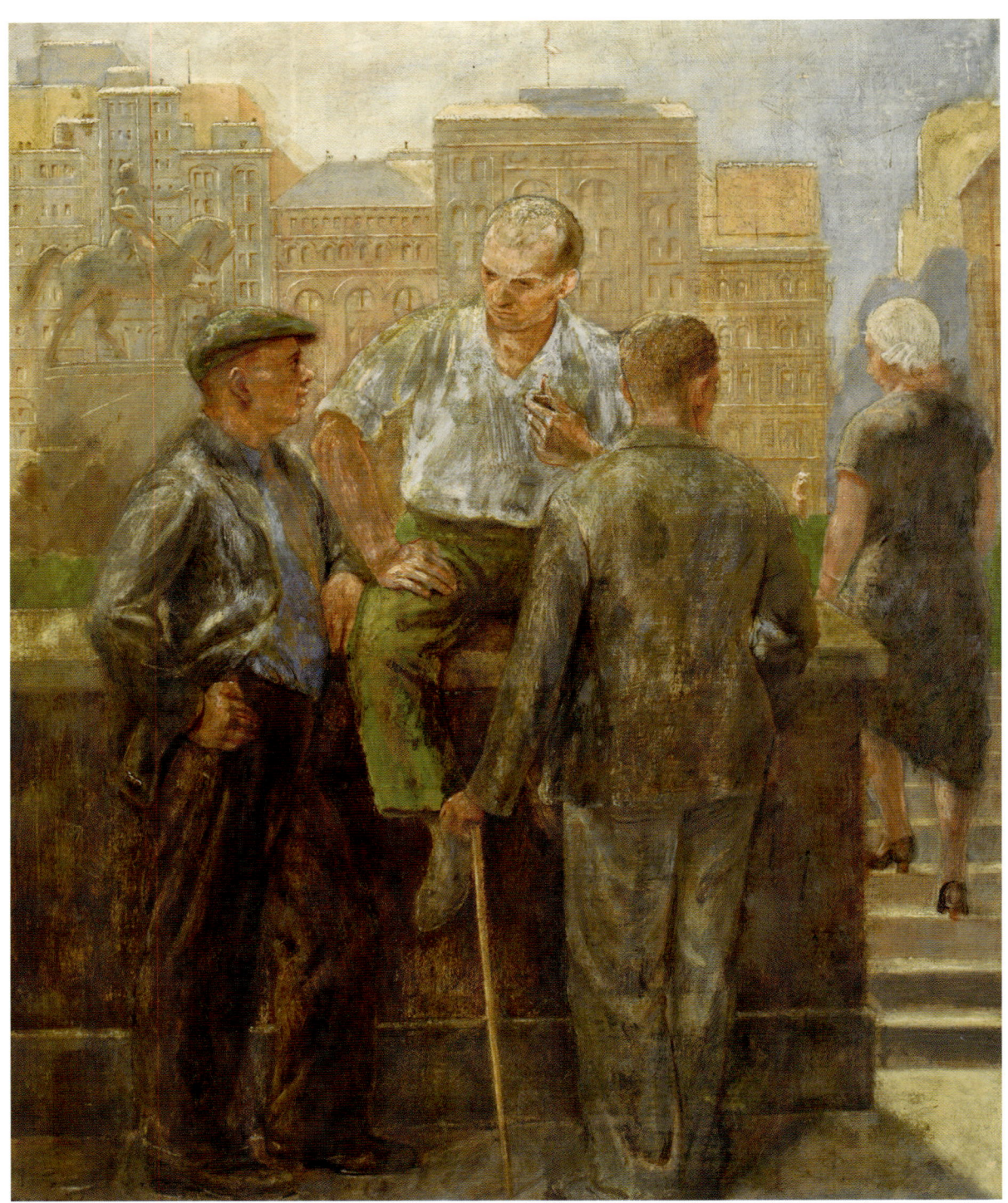

Isabel Bishop
American, 1902-1988

Three Men at Union Square
c. 1930, oil on canvas, mounted over Masonite
24 ¼ x 20 in. (61.6 x 50.8 cm)
Museum purchase, funds provided by an
anonymous donor and the Caroline Julier and
James G. Richardson Acquisition Fund
2000.10

Isabel Bishop enjoyed a reputation as a keen observer of ordinary, fleeting moments in New York City's Union Square. Born in Cincinnati, Ohio, and raised in Detroit, Michigan, Bishop left home in 1918 at age sixteen to study illustration at the New York School of Applied Design for Women. She also attended the Art Students League, where her teachers included Realist painters Guy Pène du Bois and Kenneth Hayes Miller, who encouraged her to draw inspiration from the street life of New York City. Accompanied by Miller and the artist Reginald Marsh, Bishop traveled to Europe in 1931 to study art, especially the works of the Old Masters.

Bishop possessed considerable drafting skills and a facility in massing and organizing forms that endowed her subjects with dignity and monumentality. Her influences included 17th-century Dutch and Flemish painters such as Adriaen Brouwer and Peter Paul Rubens who excelled at painting scenes with large groups of figures. She worked in a careful and painstaking manner, erasing and reworking her subjects, often spending a year or more on a single painting.

Bishop, like other artists concentrating on the urban scene, sought beauty and artfulness in everyday life. One of her favorite subjects was the daily routines of people who lived and worked in and around Lower Manhattan's Union Square, where she had a studio. In *Three Men at Union Square*, Bishop constructed a theatrical backdrop for her narrative. The specific locale is identified in the title of the work and is reinforced by the inclusion of a recognizable landmark in this well-known square—Henry Kirke Brown's 1856 equestrian statue of George Washington seen in the middle ground. In the foreground, three men are engaged in conversation as one of them is distracted by a fashionably dressed young woman ascending the stairs. A bright blue sky bathes the scene in golden light and contributes to the picture's optimistic view of life in Depression-era New York City.

DR

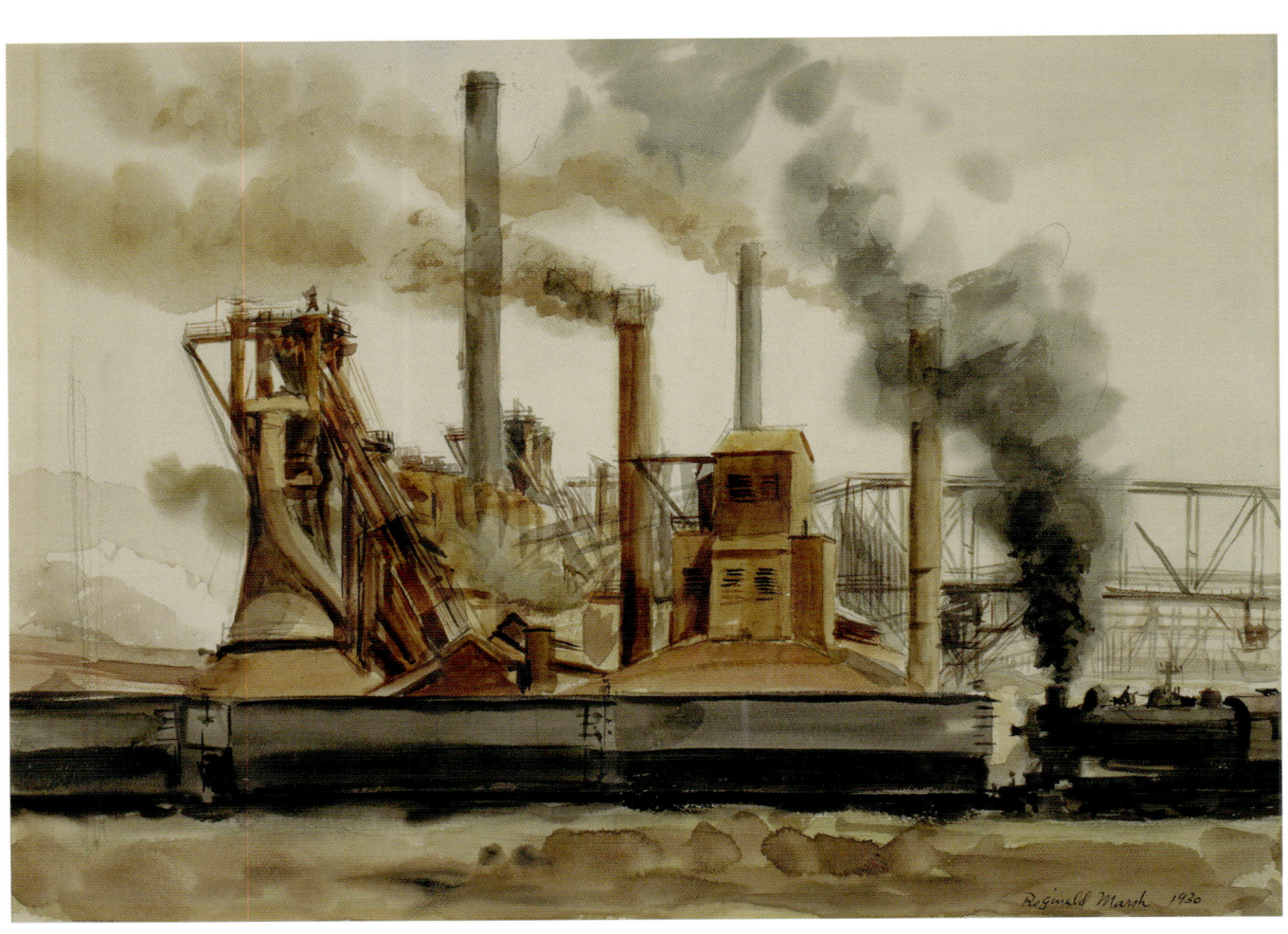

Reginald Marsh

American, born France, 1898-1954

Industrial Landscape with Railroad Cars

1930, pencil and watercolor on paper
14 x 20 in. (35.6 x 50.8 cm)
Museum purchase, funds provided
by Dr. and Mrs. David A. Cofrin
© 2009 Estate of Reginald Marsh / Art Students
League, New York / Artists Rights Society (ARS),
New York
2006.6

Reginald Marsh is best known for his depictions of the physical and social life of New York City, focusing on women shoppers, subways, rail yards, Coney Island, the Bowery, and the New York City waterfront and skyline. He also captured the urban pace of the city in the 1930s in his scenes of crowds at the beach, the movies, on the streets, in breadlines and dance halls. Born in Paris to American parents, Reginald Marsh studied at Yale Art School before moving to New York City and working as a freelance illustrator for several newspapers and magazines, including the New York *Daily News* and *The New Yorker*. Further education at the Art Students League under John Sloan and Kenneth Hayes Miller emphasized figure drawing, perspectival composition and narrative content.

In 1925 Marsh made the first of many trips to Europe, where he studied and made drawings after Old Master paintings. His study and refinement of drawing continued throughout his life and even led him to take classes in anatomy at Cornell Medical School and Columbia University. A born draftsman, he was adept at capturing essential forms within three-dimensional pictorial space. Even in his oil paintings and watercolors, Marsh often seemed to draw with a brush, building up forms with superb graphic skill.

Industrial Landscape with Railroad Cars deals with two of Marsh's favorite themes—locomotives (one dominates the foreground) and bridges (visible in the distance). Here, Marsh beautifully captures the grime and dirt of this industrial landscape in the thick smoke billowing from the passing train and the tall smokestacks of the factory. Marsh's paintings were based on firsthand observation of contemporary life in New York City. He walked the streets continually, seldom without a sketchbook, and frequented every neighborhood, sketching all aspects of the city.

DR

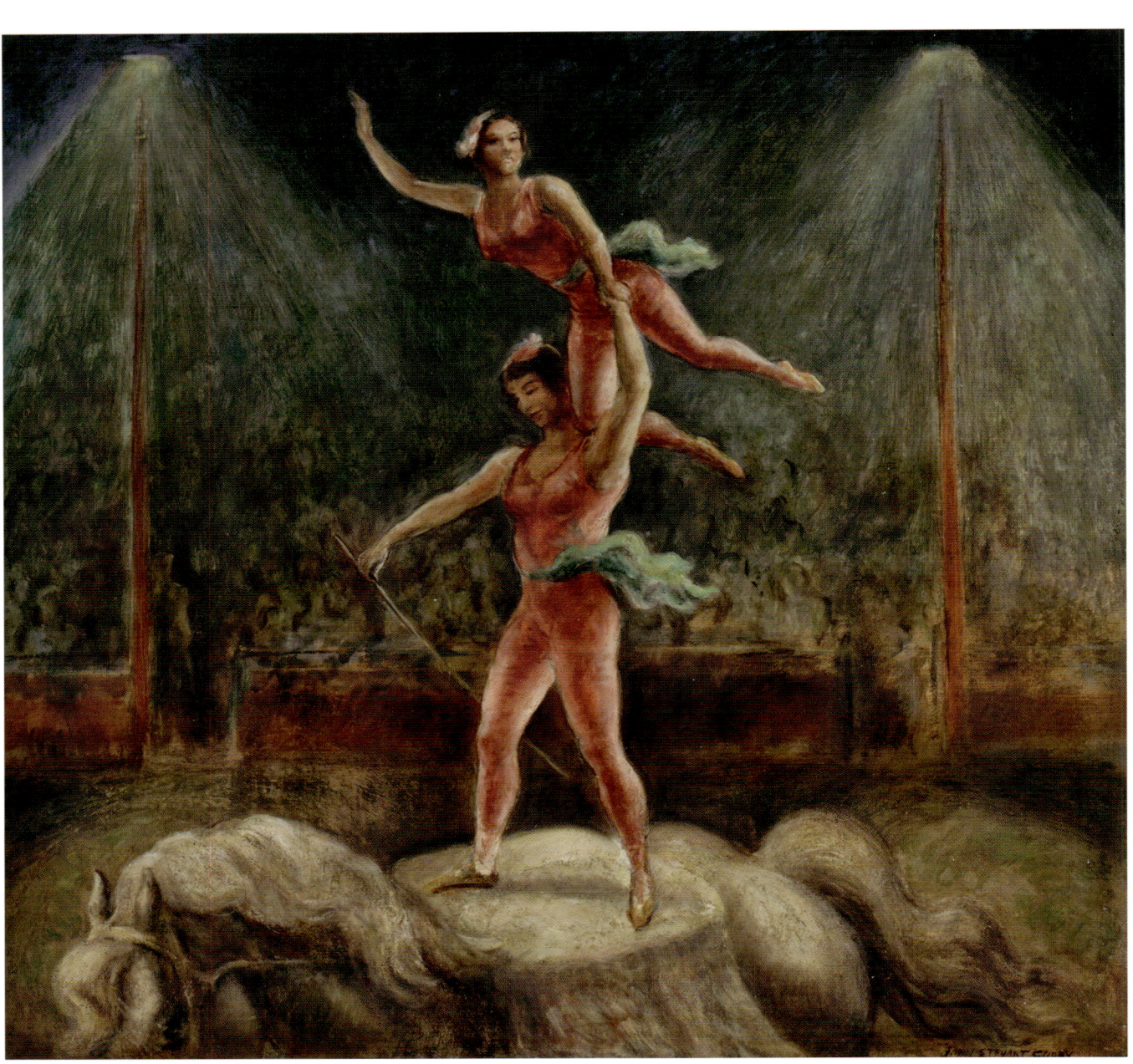

John Steuart Curry
American, 1897-1946

The Rieffenach Sisters
1932, oil and tempera on board
22 x 24 in. (55.9 x 61 cm)
Gift of Eloise R. Chandler in memory of
William H. Chandler
Image permission courtesy of the
artist's estate, Kiechel Fine Art
1993.20.1

John Steuart Curry had a long-standing interest in recording the regional and local character of the American landscape, its architecture and people. Curry's work responded to a desire for a native art at a time when the country was experiencing acute sociological and economic changes as a result of the Great Depression. Along with painters Thomas Hart Benton and Grant Wood, Curry led the Regionalist movement of the 1930s and 1940s, capturing unique and powerful images of America's heartland.

Curry was born in Dunavant, Kansas, to a hardworking farming family. Following high school, he enrolled at the Kansas City Art Institute in 1916 and the Art Institute of Chicago, where he studied for two years from 1916-1918. The following year, he began a seven-year period working as a magazine illustrator for Harvey Dunn in New Jersey. In 1926 Curry studied briefly in Paris with Russian academician, Basil Schoukhaieff. Following his return to the United States in 1927, Curry began to paint scenes of rural America that firmly established his reputation as a painter of the American Scene.

Already known for his paintings of rugged, frontier people, Curry turned to another American folk subject in 1932—the circus. Since his youth, Curry had been fascinated with the circus and enjoyed the spectacle of performances he had witnessed at rural county fairs. This interest inspired him to tour New England with the Ringling Brothers and Barnum & Bailey Circus in April 1932. Based on this experience, Curry created a series of sketches, watercolors and paintings that captured the rich pageantry of carnival life. *The Rieffenach Sisters* depicts a sister duo of horseback riders who were billed on posters as "riding beauties of international fame." *The Rieffenach Sisters* exemplifies the qualities found in much of Curry's art, most notably dramatic excitement, activated space and sculptural articulation.

DR

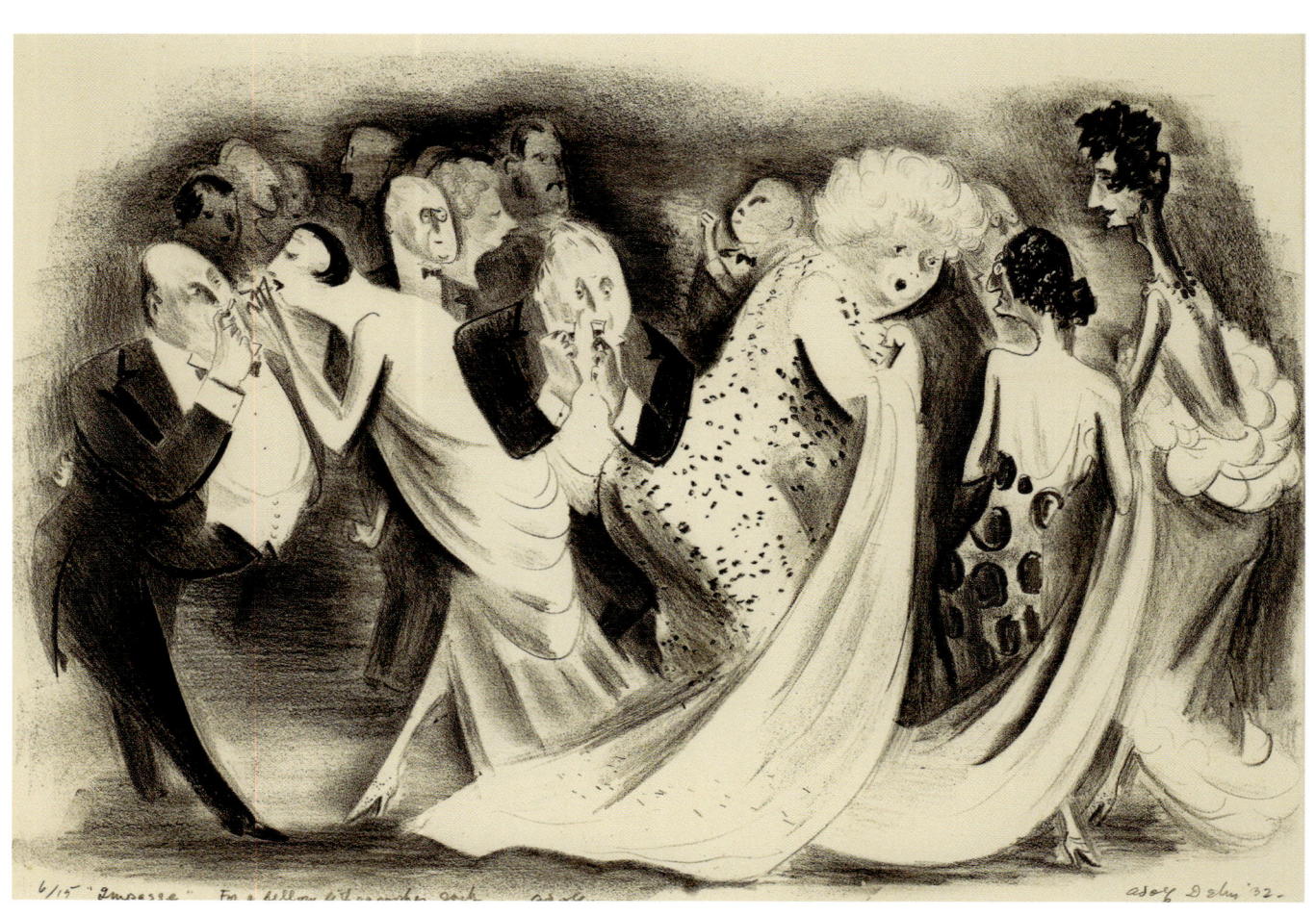

6/15 "Impasse"   For a fellow to remember Jack   Adolf Dehn '32.

ADOLF ARTHUR DEHN
American, 1895-1968

IMPASSE
1932, lithograph
image: 10 x 14 ⅞ in. (printmark) (25.4 x 37.8 cm)
sheet: 10 ⅛ x 15 in. (25.7 x 38.1 cm)
Gift of John Taylor Arms
PR-72-18

Adolf Dehn enjoyed great success both as a landscape watercolorist and a chronicler of American urban and rural life in the Depression. Active as a painter and lithographer, Dehn had a remarkable genius for caricature and a keen interest in the observation of life. Born and raised in rural Minnesota, Dehn began studies at the Minneapolis Institute of Art in 1915 and the Art Students League in New York in 1917. While a student at the Art Students League, he came to know radical artists and writers who contributed to important socialist periodicals such as *The Masses* and *The Liberator*. These friendships deepened his political consciousness and inspired his desire to become a satirical artist.

Dehn traveled in Europe from 1921 to 1929, working almost exclusively as a lithographer. The cafés, opera houses and parks of Vienna, Paris and Berlin provided ample subject matter for his satirical prints and drawings that often targeted the smugness and pretensions of the well-to-do. Settled in New York in late 1929, Dehn continued his interest in caricature of high and low life. In lively and humorous lithographs and drawings, he captured the vibrancy of the Manhattan skyline, nightclubs and cafés as well as lyrical views of Central Park and rural New York. These themes responded to the American Regionalist emphasis on subject matter drawn from the artist's everyday environment.

Impasse dates to the early years following Dehn's return to New York and captures an amusing and lively scene of local nightlife, showing his great mastery of form and space, and the utmost economy of line. With his remarkable powers of observation and keen sense of humor, Dehn describes a wide array of facial expressions and emotions in *Impasse*, from the look of amusement of the gentleman trying to squeeze between two well-dressed ladies, to the confusion of the heavy-set woman in the center and the smugness of other figures in the crowd.

DR

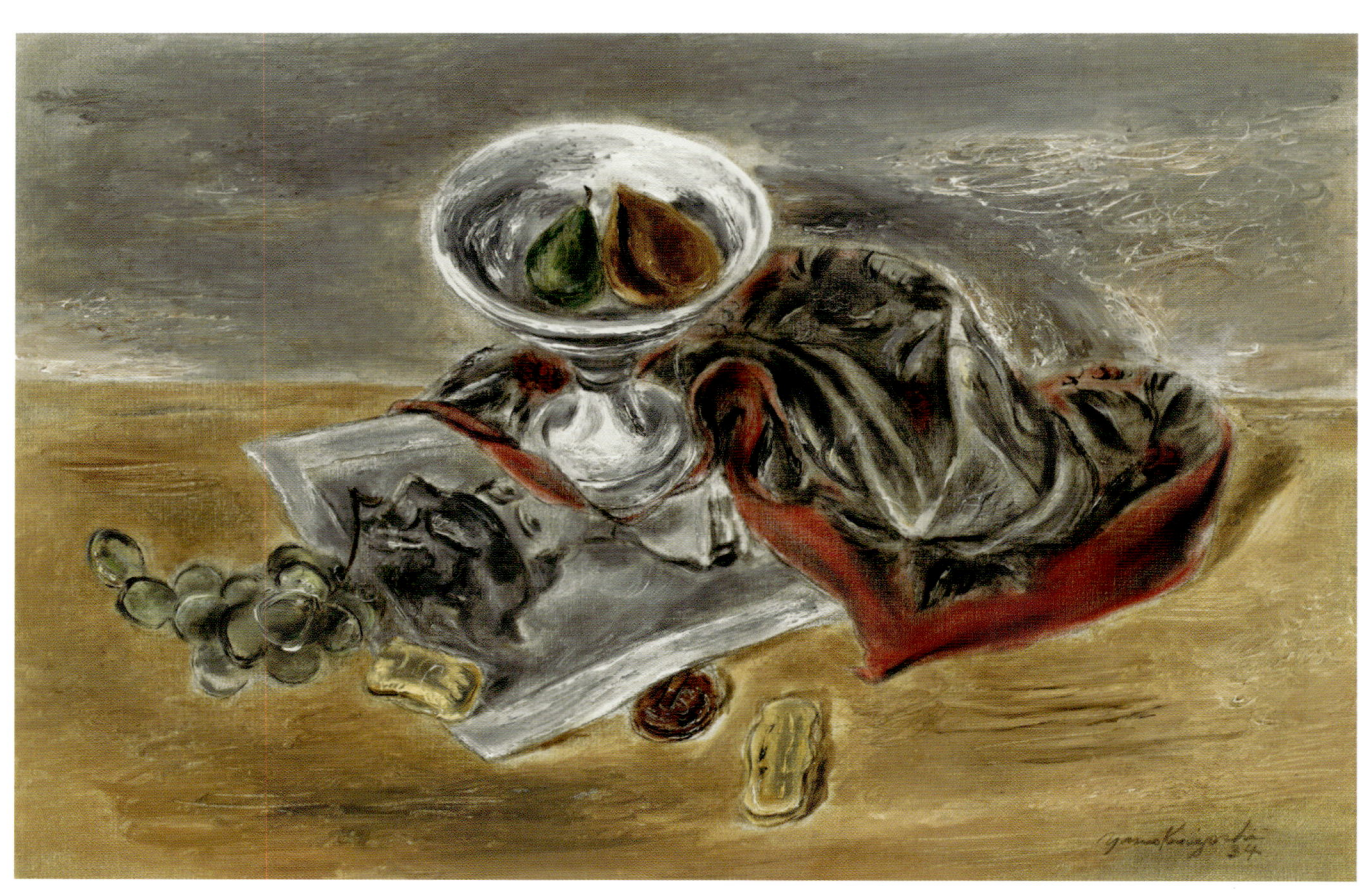

Yasuo Kuniyoshi
American, born Japan, 1889-1953

Untitled
1934, oil on canvas
18 ¼ x 28 ¼ in. (46.4 x 71.8 cm)
Gift of Eloise Ricks Chandler
Art © Estate of Yasuo Kuniyoshi/
Licensed by VAGA, New York, NY
1995.5.7

The American painter, photographer and printmaker Yasuo Kuniyoshi was known for his paintings and prints of still-life subjects, female circus performers and nudes. Kuniyoshi left his native Japan in 1906 and immigrated to the United States at age sixteen. For the next four years he worked at menial, poorly paid jobs on the West Coast. He developed an interest in drawing and studied at the Los Angeles School of Art and Design from 1907 to 1910. Kuniyoshi then moved to New York and enrolled in the National Academy of Design, studying with Realist painter Robert Henri, and the Art Students League, where he was a student of Kenneth Hayes Miller from 1916 to 1920. Kuniyoshi traveled to Europe in 1925 and 1928 and to Japan in 1931. During the Depression, he supplemented his income by working as a commercial photographer.

In his work, Kuniyoshi often combined elements of traditional Japanese painting and references to works by well-known American and European modernist artists. In addition, Kuniyoshi was drawn to early American folk art which shared stylistic elements, such as flattened perspective, with traditional Japanese woodblock prints. In this untitled still life, Kuniyoshi relies on his signature palette of subdued earth tones. The tilted picture plane recalls Japanese *Ukiyo-e* woodblock prints. The photographic image partially concealed by the base of the bowl is a reproduction of *Woman with a Hat* by French painter Henri Matisse, an artist Kuniyoshi greatly admired.

Kuniyoshi went on to achieve recognition in the 1930s and 1940s as a leading American Realist and was an important teacher at the Art Students League. Following the bombing of Pearl Harbor in December 1941 by the Japanese, Kuniyoshi's ethnicity exposed him to anti-Japanese sentiments as his legal status changed from "resident alien" to "enemy alien." At the time of his death in 1953, Kuniyoshi's citizenship papers were still in the process of completion. Kuniyoshi's life and art exemplify the successful cross-fertilization of Japanese and American cultures. By referencing American, European and traditional Japanese art in his work, Kuniyoshi sought to fuse influences from both the East and the West into a new cultural identity.

DR

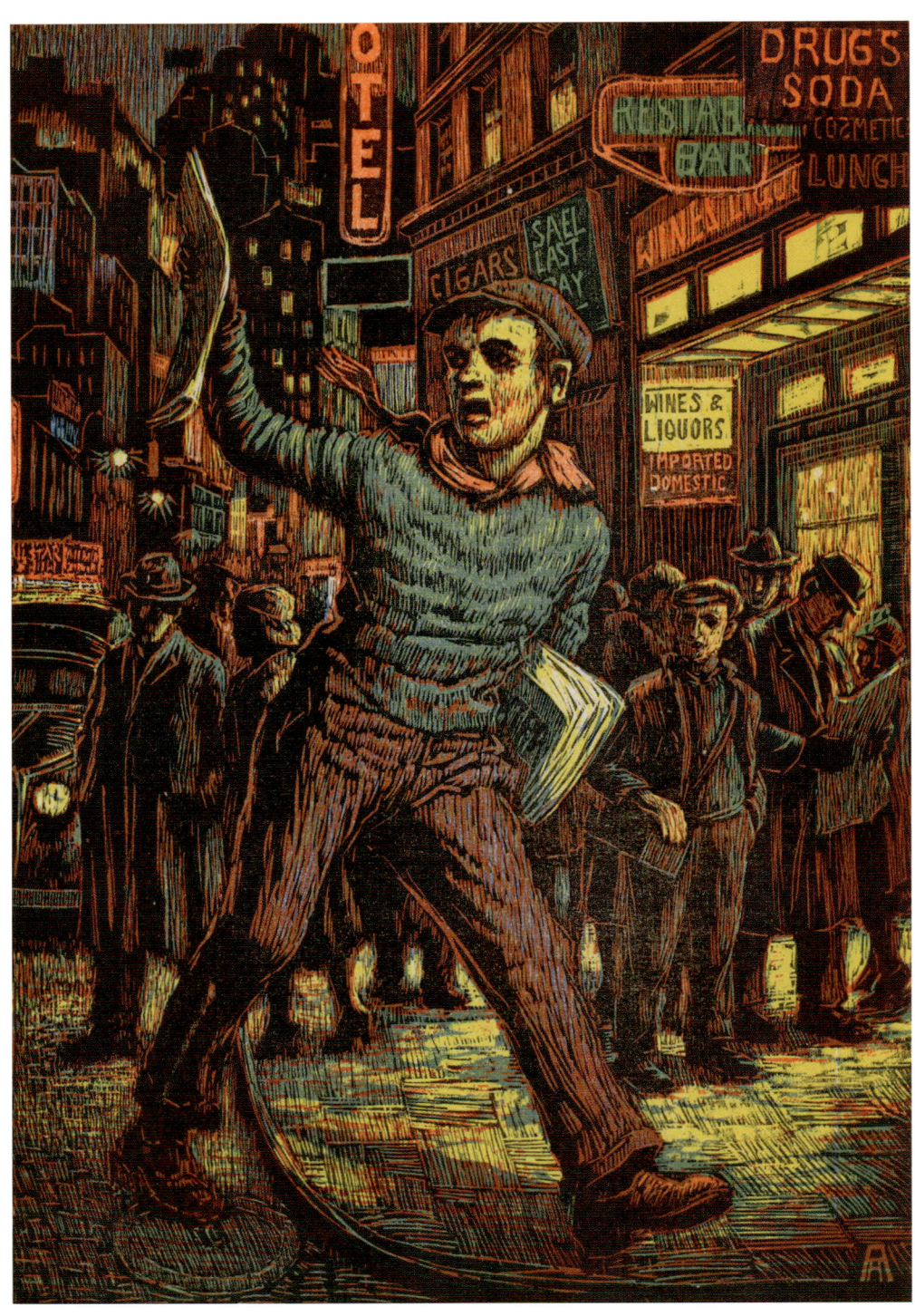

ALBERT ABRAMOVITZ

American, born Russia, 1879-1963

WUXTRY!

c. 1935-1939, color woodcut
image: 14 ⅛ x 9 ¹⁵⁄₁₆ in. (35.7 x 25.2 cm)
sheet: 18 x 13 in. (45.7 x 33 cm)
Gift of Dr. and Mrs. Corbin S. Carnell
in memory of E. Muriel Adams
1992.11.3

Albert Abramovitz is best known for his paintings and prints commissioned by the Works Progress Administration's Federal Art Project (WPA/FAP). Established in 1935, the Federal Art Project had two goals—to provide work relief for artists and to supply works of art for public places. Prints were identified as a valuable tool for addressing this goal of supplying art for the people, because they could be printed in multiples and would presumably reach a larger viewing public. A total of sixteen workshops located in nine states made up the Graphics Division of the FAP. The first and largest of these was established in New York City. Together, these workshops employed more than 250 artists and produced nearly 11,000 designs from which more than 300,000 prints were pulled. Printed in small editions, usually numbering 25, the prints were allocated to tax-supported institutions such as museums, libraries, schools, hospitals and prisons.

Encouraged by the WPA to observe and record popular culture, printmakers also were concerned with representing important societal issues of the day, especially the effects of economic upheaval. Like many WPA artists, Abramovitz addressed the hardships of the Depression such as homelessness and unemployment, and included images of everyday people. The title of this print is taken from the typical newsboy's cry: Wuxtry! Wuxtry! or Extra! Extra! The curious misspellings on the storefronts in the background such as "sael last day" and "Restarant Bar" speak to the immigrant experience in New York City.

Abramovitz was born in Riva, Latvia, and received his artistic training at the Imperial Art School in Odessa and the Académie de la Grande Chaumière in Paris. Abramovitz immigrated to the United States in 1916 and lived in New York City and Los Angeles before settling down in Brooklyn, New York, in the 1930s. During the Depression, Abramovitz found employment in the graphics workshop of the New York City WPA/FAP, where he completed eighteen prints between November 1935 and April 1939.

DR

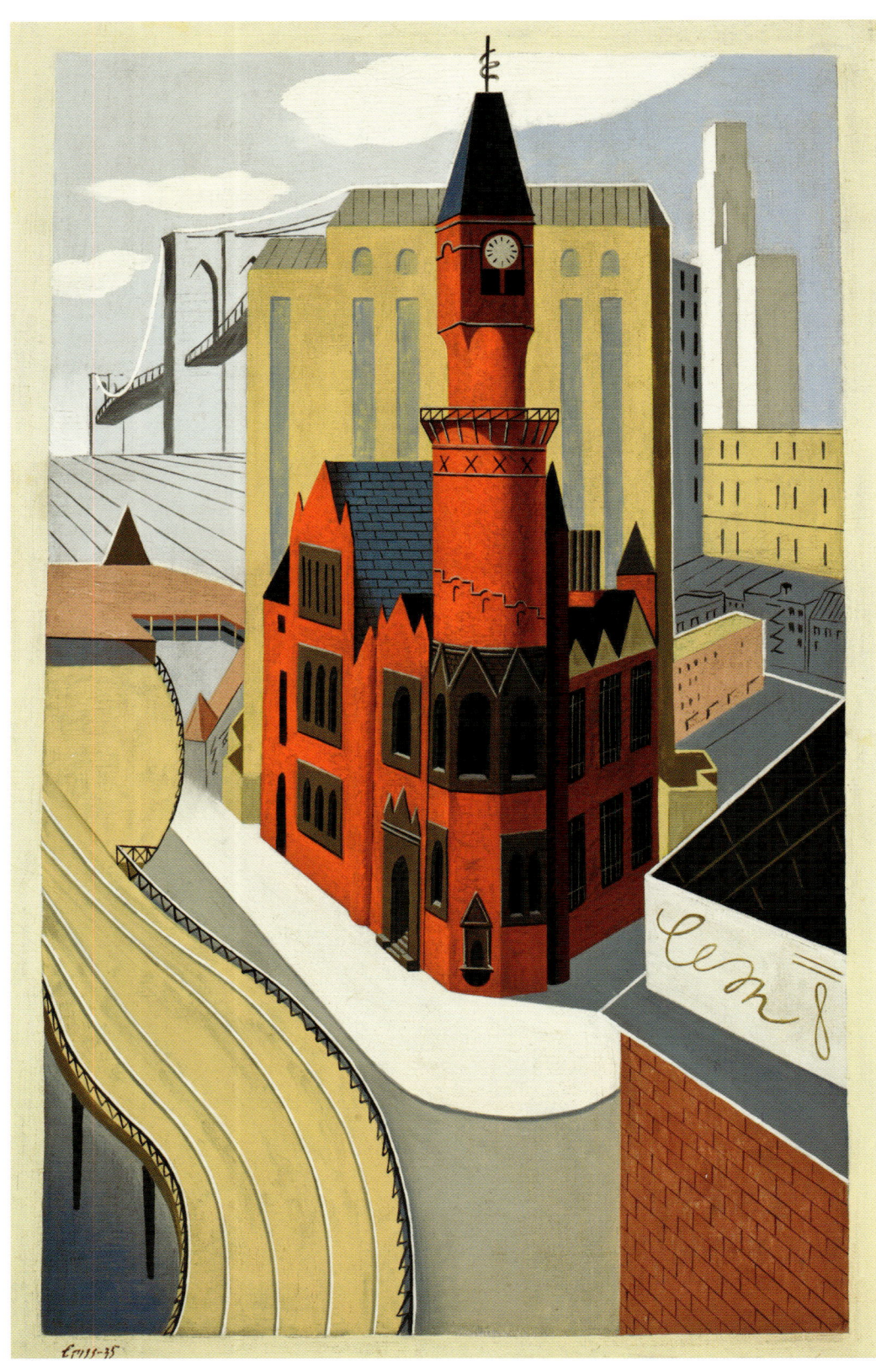

FRANCIS CRISS
American, born England, 1901-1973

JEFFERSON MARKET COURTHOUSE
1935, oil on canvas
35 ⅛ x 23 ⅛ in. (89.2 x 58.7 cm)
Gift of William H. and Eloise R. Chandler
PA-83-122

Francis Criss made a significant contribution to American art in the 1930s with his cityscapes and portraits that form a unique blend of Precisionism and Surrealism. Born in London into a Jewish family of Russian descent, Criss immigrated with his family to the United States in 1903 and settled in Philadelphia. Criss was educated at the Pennsylvania Academy of the Fine Arts (1917-1921) and the Art Students League in New York (1926-1929). Throughout the 1930s, Criss' work was included in major exhibitions of contemporary art, his paintings widely praised by critics. Beginning in the late 1930s, Criss became increasingly preoccupied with teaching and commercial art projects as a means to support his family, leaving little time for painting.

Jefferson Market Courthouse belongs to a series of three views depicting the courthouse at the corner of Sixth Avenue and West 10th Street in New York City. Each version shows Criss experimenting with different presentations of the same view with varying degrees of detail. In this work, Criss used hard edges and severe planes to depict the rectilinear forms of the city. Despite the absence of figures, Criss suggests the frenzy of urban life through the dynamic interplay of lines and shapes. His use of color and linear design give the painting a stark yet decorative quality. The calligraphic elements suggest the influence of Stuart Davis, who often included text in his work of the 1930s.

Jefferson Market Courthouse demonstrates Criss' merger of Precisionism with the vaguely disquieting imagery and fantastic composition that have come to be known as hallmarks of Surrealism. Like the precisionist paintings of artists such as Niles Spencer and Charles Sheeler, Criss' cityscapes embody crisp lines, simplified forms and flat color. An eerie stillness and quiet permeate much of Criss' work, drawing comparison with the cityscapes of Surrealist artists such as O. Louis Gugliemi or Peter Blume.

DR

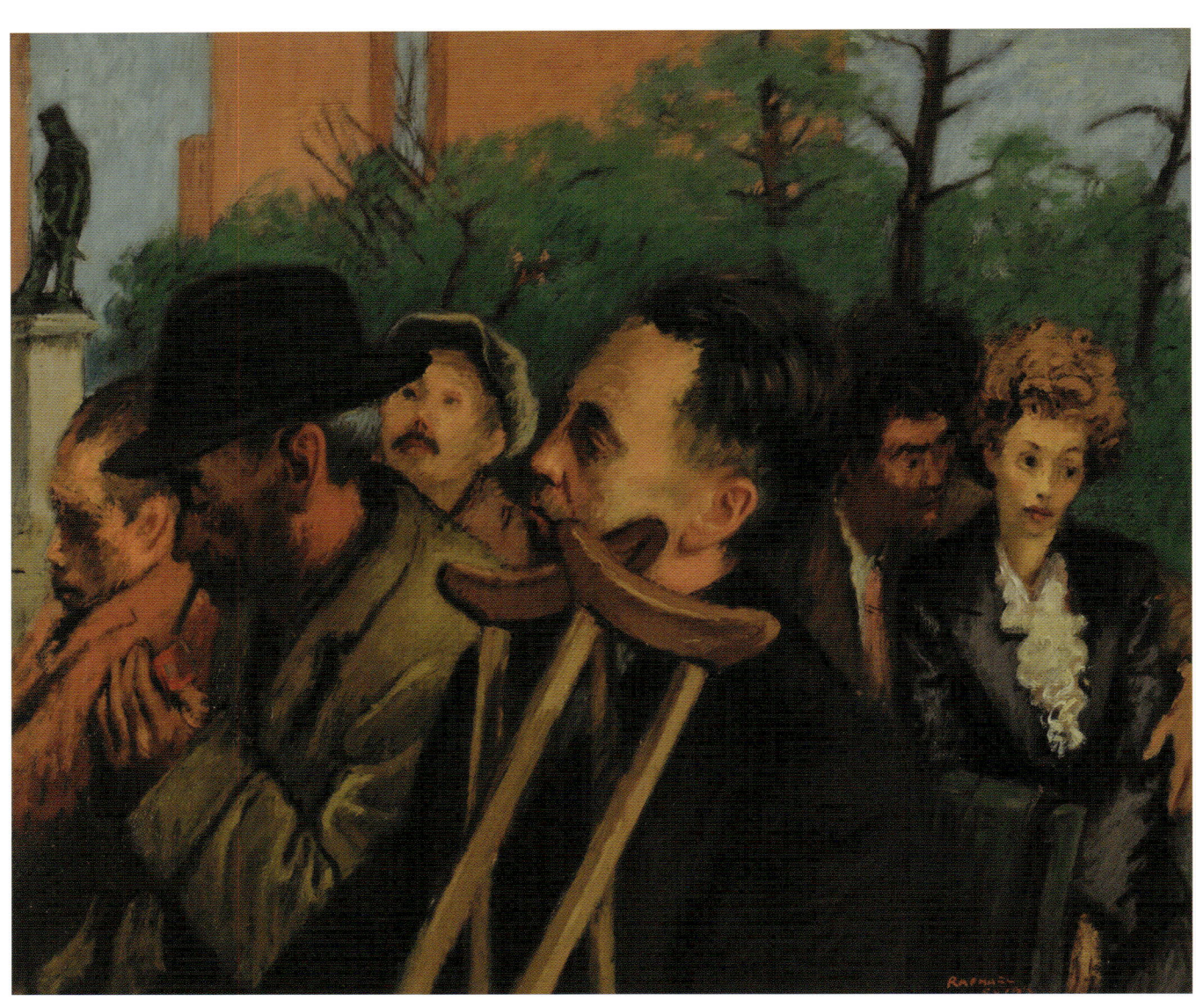

Raphael Soyer

American, born Russia, 1899-1987

In Washington Square

c. 1935, oil on canvas
20 x 24 ½ in. (50.8 x 62.2 cm)
Museum purchase by exchange, gift of
William H. and Eloise R. Chandler
© Raphael Soyer, courtesy of Forum Gallery,
New York, NY
1996.2

Raphael Soyer's urban subjects were motivated by his experiences in New York City after emigrating with his family from Russia in 1913. Soyer studied painting in New York at Cooper Union, the National Academy of Design and the Art Students League, where he also taught intermittently from 1933 until 1942. By the mid-1930s, he was a leading advocate of Realism and captured scenes of ordinary city life in his paintings, watercolors, lithographs and book illustrations. Along with other Realist artists such as Edward Hopper, Ben Shahn and Yasuo Kuniyoshi, Soyer founded *Reality*, an influential art magazine in the early 1950s.

Soyer and his brothers Moses and Isaac, who were also painters, were prominent in the Fourteenth Street School of painters working and living in Greenwich Village in the 1920s. This group of Social Realist artists was interested in capturing men and women in contemporary settings such as the parks, streets and subways of New York City. Yet unlike the painters of the Ashcan School several decades earlier, Soyer and his contemporaries approached these themes not as picturesque spectacle but with greater attention to social concerns. With his brother Moses, Raphael also painted for the Works Progress Administration's Federal Art Project in the 1930s. These projects included two murals painted in 1939 for the Kinglessing Post Office in Philadelphia.

As a witness to the Depression, Soyer explores the lives of the working class and the unemployed in his Social Realist works. *In Washington Square* depicts a crowded urban setting, yet the artist has taken great care to portray the individualized character of his subjects who often came from the rather poor neighborhoods where his family lived. In fact, these portraits are likely derived from his many studies of the unemployed executed during the Depression. Caught in moments of quiet self-absorption, his figures are conveyed with great sensitivity and humanity.

DR

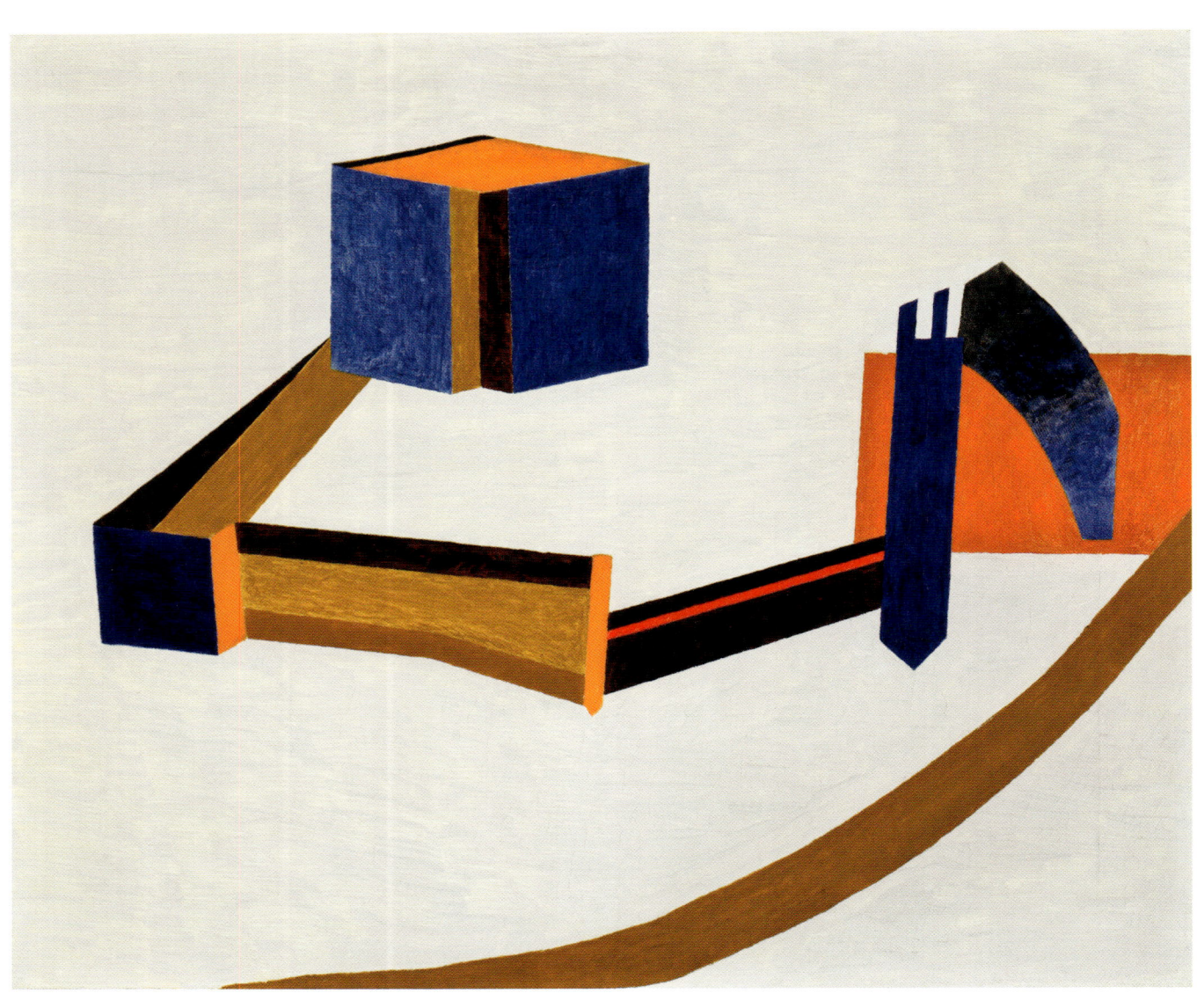

ALBERT E. GALLATIN
American, 1881-1952

KENILWORTH CASTLE-AERIAL VIEW
1937, oil on canvas
16 ¼ x 20 ¼ in. (41.3 x 51.4 cm)
Museum purchase by exchange, gift of
Helen Sawyer Farnsworth and
Louise H. Courtelis
2007.9

Albert E. Gallatin was an important promoter of abstract art in the United States at a time when Realism dominated American painting. Through his Gallery of Living Art, founded in 1927 at New York University, Gallatin introduced the American public to Cubism and other European avant-garde styles. Gallatin's museum also provided an important venue for the work of American abstract artists including his closest associates, George Morris, Suzy Frelinghuysen and Charles Shaw, also known as the Park Avenue Cubists.

Gallatin increasingly dedicated himself to painting his own abstractions in the 1930s. By the mid-1930s, he was incorporating Cubist elements in his paintings, featuring bright and sharply contrasting colors set against open backgrounds. In *Kenilworth Castle-Aerial View*, Gallatin transforms an observed subject (the castle) into an abstract composition, demonstrating his unique blending of representation with pure abstraction, and looks back to Picasso's work of the early 1900s. Instead of depicting the castle from a specific viewpoint, Gallatin presents different aspects of the castle simultaneously, its parts appearing as geometric planes.

When his father died in 1902, Gallatin inherited a family fortune developed by his great-grandfather and namesake, Albert Gallatin, who served as U.S. Secretary of the Treasury under Presidents Jefferson and Madison. Gallatin began collecting art in the 1920s and soon acquired works by Pablo Picasso, Georges Braque, Juan Gris, and Fernand Léger, among many others. In 1927, his Gallery of Living Art (later renamed the Museum of Living Art) became the first museum of contemporary art in the United States, predating the Museum of Modern Art by two years and the Whitney Museum of American Art by four. During his museum's fifteen-year existence, Gallatin also acquired works by American artists such as Alexander Calder, Ad Reinhardt and the Park Avenue Cubists. With its unparalleled quality and its location on Washington Square near many artists' studios, Gallatin's collection inspired a younger generation of artists. In 1975, Gallatin's Museum of Living Art was renovated and reopened as the Grey Art Gallery.

DR

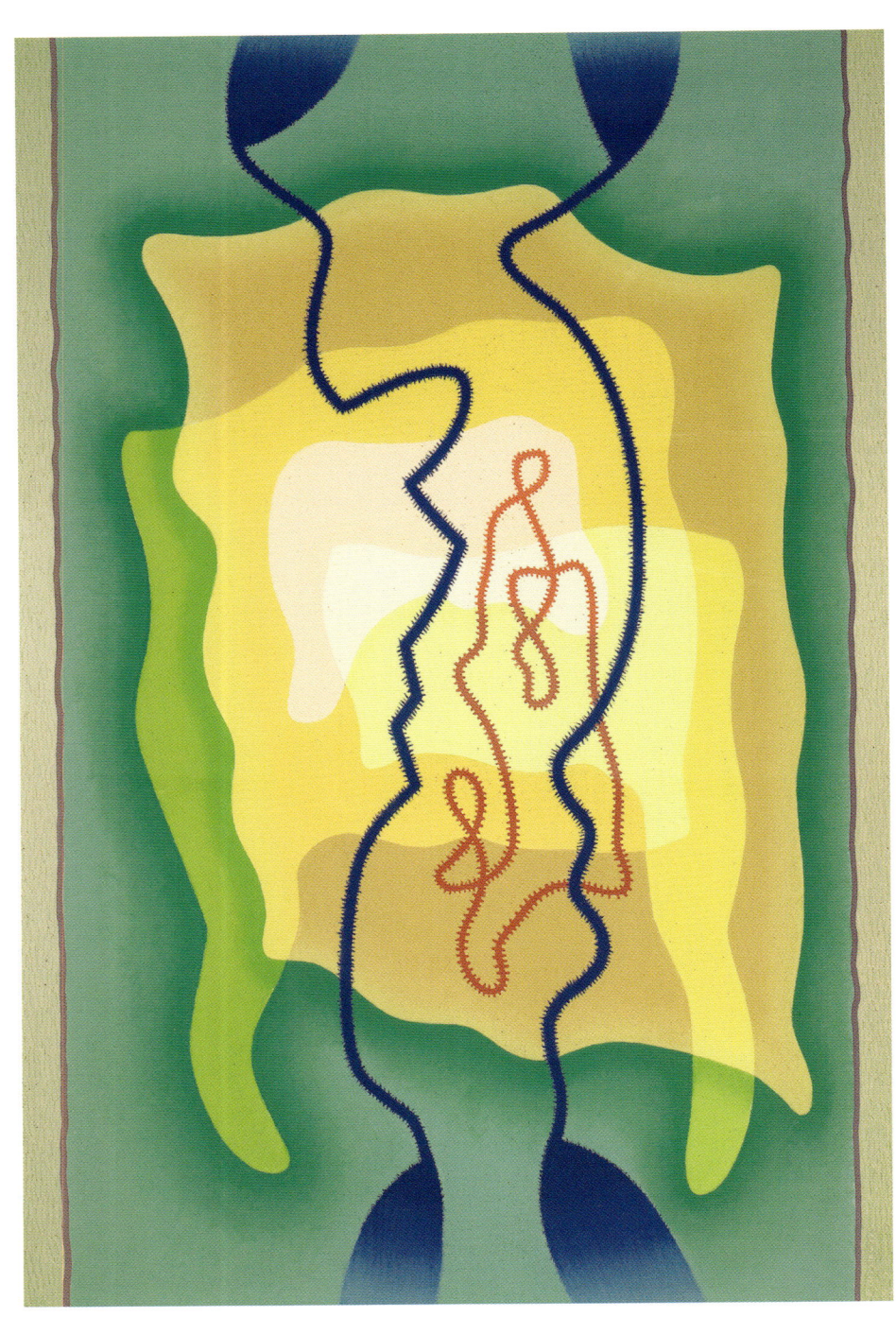

Raymond Jonson
American, 1891-1982

Transparencies with Blue Movement
1937, oil on canvas
35 ⅛ x 24 ⅛ in. (89.2 x 61.3 cm)
Gift of Charles Morris
PA-79-27

Raymond Jonson was a leader among American abstract artists and a proponent of modernism in New Mexico, where he was an influential teacher. Born in Iowa and raised in the Midwest and the West, Jonson moved to Chicago in 1910, where he enrolled at the Chicago Academy of Fine Arts and the Art Institute of Chicago. In 1913 the landmark Armory Show traveled from New York to Chicago, exposing Jonson to European modernism. He was especially drawn to the purely non-objective paintings of Russian avant-garde artist Wassily Kandinsky, who sought a universal language for expressing emotional experience. In 1924, Jonson moved to New Mexico and in 1934, accepted a teaching position at the University of New Mexico in Albuquerque.

Searching for a personal abstract style of his own that expressed universal order and harmony, Jonson experimented with various styles and techniques. Influenced by the art and artistic philosophy of Kandinsky, Jonson believed the purpose of art was to provide a vehicle for spiritual exploration and fulfillment rather than an illusionistic rendering of the physical world. By the mid-1930s, Jonson had developed a unique non-objective style marked by simplicity of design, expressive and harmonious color, and idiosyncratic imagery of floating organic shapes. In 1938, Jonson and fellow abstract artists working in New Mexico formed the Transcendental Painting Group which promoted purely non-objective art.

For Jonson, the sensations associated with light and color best expressed the spiritual forces and feelings that he sought to convey in his art. Music was another sensation that Jonson turned to as an abstract means of expression. *Transparencies with Blue Movement* illustrates Jonson's use of transparent shapes and luminous colors to give the illusion of shifting space and the interpenetration of forms. The rhythmic interplay of colors and forms creates a vibration of luminosity that for Jonson was akin to the rhythmic patterns found in music.

DR

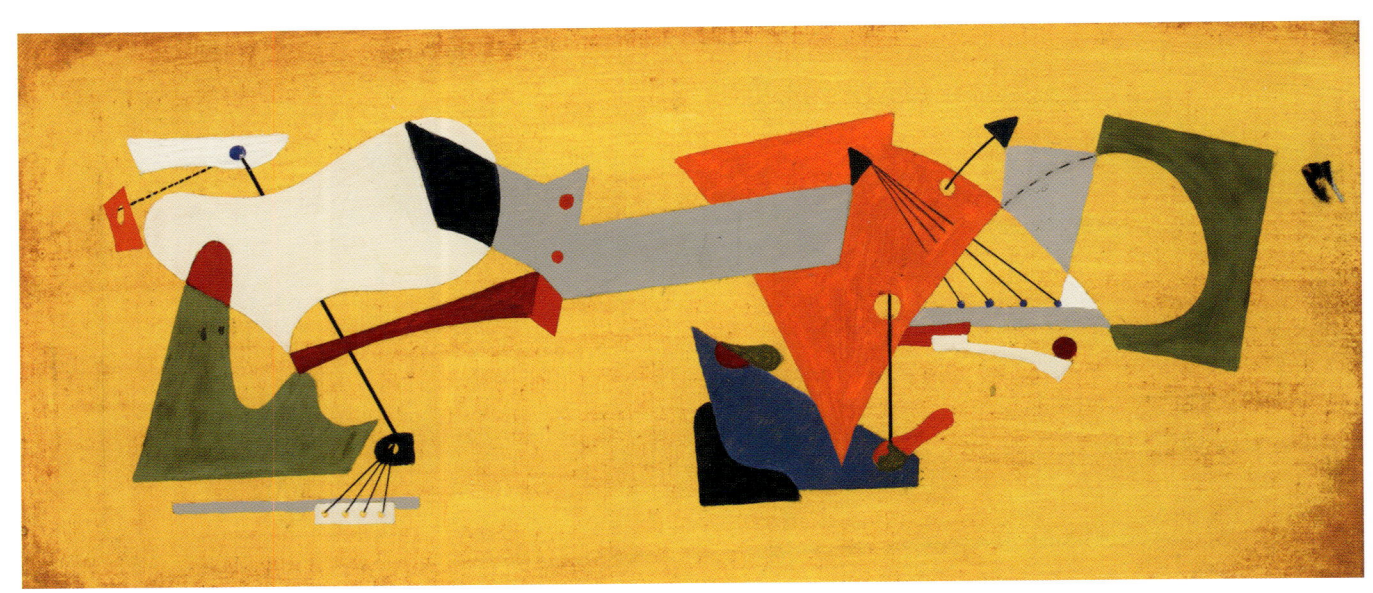

Esphyr Slobodkina
American, born Russia, 1908-2002

Mural Sketch #1
1937, oil on gessoed Masonite
9 ½ x 22 ½ in. (24.1 x 57.2 cm)
Museum purchase, funds provided by the
Caroline Julier and James G. Richardson
Acquisition Fund
2007.36

Esphyr Slobodkina was a pioneer in the development of abstract art in the United States. Born in Siberia, Slobodkina and her family were displaced during the civil war that followed the Bolshevik Revolution. At age thirteen, she left Russia with her mother and sister and joined a community of prosperous Russian émigrés in Harbin, Manchuria. She first learned design from her mother who established a dressmaking salon in Harbin. Intent on becoming an architect, Slobodkina studied engineering and architecture at the First Harbin Public Commercial School. Following her graduation in 1927, she and her sister joined their brother in New York City and enrolled at the National Academy of Design. In 1931 Slobodkina met fellow Russian artist Ilya Bolotowsky, whom she later married, and quickly absorbed abstract styles under his tutelage.

During the Depression, Slobodkina worked as a dressmaker and textile designer and incorporated this experience into her work. Her paintings from the 1930s reflect her interest in collage with flat, layered forms and carefully constructed arrangements inspired by textile designs. In the mid-1930s, Slobodkina joined the Artists' Union and found employment with the Works Progress Administration's Federal Art Project. By 1938 she had produced five mural sketches depicting interlocking shapes of bright colors. *Mural Sketch #1* represents one of these early mural projects for an unidentified site and shows Slobodkina's mature style with its basis in collage and assemblage. The flattened, abstracted style with interlocking forms and pure color reveals a highly refined sense of artistic style and astute sensitivity to color.

Slobodkina's unique style was embraced by members of the American Abstract Artists group founded in 1937. She exhibited regularly in their annual exhibitions and was a close associate of artist and gallery owner Albert Gallatin who gave Slobodkina her first one-person exhibition at his Gallery of Living Art in New York City in 1940. During her long career as an artist, Slobodkina created a substantial body of work that reflects her diverse interests in painting, collage, jewelry design and sculpture. She was also a noted author and illustrator of children's books such as her acclaimed book *Caps for Sale*, first published in 1940.

DR

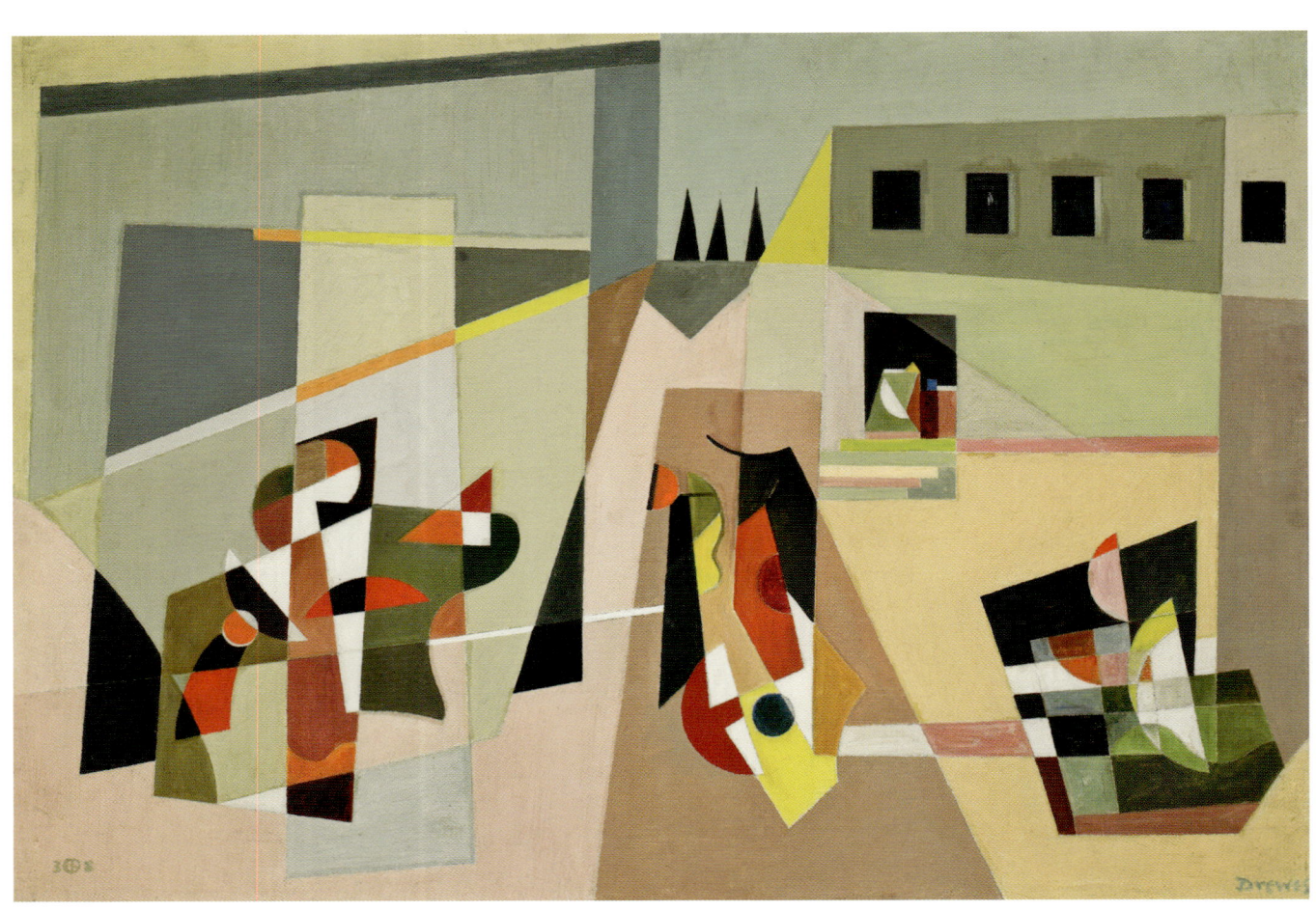

WERNER DREWES
American, born Germany, 1899-1985

COMPOSITION AFTER BOTTICELLI
1938, oil on canvas
20 x 30 in. (50.8 x 76.2 cm)
Museum purchase, funds provided
by Dr. and Mrs. David A. Cofrin with
additional funds provided by exchange,
gift of Helen Sawyer Farnsworth
2006.5

Werner Drewes was a renowned painter, printmaker and teacher who had an important impact on 20th-century American art. Born in Canig, Germany, Drewes served for two years on the Western Front as a soldier in the German Army. In 1921 he was admitted to the Staatliches Bauhaus, an art and architecture school in Germany, where he was a student of Paul Klee and Wassily Kandinsky. Under political pressure from the Nazis who strongly objected to abstract art, Drewes left Germany in 1930 and settled in New York City.

Drewes enjoyed a successful career as an artist and an influential teacher in New York. Employed by the Federal Art Project (FAP), Drewes taught printmaking at the Brooklyn Museum and also served as technical supervisor of the FAP's Graphics Division, based in New York City, from 1941 to 1942. Drewes was a founding member of the American Abstract Artists Group which promoted abstract art at a time when the realism of American Scene painting and Regionalism prevailed. In the 1930s, the American public and most art critics dismissed abstract art as merely decorative and concluded that art influenced by European abstraction was derivative and downright un-American.

As its title suggests, *Composition after Botticelli* was inspired by the paintings of the Florentine Renaissance master Alessandro Botticelli (1444/45-1510). Drewes' tribute to Botticelli is most likely a loose interpretation of the Italian painter's *Three Miracles of Saint Zenobius* (1500-1510) in the collection of the Metropolitan Museum of Art, New York. Drewes' composition bears striking similarities with Botticelli's panel painting depicting various scenes in the life of the 5th-century bishop of Florence. The two works share numerous compositional elements such as the three main groupings of figures before a perspectival architectural study, the horse in the middle foreground, the view into a darkened room in the right background, and the stand of cypress trees in the middle distance.

DR

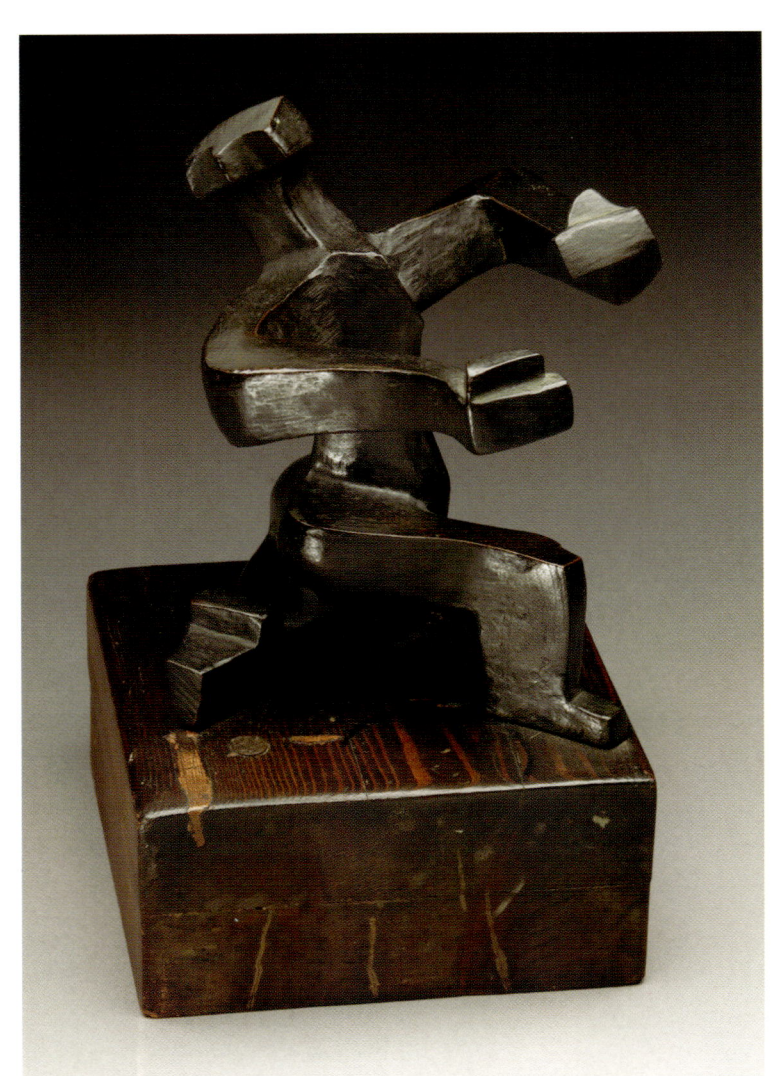

Louise Nevelson
American, born Ukraine, 1899-1988

Untitled
c. 1940, bronze
8 ¾ x 9 ½ x 7 in. (22.2 x 24.1 x 17.8 cm) exclusive
of base
Gift of Dr. and Mrs. David A. Cofrin
© 2009 Estate of Louise Nevelson /
Artists Rights Society (ARS), New York
2003.9

Known for her inventive and dynamic compositions, Louise Nevelson has long been celebrated as one of America's leading and most innovative sculptors. Born in Kiev, Russia (now Ukraine), Nevelson immigrated with her family to the United States in 1905 and settled in Rockland, Maine, where her father ran a lumberyard. After her marriage to cargo ship owner Charles Nevelson in 1920, she moved to New York and began to study acting, piano, voice, dance, painting and sculpture. From 1928 to 1930, she studied at the Art Students League and in 1931 traveled to Munich to study painting with Hans Hofmann, whom she credited with introducing her to Cubism and the dichotomy of negative and positive space.

Throughout the 1930s and 1940s, Nevelson continued to practice both painting and sculpture. Her early experiments in sculpture included semi-abstract animals and figures in terra-cotta, plaster, wood and cast stone. In these small-scale simplifications of figures, Nevelson explored her interests in scale, light, shadow, surface texture and depth—qualities that continued to preoccupy Nevelson her entire life. This untitled piece, one of the few examples of her early sculpture to be cast in bronze, shows a preoccupation with blockish, interlocking masses and Nevelson's strong appreciation for the Cubist sculpture of Jacques Lipchitz, Pablo Picasso and others.

By the mid-1950s, Nevelson had begun to produce the monumental works for which she is best known today. These box-like wood assemblages of found objects were transformed by Nevelson with monochromatic spray paint, typically all black, and later white or gold as well. In the mid-1960s Nevelson experimented with new materials such as aluminum, Lucite and Plexiglas for her assemblages that now involved fewer elements and a more rigidly controlled space. During the last two decades of her life, she began to fabricate free-standing constructed steel sculptures based on botanical shapes. One of her latest works was Louise Nevelson Plaza, completed in 1979, an outdoor environment of seven sculptures in New York City's financial district.

DR

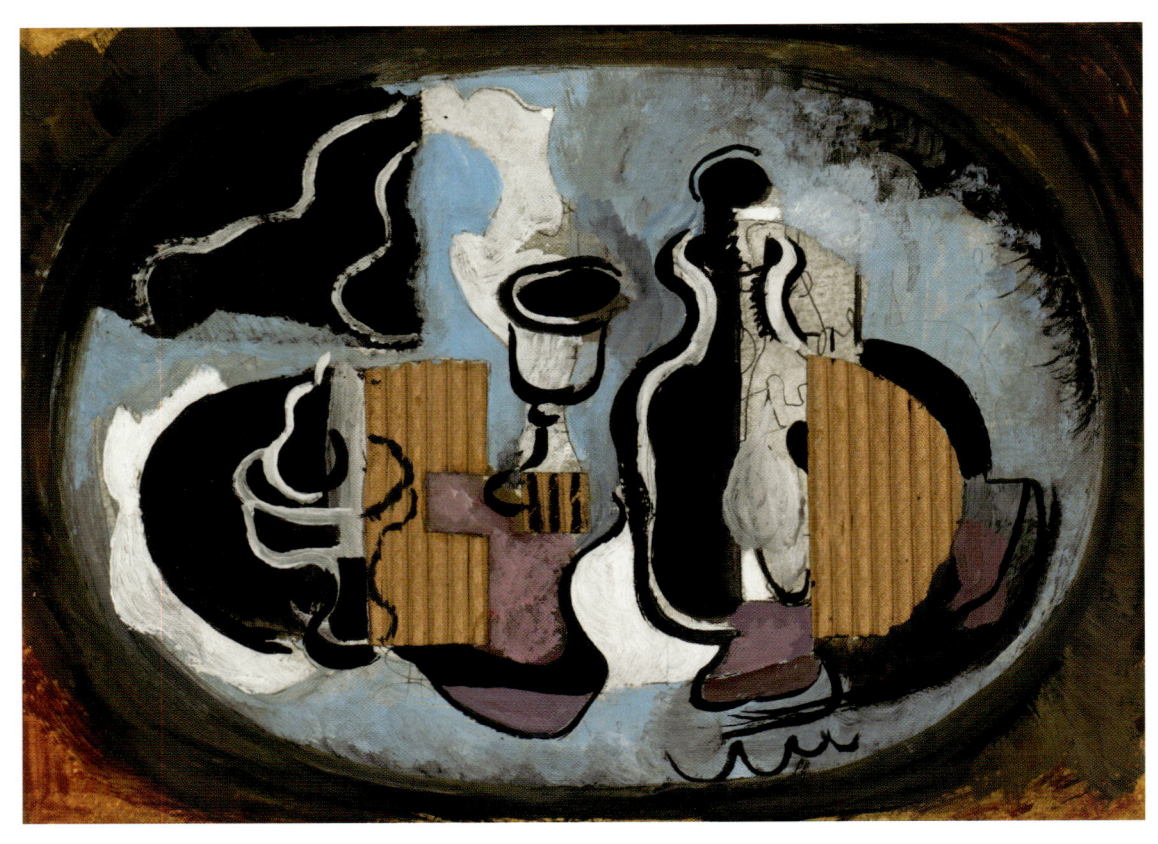

SUZY FRELINGHUYSEN
American, 1911-1988

CUBIST STILL LIFE
c. 1943, oil and collage on board
9 x 13 in. (22.9 x 33 cm)
Museum purchase, funds provided by the
Caroline Julier and James G. Richardson
Acquisition Fund, with additional funds
provided by exchange, gift of
Helen Sawyer Farnsworth
© Frelinghuysen Morris Foundation
2007.10

Suzy Frelinghuysen and her closest colleagues, artists Albert Gallatin, Charles Shaw, and George Morris, formed a significant niche in American art during the 1930s and 1940s. Known as the Park Avenue Cubists, this group introduced the American public to Cubism and the art of Pablo Picasso at a time when Realist painting was the favored style in American art. Born Estelle Condit Frelinghuysen, Suzy—as she was known in the art world and to friends—was the granddaughter of Frederick T. Frelinghuysen, who served as U.S. Secretary of State under President Chester A. Arthur. Raised in Elberton and Princeton, both in New Jersey, she moved to New York City in her late teens.

As a child, Frelinghuysen developed an interest in the arts, especially opera and painting. She had no formal art training, although she took private lessons in her youth. In 1935, she married fellow artist George Morris who encouraged her interest in painting. Soon afterwards, she began producing Cubist collages, often incorporating fragments of newspapers or opera librettos. Her playful references to works by Pablo Picasso and Georges Braque reveal a sophisticated knowledge and understanding of abstract art. In *Cubist Still Life*, Frelinghuysen layered collage elements with paint to represent a still life, including a wine glass, bottle and other objects set against a bright blue background.

Frelinghuysen joined the American Abstract Artists group soon after its founding in 1936 and participated in its annual exhibitions. Yet her artistic production slowed down after 1947, when she began a second career as a singer in the New York City Opera. She became an instant success, singing the lead roles as a dramatic soprano in *Tosca* and *Ariadne auf Naxos* under the name Suzy Morris. Frelinghuysen's opera career was cut short in 1951 following a bout of bronchitis, and she returned once again to painting full-time.

DR

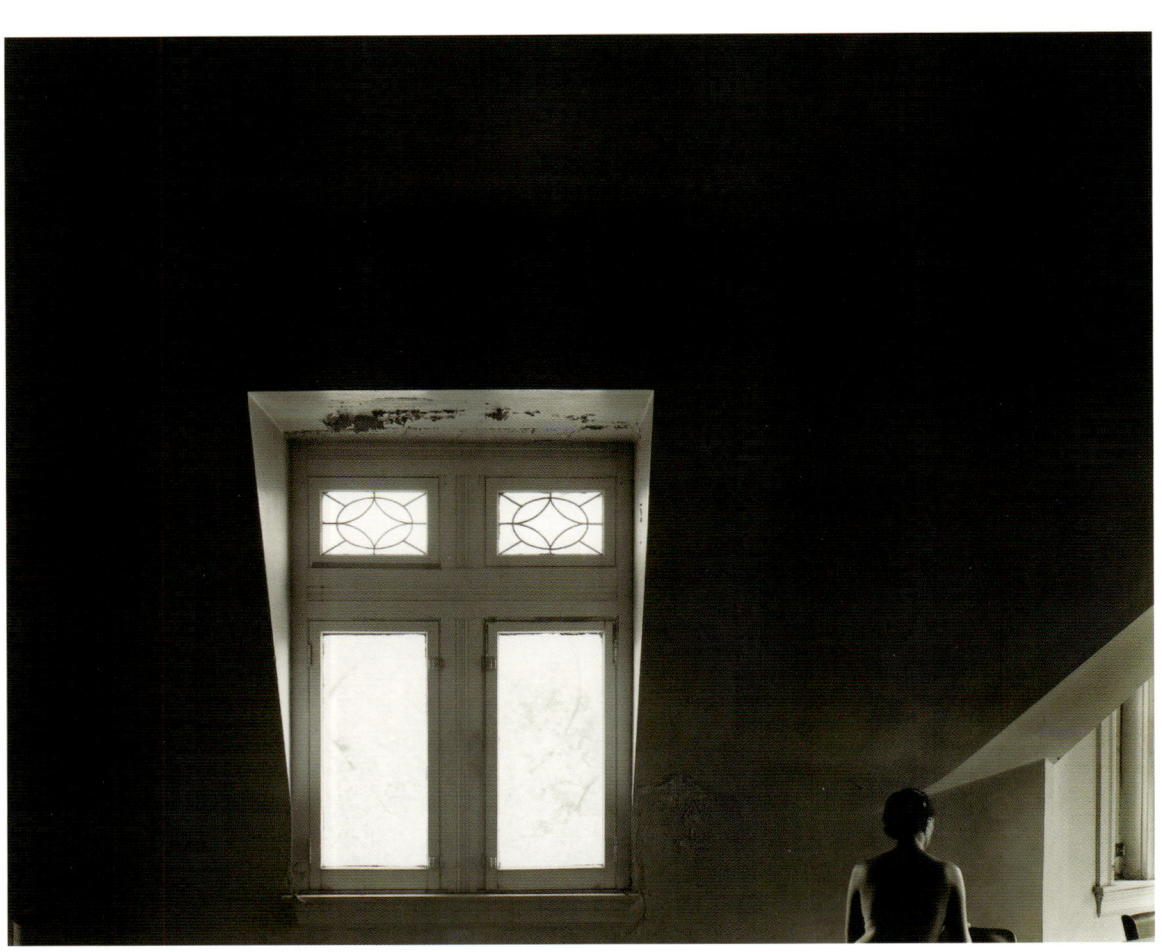

Harry Callahan
American, 1912-1999

Eleanor, Chicago
1948, gelatin silver print
image: 7 9/16 x 9 1/2 in. (19.2 x 24.1 cm)
Museum collection, University Gallery purchase,
President's Special Purchase Fund
© Estate of Harry Callahan;
courtesy Pace / MacGill Gallery, New York
PH-71-45

Harry Callahan was one of the most important American photographers of the mid-20th century. Despite being self-taught, he became renowned for his ability to transform his subjects into arresting compositions with a characteristic sharpness and a strong sense of design. Among Callahan's best known subjects are landscapes, city streets and pedestrians, and his much celebrated portrait series of his wife, Eleanor. This photograph of Eleanor is defined by the geometry of the room and most notably the large window that dominates the composition. Although this work is highly abstracted, Callahan does not lose his subject entirely. It is a deeply personal study of form and light in which the nude body of his wife forms a seemingly small detail yet is the central subject of the composition.

Callahan was born and raised in Detroit, Michigan. Beginning in 1934, he studied engineering at Michigan State University but left after three semesters and took a job as a clerk in the accounting department at Chrysler Motors in Detroit. He purchased his first camera in 1938 and joined the Chrysler Camera Club, a group of Chrysler employees who were interested in photography. He joined the Detroit Photo Guild in 1940 and attended a lecture and workshop by seminal photographer Ansel Adams the following year. Inspired by Adams' ideas, Callahan purchased an 8 x 10 view camera and took a leave from his job to concentrate on his photography. His 1942 visit to New York City where he met Alfred Stieglitz further encouraged his experimentation and his interest in pursuing photography as a serious endeavor.

Callahan's first one-person exhibition was in the form of a small two-week installation at the 750 Studio Gallery in Chicago in 1947. His strikingly original photographs caught the attention of Edward Steichen, director of the photography department at New York City's Museum of Modern Art, who regularly exhibited Callahan's work in group exhibitions thereafter. Callahan was also an important teacher of photography at the Institute of Design in Chicago where he was also head of the photography program. Under the influence of the Institute's founder, Bauhaus artist Lázló Maholy-Nagy, Callahan continued his interests in abstraction and experimentation with collage, color and multiple exposures.

DR

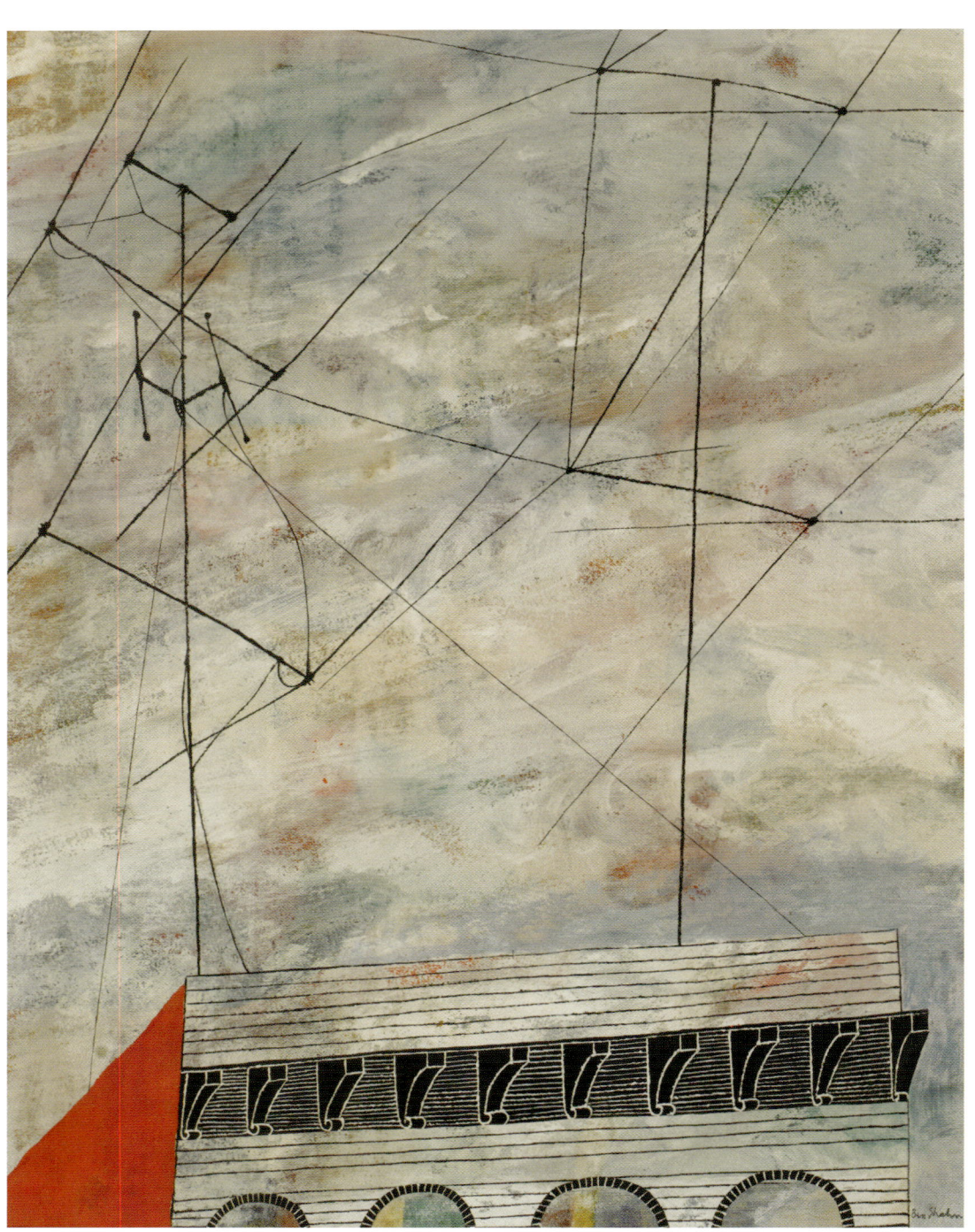

Ben Shahn
American, born Lithuania, 1898-1969

Television #2
1949, tempera and ink on paper
19 ½ x 15 ¾ in. (49.5 x 40 cm)
Museum purchase, funds provided by the
Caroline Julier and James G. Richardson
Acquisition Fund
Art © Estate of Ben Shahn/
Licensed by VAGA, New York, NY
1997.20

The highly-acclaimed Social Realist painter Ben Shahn was born in Kovno, Lithuania, and immigrated to Brooklyn, New York, in 1906. From 1913 to 1917, he worked as a lithographer's apprentice while attending high school and supported himself through commercial lithography until around 1930. Shahn enrolled at the Art Students League in 1916 and the National Academy of Design in 1921. Between 1925 and 1929, he traveled extensively in North Africa, Spain, Italy and France and was exposed to recent developments in European art. He was especially impressed with works by French artists Raoul Dufy, Georges Rouault and Pablo Picasso.

Shahn became increasingly interested in the causes of labor and social reform in the 1930s, executing some of his most famous works. In 1931 he began a series of drawings and gouaches based on the trial of Nicola Sacco and Bartolomeo Vanzetti, Italian-American anarchists convicted of killing two bank guards. The exhibition of his *Sacco and Vanzetti* series at Downtown Gallery in 1932 was a critical and commercial success. Between 1933 and 1942, Shahn worked on a series of public art projects that treated American life through allegory. A few examples include his paintings on the theme of Prohibition for a proposed mural in Central Park, a fresco at a federal housing development for garment workers in New Jersey, and a mural series on agriculture and industry for the Bronx Central Post Office.

Television #2 exemplifies the immediacy and direct appeal of Shahn's style, incorporating simplified forms and broad, flat areas of color overlaid with a network of bold lines. As with his mural projects, Shahn applied symbolism and allegory to his smaller and more intimate works reflecting a more personal observation of people and places. In *Television #2*, the series of TV antennae dominating the rooftops symbolizes massive changes taking place in American culture in the years immediately following World War II. In the late 1940s, Americans had additional disposable income and increased leisure time, paving the way for a boom in popular consumption of TV sets. By 1949, almost all major cities had at least one TV station, and about three million households in the United States had TVs.

DR

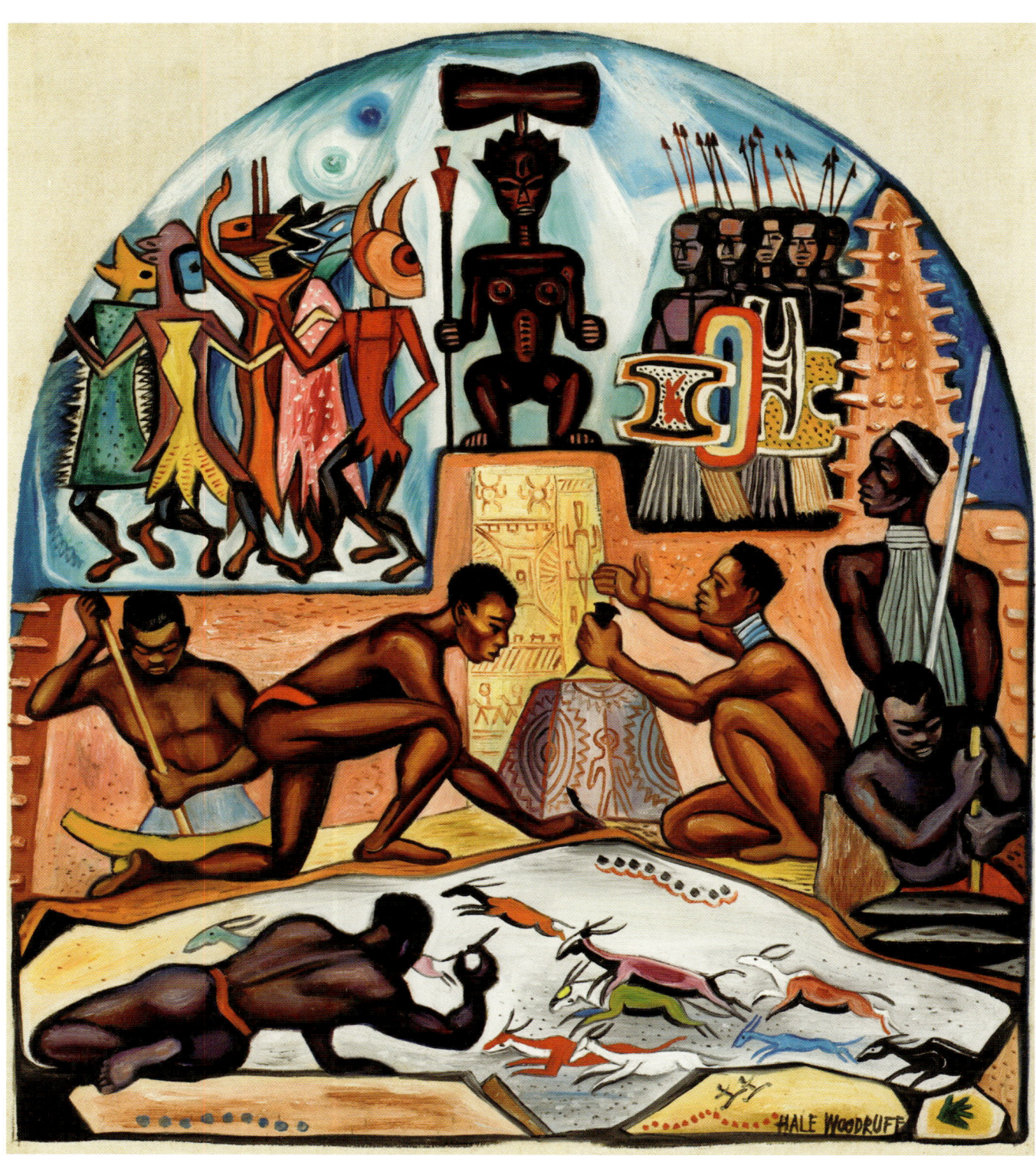

HALE ASPACIO WOODRUFF
American, 1900-1980

THE ART OF THE NEGRO: NATIVE FORMS (STUDY)
1950, oil on canvas
23 x 21 in. (58.4 x 53.3 cm)
Museum purchase, gift of an anonymous
donor with additional funds provided by
exchange, gift of Helen Sawyer Farnsworth
© Estate of Hale Woodruff / Elnora, Inc.;
Courtesy of Michael Rosenfeld Gallery, LLC,
New York, NY
2005.17

A pioneering artist and educator, Hale Woodruff is best known for his mural series on the *Amistad* slave ship mutiny of 1839, executed for Talladega College in Alabama, and his *Art of the Negro* series at Atlanta University (now Clark-Atlanta University) in Georgia. Still in its original location in the Trevor Arnett Library rotunda, Woodruff's *Art of the Negro* series comprises six canvases celebrating African art as a major influence on 20th-century aesthetic production. *Native Forms* is a study for the first canvas in the series. On the border between abstraction and figuration, the six compositions in the series respond to a shift in Woodruff's style in the mid-1940s away from his earlier Regionalist style toward greater abstraction.

Born in Cairo, Illinois, Woodruff studied at John Herron Art Institute in Indianapolis, the Art Institute of Chicago and Harvard University's Fogg Museum School. Beginning in 1927, he studied modern art theory and technique in Paris at the Académie Moderne. After four years of study in France, Woodruff returned to the United States in 1931 and joined the faculty of Atlanta University, a new school for African American students. In the mid-1940s, Woodruff moved to New York and taught art education for more than twenty years at New York University.

In his study for *Native Forms*, Woodruff includes references to the artistic production of various African peoples, both ancient and contemporary, to establish the cultural bonds between African and African American artists. The upper zone is dominated by an imposing figural staff dedicated to Shango, the deity of lightning and thunder in the Yoruba culture of western Nigeria. To the left of this staff, the brightly colored masked figures evoke images from ancient rock paintings in southwestern Africa. On the right of the staff, African warriors bearing colorful shields allude to the Zulu people of South Africa. In the lower half of the panel, prehistoric artists mix pigments, carve reliefs and paint wall paintings. The other works in the series provide additional links between traditional African Arts and 20th-century modernism, emphasizing Woodruff's belief that African art was one of the core cultural traditions that shaped the history of Western art.

DR

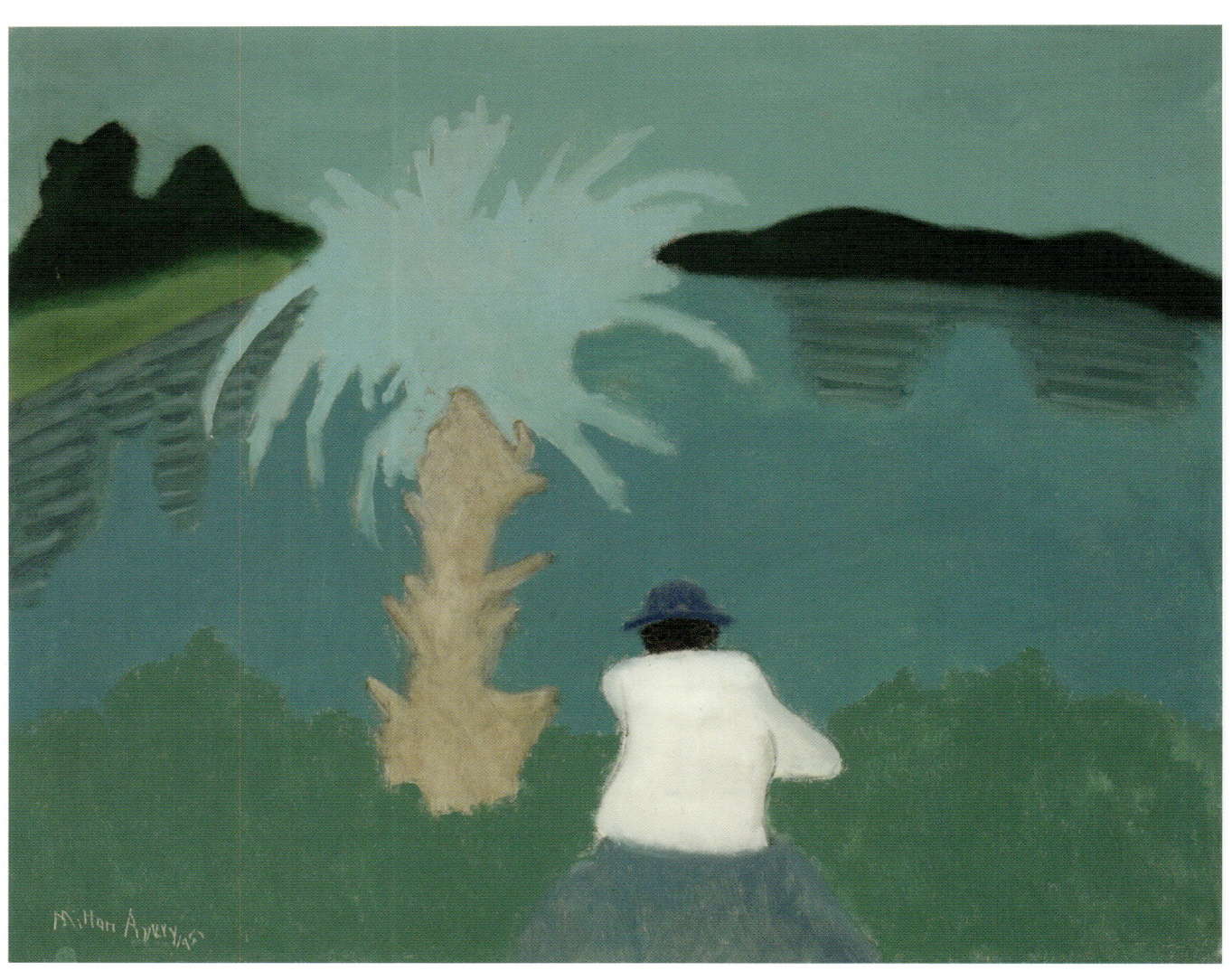

Milton Avery
American, 1885-1965

Florida Lake
1951, oil on canvas
26 x 36 in. (66 x 91.4 cm)
Museum purchase by exchange, gift
of William H. and Eloise R. Chandler
© 2009 Milton Avery Trust / Artists Rights
Society (ARS), New York
1995.30

Milton Avery worked in a series of Connecticut factories from age sixteen until age forty to support his family while taking evening classes at a local school for the arts. He enrolled in New York's Art Students League in 1926 and devoted himself full-time to his art. During the 1930s, Avery began to move away from his earlier detailed and illusionistically modeled forms in favor of simplified shapes and flat harmonious color. This new and more abstract way of painting was inspired by avant-garde European artists such as Pablo Picasso and Henri Matisse who were more interested in the general nature of a subject rather than its details.

Avery's approach to painting landscapes involved simplifying, flattening and distorting the original source. He also introduced colors that were not necessarily naturalistic such as pink for the sky or red and blue for a field. These color changes were motivated by his desire to reflect a particular mood rather than a naturalistic representation of color. Following the artist's major heart attack in 1948, Avery's style underwent a subtle shift toward softer color harmonies and a greater use of thin veils of color that reinforced the flatness of the canvas.

Florida Lake is an excellent example of Avery's integration of figurative subject and abstracted form and is conceived as a series of flat, interlocking shapes of homogenous color. This landscape was painted shortly after a trip to Maitland, Florida, where Avery spent winters at the Research Studio artist colony, now the Maitland Art Center. To recreate this scene on canvas, Avery conceived the composition in terms of large simple masses and treated each shape as a single color area, omitting details that he considered unnecessary to the overall design. Avery reduced his subject to its bare essence in an effort to communicate, in formal terms, his emotional response to the original source.

DR

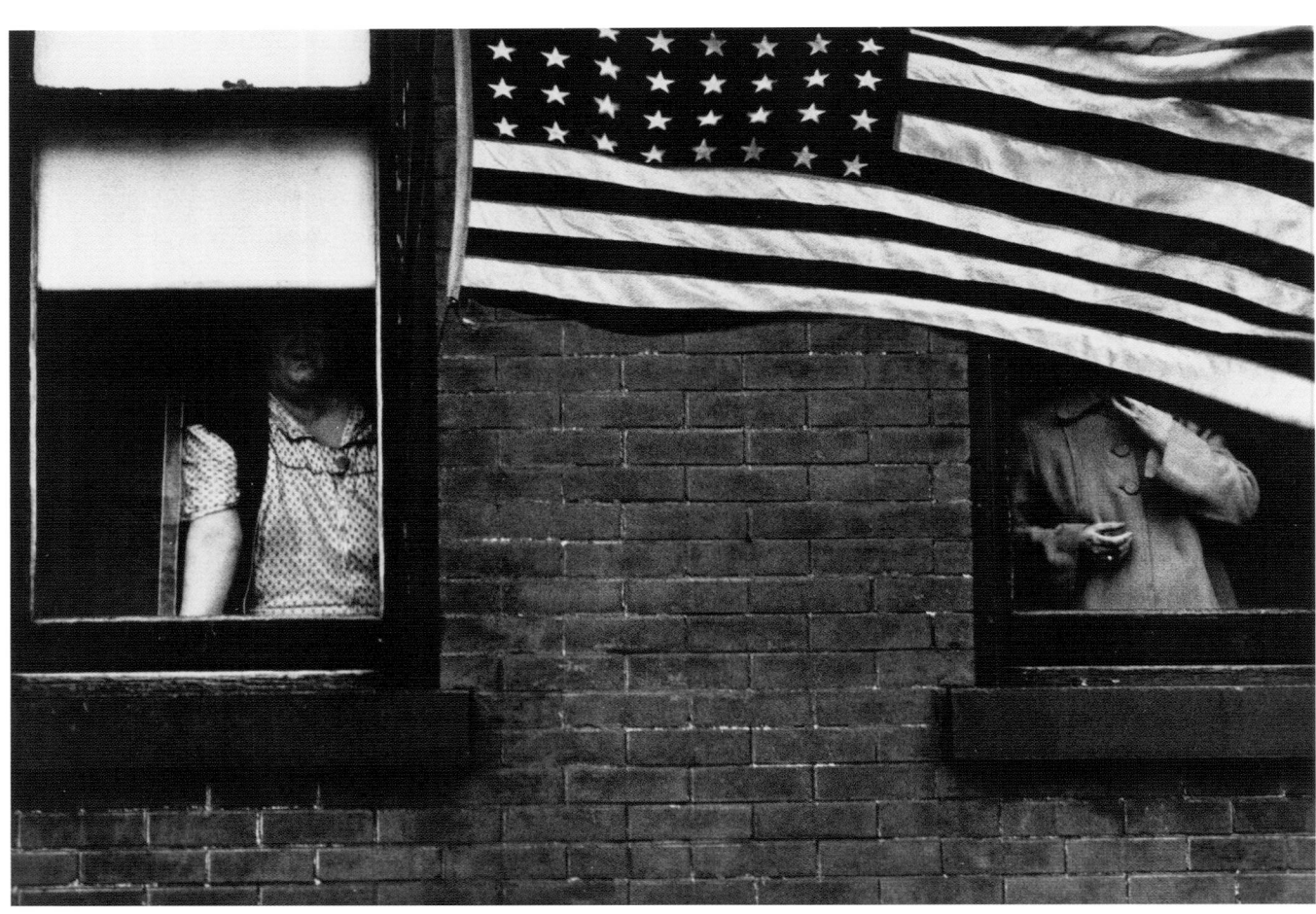

ROBERT FRANK
American, born Switzerland, 1924

PARADE, HOBOKEN, NEW JERSEY
c. 1955, gelatin silver print
image: 13 x 19 ⅛ in. (33 x 48.6 cm)
sheet: 16 x 20 in. (40.6 x 50.8 cm)
Museum purchase, transfer from
University Gallery
© Robert Frank, from *The Americans*
PH-71-43

Robert Frank's book *The Americans* opened with this image taken at a parade in Hoboken in 1955. The image of faces obscured behind an American flag set the tone for his seminal book and led to a new way of making and understanding documentary photography. Born in Switzerland, Robert Frank was relatively new to America in 1955 when he was awarded a Guggenheim grant to photograph America during the Cold War, Eisenhower years. Compared to picture story narratives that had become common in *Life* and other contemporary magazines, Frank's less literal style is evident in the powerful ambiguity of this flag image, which leaves viewers with mixed feelings and questions about both the parade watchers and the intentions of the photographer.

Much of the critical and historical response to Frank's work attributes its strength to his fresh perceptions as an outsider, new to American popular culture and therefore, able to focus on common things that might seem inconsequential. As a mirror of American culture, Frank's photographs are both an echo of Walker Evans' Depression-era documentary and also a precursor to Pop art of the next decade such as Andy Warhol's deadpan representation of American products and people or Jasper John's exploration of the flag motif.

Contemporary reviewers of Frank's book generally recognized the distinct character of his style. But many—most notably a series of short reviews in *Popular Photography* (May, 1960, p. 106)— were critical about what they perceived as a negative attitude toward America. James M. Zanutto called the book "A sad poem for sick people …The serious question is this: do such personal statements merit publication?" But this defensive response to Frank's openly subjective style was anticipated and already addressed by Jack Kerouac in his introduction to the American edition of *The Americans* (1959) featuring his "beat" misspellings: "Anybody doesnt like these pitchers dont like potry, see? Anybody dont like potry go home see Television shots of big hatted cowboys being tolerated by kind horses." [sic] Perhaps the real measure of Frank's achievement is that his images continue to provoke and inspire reflection.

TS

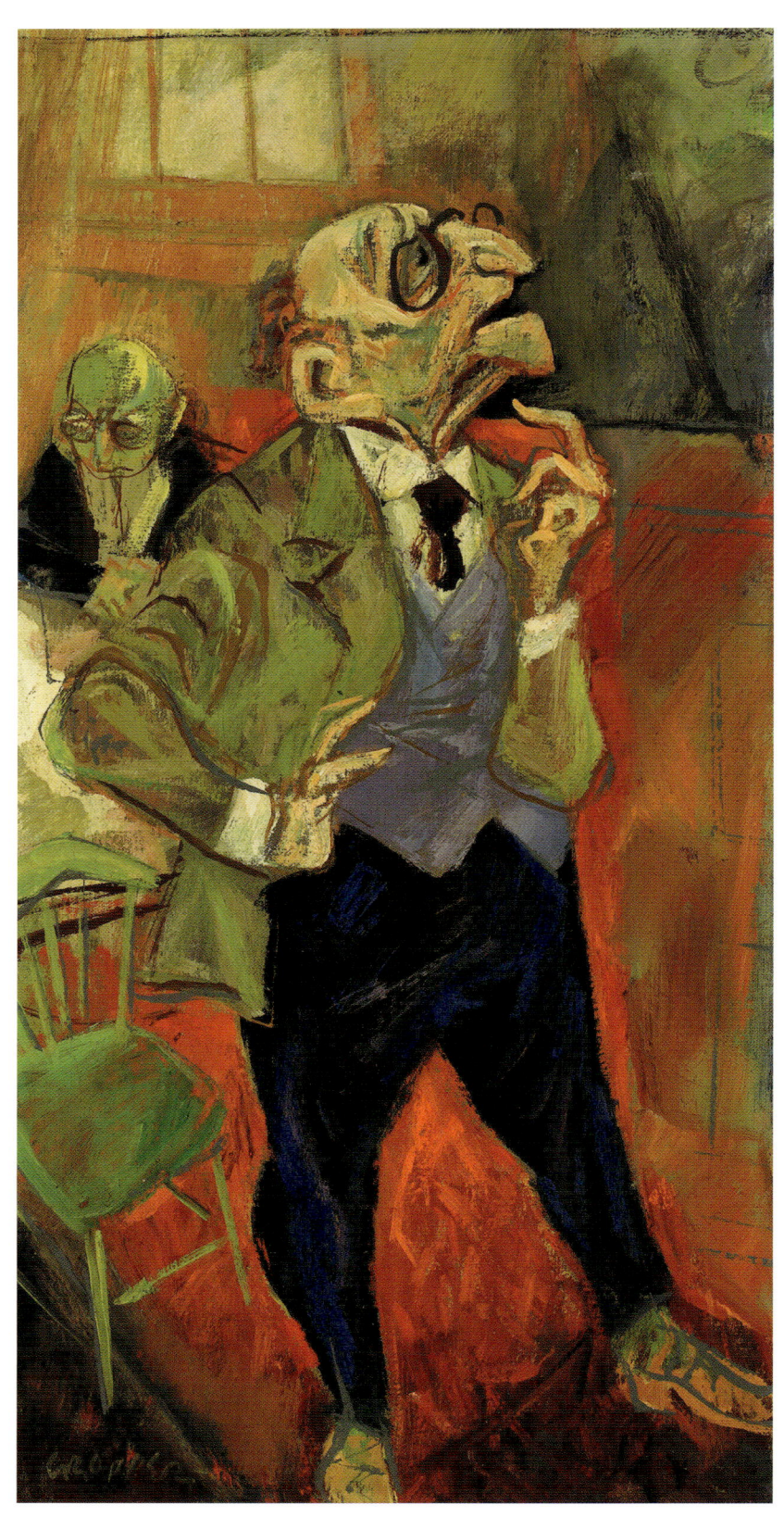

WILLIAM GROPPER
American, 1897-1977

ATTORNEY
c. 1955, oil on canvas mounted on board
25 ¼ x 13 ¼ in. (64.1 x 33.7 cm)
Gift of Eloise R. Chandler in memory of
William H. Chandler
Image permission courtesy of the
Gropper Family
1993.20.2

Cartoonist, lithographer and painter William Gropper was born on the Lower East Side of New York City into a working-class family that labored in the sweatshops of the garment industry. Although he left high school at the age of fourteen to help support his family, Gropper became interested in drawing and enrolled at the Ferrer Modern School between 1912 and 1915. Here Gropper received his first formal art training under Robert Henri and George Bellows, leaders of the Realist Ashcan School of painters. After briefly attending the National Academy of Design, Gropper was offered a scholarship to attend the New York School of Fine and Applied Arts (now the Parsons School of Design).

Soon after his graduation in 1917, Gropper was hired by the *New York Tribune* to create cartoons and illustrations for human-interest stories. By the late 1920s, Gropper was an accomplished cartoonist and draftsman and had established himself as a major satirical artist contributing to numerous newspapers and magazines including *The New Yorker*, *Vanity Fair*, the *New York Post* and *The New Masses*. Gropper began painting seriously in the 1920s and by the early 1930s began receiving commissions for public art projects funded by the New Deal Works Progress Administration (WPA) including murals for the Detroit and Freeport, Long Island post offices.

Throughout his career, Gropper was actively engaged in support of the organized labor movement, producing some of the most compelling works of social protest during the period. Common themes in his paintings and prints include people working in sweatshops, farm workers picking crops, and images of pompous politicians and the wealthy. *Attorney* is a satirical painting of an elderly lawyer gazing upward with mouth open as if searching for the right words to convince the court of his argument. Works such as this expressed Gropper's disdain for the American ideological culture of the 1950s, and his more caustic satirical works often provoked controversy. In 1953 Gropper was one of the first American artists to be blacklisted by Senator Joseph McCarthy's Permanent Subcommittee on Investigations. As a result, Gropper's active schedule of commissions and exhibitions slowed down for the next ten years.

DR

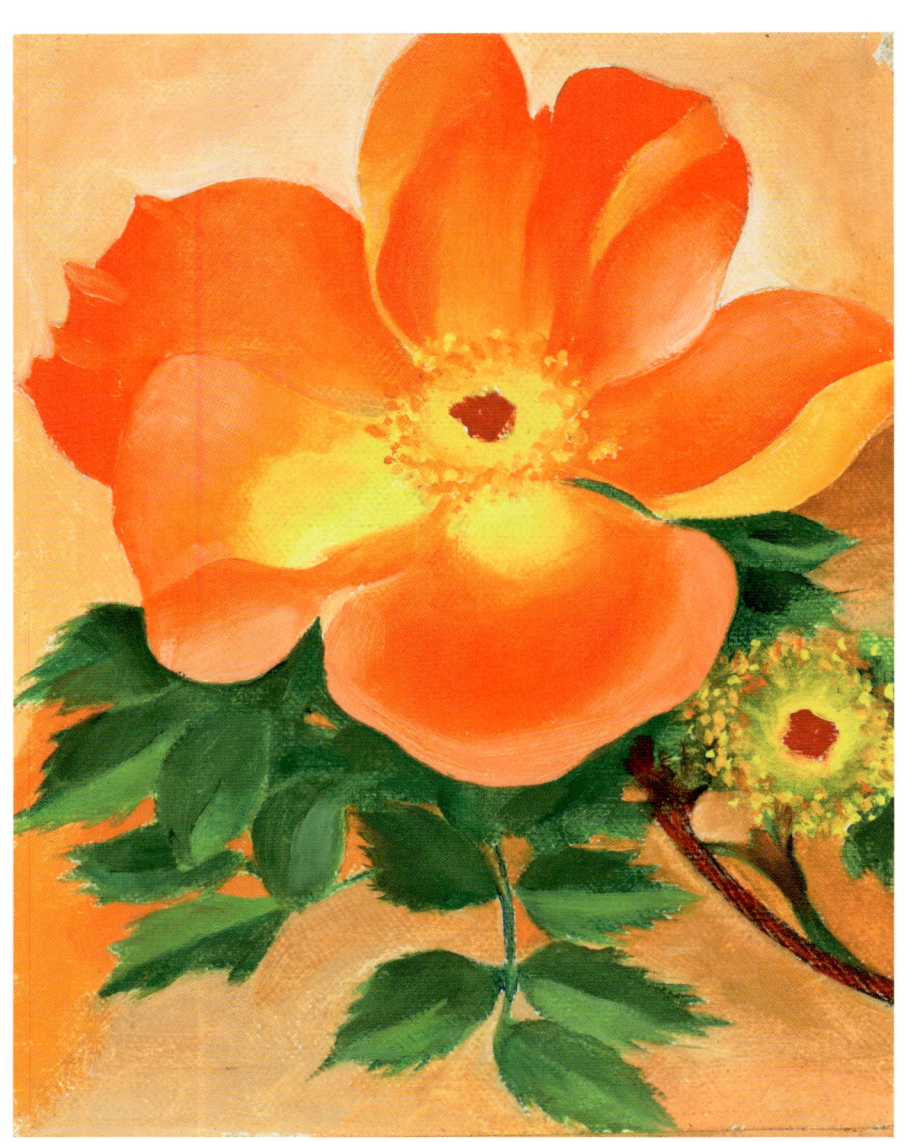

GEORGIA O'KEEFFE
American, 1887-1986

AUSTRIAN COPPER ROSE IV
1958, oil on canvas
8 ½ x 6 ¾ in. (21.6 x 17.1 cm)
Bequest of Ruth Pruitt Phillips
© 2009 Georgia O'Keeffe Museum /
Artists Rights Society (ARS), New York
2005.23.7

A major figure in American art, Georgia O'Keeffe created a highly individual style of painting, synthesizing the formal language of modern European abstraction with American subject matter. O'Keeffe's boldly original works span a period of nearly 70 years from her earliest abstract charcoal drawings to her late experiments in clay made a few years before her death at the age of 98. Born in Wisconsin, O'Keeffe studied at the School of the Art Institute of Chicago (1905-1906), and the Art Students League (1907-1908) in New York City, where she studied with William Merritt Chase. In 1914 she enrolled at Columbia University Teachers College in New York to study art with painter Arthur Wesley Dow. While living in New York, O'Keeffe met Alfred Stieglitz, the photographer and art dealer who was primarily responsible for introducing modern art to American audiences and who later became her husband and greatest promoter.

O'Keeffe credited her introduction to modernism to the early work of American painter Arthur Dove, whom she met in 1917. The two artists shared a mutual interest in capturing the fleeting aspects of nature through a language of dynamic, abstract shapes. O'Keeffe's formal vocabulary for expressing the essence of her subjects included sweeping organic forms, stylized designs, spatially ambiguous forms and complex patterns of flattened color that obliterate any illusion of depth.

O'Keeffe painted almost exclusively the flowers, animal bones and landscapes surrounding her studios in Lake George, New York, and New Mexico. Among her most famous and celebrated subjects are the paintings of flowers, which have been interpreted by some scholars as symbolic representations of the cycle of life, while others have analyzed them as symbols of sexuality. Although most of her flower paintings date to the 1920s and 1930s, O'Keeffe continued to paint flowers through the 1950s. *Austrian Copper Rose IV* is at once an objective interpretation of a rose and a meditation on form and color. The image is both realistic and abstract as O'Keeffe describes the petals, stamens and pistils of the rose as a graceful study of gentle curves, shapes and hues.

DR

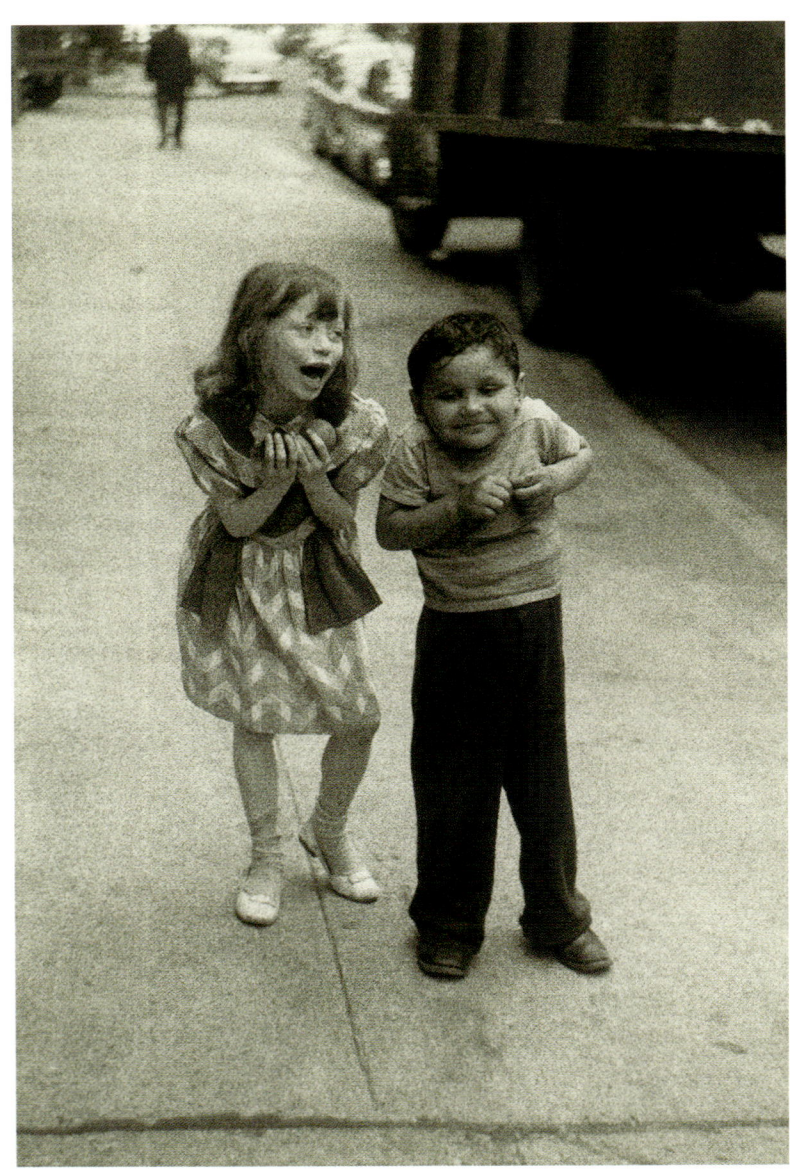

Diane Arbus
American, 1923-1971

Child teasing another, N.Y.C.
1960, gelatin silver print by Neil Selkirk, 1990s
image: 8 ⅞ x 6 in. (22.5 x 15.2 cm)
sheet: 14 x 10 ⅞ in. (35.6 x 27.6 cm)
Museum purchase with funds provided by the
Melvin and Lorna Rubin Fund
2005.42

A major figure in American documentary photography, Diane Arbus produced a vast body of compelling and often disturbing photographs before her suicide in 1971. Her sharply rendered and somewhat confrontational photographs of nudists, street people, transvestites, twins, performers and the developmentally disabled remain as controversial today as at the time of their creation. Arbus was born Diane Nemerov to an upper-middle-class family that owned Russek's, a fashionable Fifth Avenue department store in New York City. She attended the Ethical Culture and Fieldston Schools where she received a progressive education and developed an interest in painting. In 1941 at age eighteen, she married Allan Arbus, and together they ran a successful commercial fashion photography business until 1956, when she decided to focus on her own fine art photography.

In 1941 Arbus studied briefly under Berenice Abbott, and between 1956 and 1957 she studied under Lisette Model who encouraged her to capture personal images with a documentary eye. Beginning in 1960, Arbus' photo essays depicting marginal characters and public spectacles appeared in magazines such as *Esquire* and *Harper's Bazaar*. Although appearing casual and spontaneous, Arbus' subjects were often posed and participated actively in the photographic process. *Child teasing another, N.Y.C* is one of her many depictions of children. In this charming yet somewhat unsettling image, Arbus avoids a romanticized view of childhood and instead presents playtime as an outlet for aggressive social interaction.

Arbus' photographs received critical praise from the international artistic community. In 1963 and 1966 she was awarded John Guggenheim Fellowships, and in 1967 her work was included in the *New Documents* exhibition at the Museum of Modern Art. In 1972, the year following her death, Arbus became the first American photographer to be represented at the Venice Biennale. That same year, a major retrospective of her work was held at the Museum of Modern Art and also traveled to venues throughout the United States and Canada until 1975. Between 2003 and 2006, *Diane Arbus Revelations*, an exhibition of more than 200 photographs plus a great deal of biographical material, toured major museums in the United States and Europe.

DR

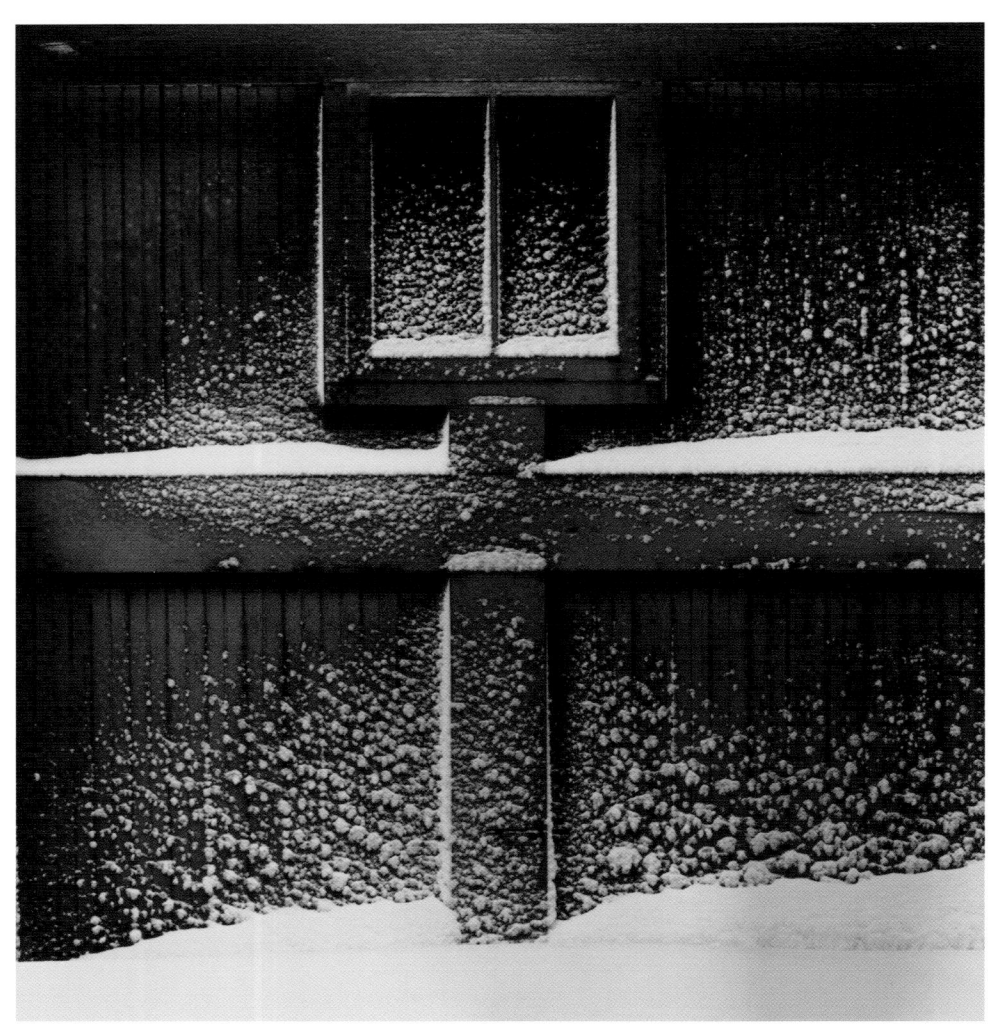

MINOR WHITE
American, 1908-1976

HAGGS ALLEY, ROCHESTER
1960, gelatin silver print
image and sheet: 9 ⅝ x 9 ⅜ in. (24.4 x 23.8 cm)
Museum collection, University Gallery Purchase
© Trustees of Princeton University
PH-71-50

The photographer, poet and teacher Minor White is best known for his sharply detailed photographs exploring landscapes and architectural themes with disorienting qualities of light. White was born in Minneapolis, Minnesota, the only child of a bookkeeper and dressmaker. Following his graduation in 1934 from the University of Minnesota, where he studied botany and poetry, White lived briefly in Portland, Oregon. White moved to New York City in 1945 and briefly studied art history and aesthetics with Meyer Shapiro at Columbia University. In New York, he studied museum methods at the Museum of Modern Art, met fellow photographers such as Edward Steichen, Harry Callahan, Paul Strand and Edward Weston, and joined the Photo League.

While living in New York, White also met Alfred Stieglitz whose ideas about photographic equivalents influenced White's use of photography as a vehicle for expressing his inner feelings and beliefs. White's introspective approach to photography was heightened in the 1950s when he became interested in mysticism, Eastern philosophy and Gestalt psychology. *Haggs Alley*, *Rochester*, White's photograph of a snow-covered garage wall, incorporates an abstracted version of a cross. Although White did not adhere to any specific Christian theology, he was captivated by the cross motif which he treated many times throughout his career in various pictorial forms, sometimes quite literal and at other times very abstracted.

White contributed a great deal to art criticism and teaching. In the 1940s, he taught at Ansel Adams' California School of Fine Arts, today the San Francisco Art Institute. He later taught courses and workshops at the Society for Photographic Education, Rochester Institute of Technology, and Massachusetts Institute of Technology. In 1952 White helped found the journal *Aperture*, served as assistant curator of exhibitions at George Eastman House in Rochester from 1953 to 1957, and was editor for the museum's publication, *Image*, from 1956 to 1957.

DR

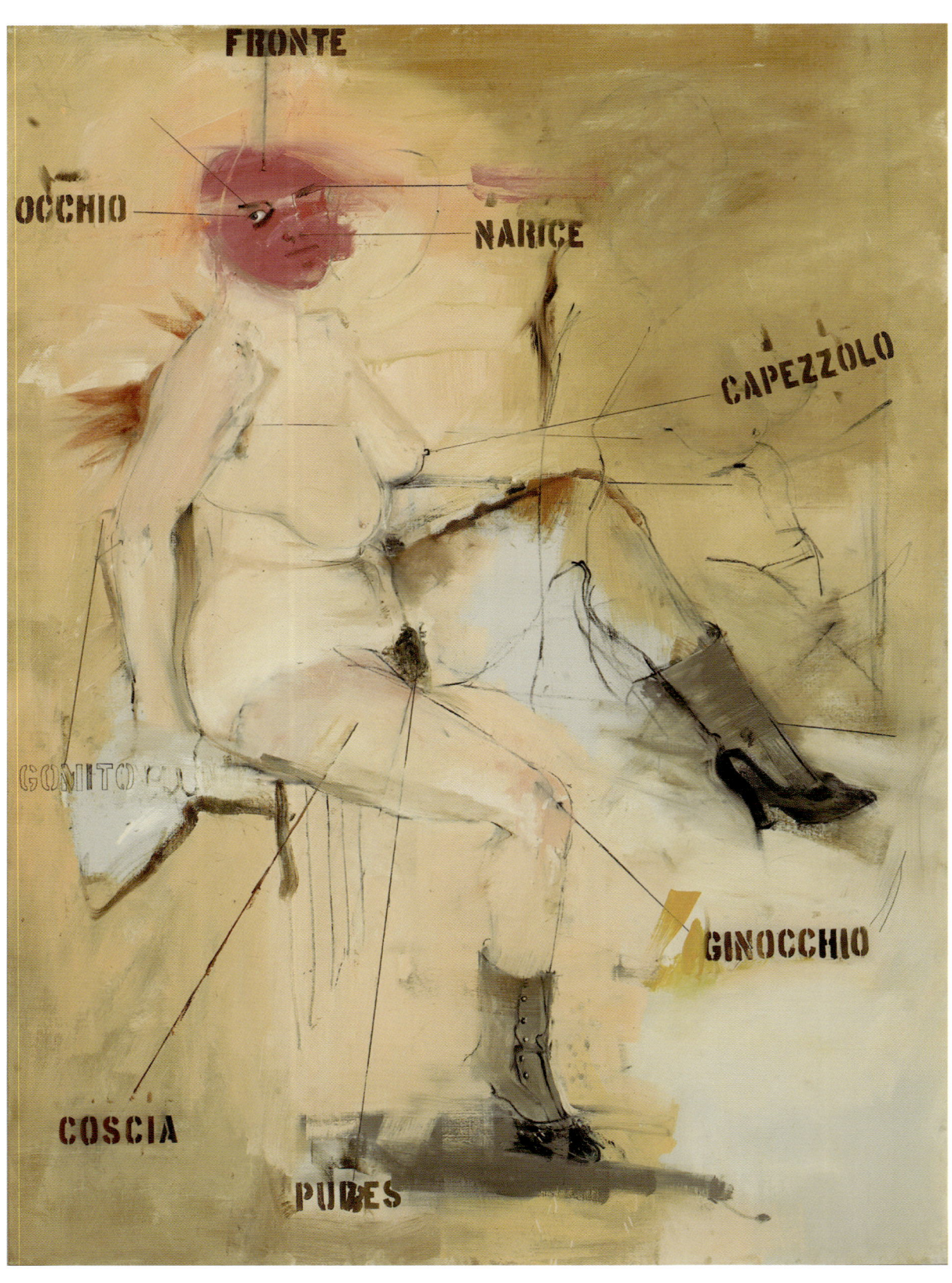

Larry Rivers
American, 1923-2002

Parts of the Body:
Italian Vocabulary Lesson

1963, oil on canvas
69 x 52 in. (175.3 x 132.1 cm)
Gift of Dr. and Mrs. Robert C. Magoon in honor
of Sam and Bessie Proctor
Art © Estate of Larry Rivers /
Licensed by VAGA, New York, NY
2005.38

Born as Yitzroch Loiza (Irving) Grossberg in the Bronx, New York, Larry Rivers was a painter, sculptor, jazz musician, actor, filmmaker and self-styled provocateur. Known for his humor and bad-boy persona, Rivers reflected a tumultuous era in American culture and politics. Rivers began his career as a musician and studied as a jazz saxophonist at the Julliard School of Music before changing his focus to painting in 1945. He trained under Hans Hofmann and at New York University, and initially was strongly influenced by Abstract Expressionism, particularly through the work of Jackson Pollock and Willem de Kooning.

Rivers rebelled against the constraints of pure abstraction and became increasingly drawn toward figuration, linear depiction and narrative subject matter. In 1953 he garnered considerable attention for the irreverent painting, *Washington Crossing the Delaware*. Strikingly different from the original painting, Rivers' work was created with charcoal, thin washes and vigorous strokes of paint brushed and wiped on the canvas. By 1957 he was integrating images from history, art history and popular culture to create a unique style that combined abstraction and realism.

Parts of the Body: Italian Vocabulary Lesson combines Rivers' interest in the conventional nude subject with his proclivity for parody and pastiche. The work serves as both homage and critique of the 19th-century European tradition of figurative painting inspired by Jacques-Louis David and Gustave Courbet. The less-than-idealized figure of a mature woman wears a mask and high heels with leggings that humorously lampoon conventional attributes of erotica. *Parts of the Body: Italian Vocabulary Lesson* is related to an earlier series focusing on French vocabulary. In each case, parts of the woman's body are identified by stenciled words in the manner of a manual. Reflecting the work of Jasper Johns, the words function as "realistic" signs indicating a conceptual notion of representation.

KO-S

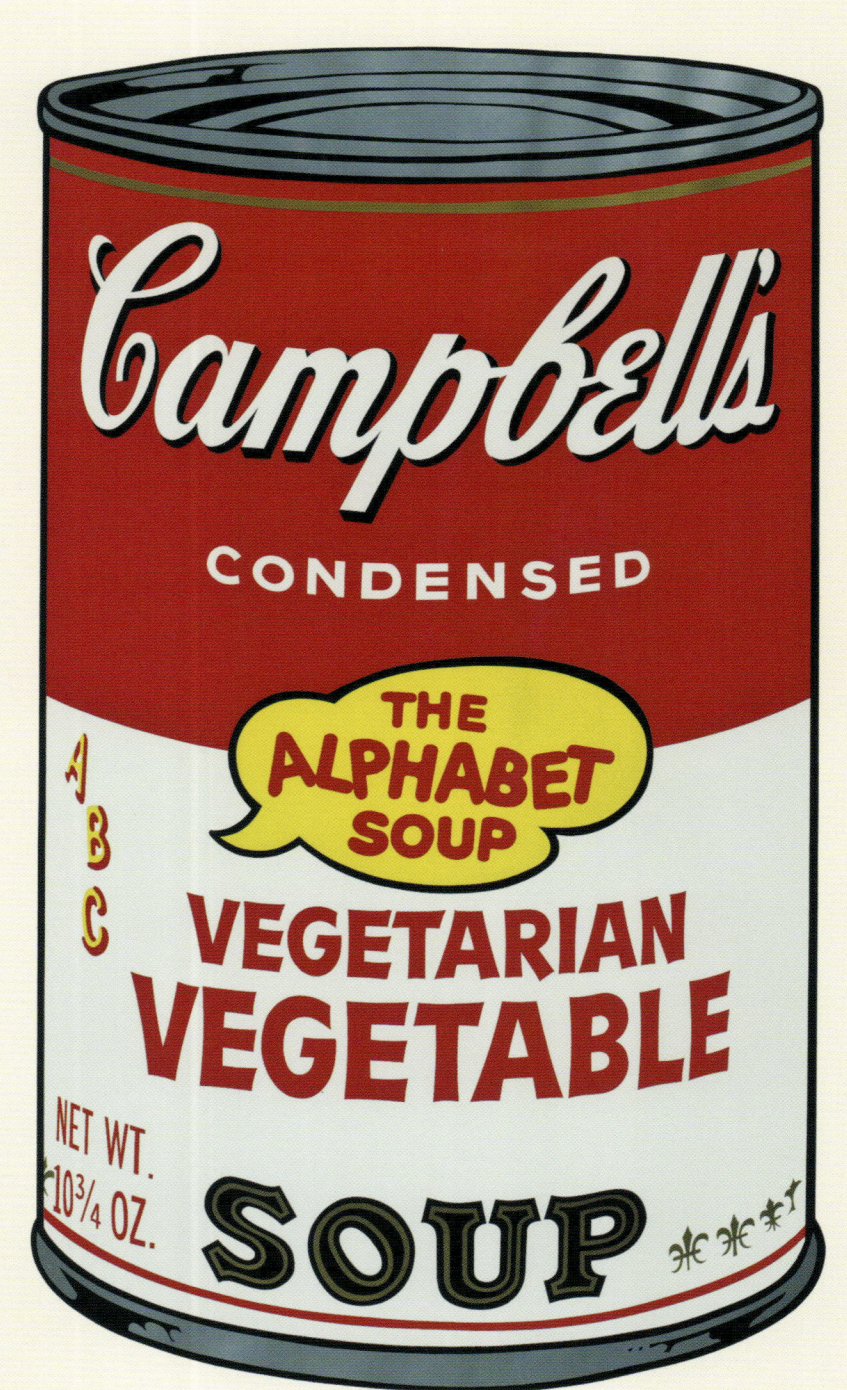

Andy Warhol
American, 1928-1987

Soup Can, Vegetarian Vegetable
1964, silkscreen print
image: 32 x 18 ¾ in. (81.3 x 47.6 cm)
Gift of Richard Anuszkiewicz
© 2009 The Andy Warhol Foundation / ARS,
New York / Trademarks, Campbell Soup Company.
All rights reserved.
1989.12.1

Andy Warhol is considered one of the most influential and iconic artists of the 20th century. He was a key figure in art, fashion, underground music, independent filmmaking and celebrity culture. A native of Pittsburgh, Warhol was born with the name Andrew Warhola. He studied design at the Carnegie Institute of Technology, moving to New York in 1949, where he worked as a commercial artist and illustrator for magazines such as *Vogue*, *Harper's Bazaar* and *The New Yorker*. Eventually he began to use product logos and newspaper images of celebrities as a source for his pictures.

Warhol produced his first *Campbell's Soup Cans* in 1962-1963, during the same time period that he created his first *Disaster*, *Elvis* and *Marilyn* paintings. Subsequently he began to mass produce his images in an assembly-line process in his famous studio known as The Factory. The *Campbell's Soup Can* paintings were first exhibited in 1962 at the Stable Gallery with the paintings arranged on a shelf to mimic the display of soup cans in a grocery store. Warhol produced 32 canvases, each representing the soups produced by the soup company at the time. Since then, the paintings and prints have become his most iconic and famous works.

Repetition was central to Warhol's work. He consistently incorporated a mechanical and impersonal character as he began to adopt silkscreen printing and the use of assistants to increase his production. Warhol's inexpressive paintings and prints challenged prevailing notions of artistic subjectivity and originality. Warhol was interested in everyday and popular objects that would appeal to the masses. His work has been interpreted by some as a mirror and/or critique of a society obsessed by serial production and consumption. Others view his work as a way to both screen against and point to the trauma and disasters of contemporary life.

KO-S

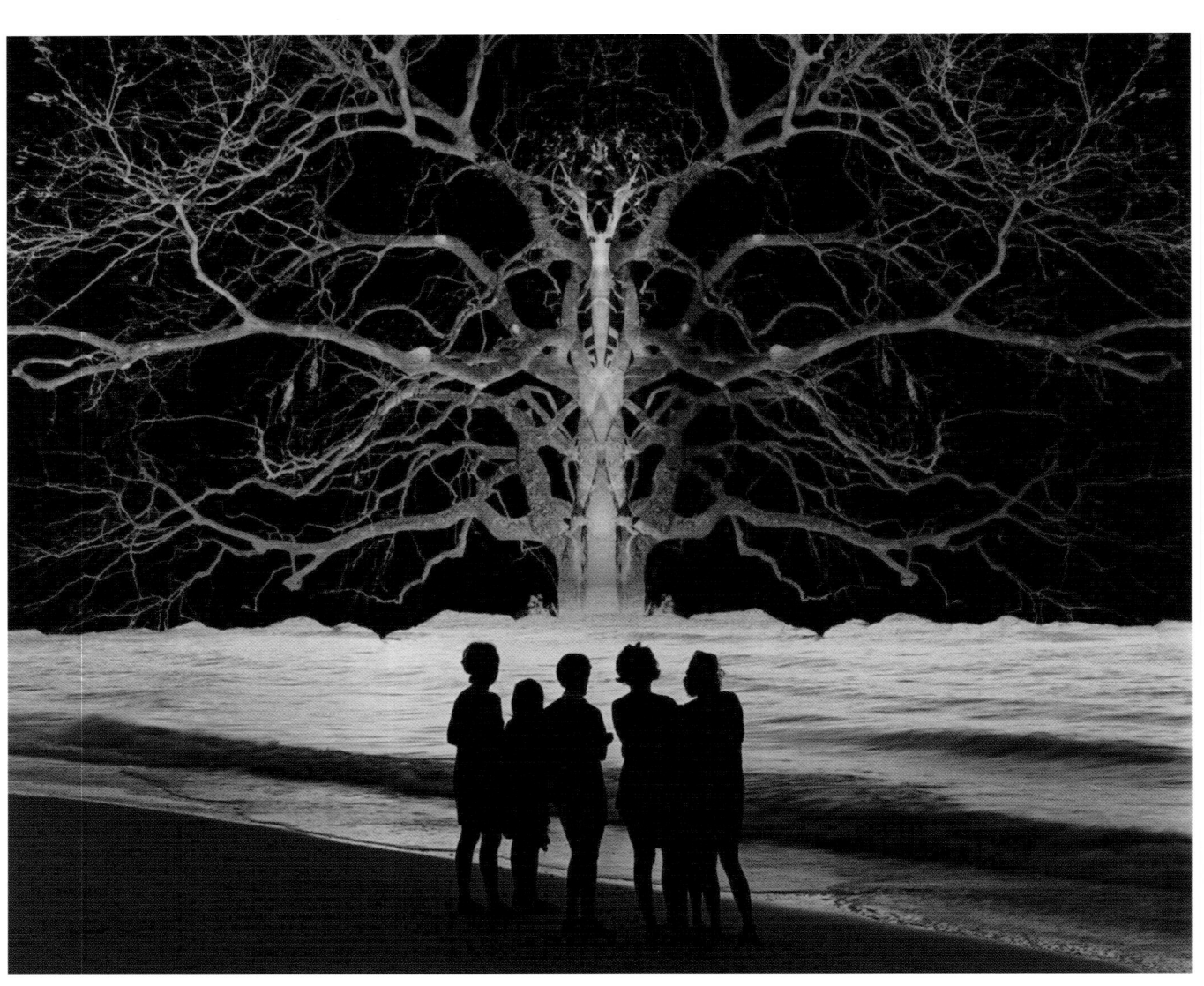

Jerry N. Uelsmann
American, born 1934

Apocalypse II
1967, printed 1972, gelatin silver print
image and sheet: 10 ¾ x 13 ½ in. (27.3 x 34.3 cm)
Gift of the artist
PH-72-47-I

Apocalypse II is one of those rare masterpieces of contemporary art that retains a sense of surprise and mystery even after repeated viewing—in this case more than four decades after its creation in the late 1960s. When Jerry N. Uelsmann began his teaching career at the University of Florida in 1960, he had already earned a reputation for his surreal montages created by his innovative darkroom techniques. He became a master at combining negatives of different subjects and scenes into seamless photographic montage. Some of his most complex works involved numerous negatives using more than a half dozen enlargers and complicated darkroom burning and dodging.

Part of the magic and power of *Apocalypse II* is the simplicity of Uelsmann's manipulations. The view of the beach with silhouetted figures looking out into the receding water is probably from a single negative. Yet what starts as a serene, almost clichéd scene is totally transformed by the tree form printed into the sky. This tree-cloud was created in just a couple of easy-to-decipher steps: Uelsmann double-printed his negative to create an impossible symmetrical pattern of branches and printed it into the sky to create a tonally-reversed negative image. The result is a powerful demonstration of Uelsmann's unconventional approach that understands light sensitive paper as receptive to a layering of exposures and multiple images, not just a mirror of a single negative.

Ueslmann's title for this work directs our interpretation toward the obvious reading of the tree form as an atomic mushroom cloud. His symbol-laden work has been fruitful territory for interpretive readings such as William Parker's discussion of Uelsmann's strange juxtapositions and imagery in relation to Carl Jung's writing on symbols and archetypes (*Aperture*, Vol. 13, no. 3, 1967). The greater enduring value of *Apocalypse II* may be that it does not need a deeper reading. It is both a comment on the anxiety of the Cold War era and an artifact, even satire, of that time.

TS

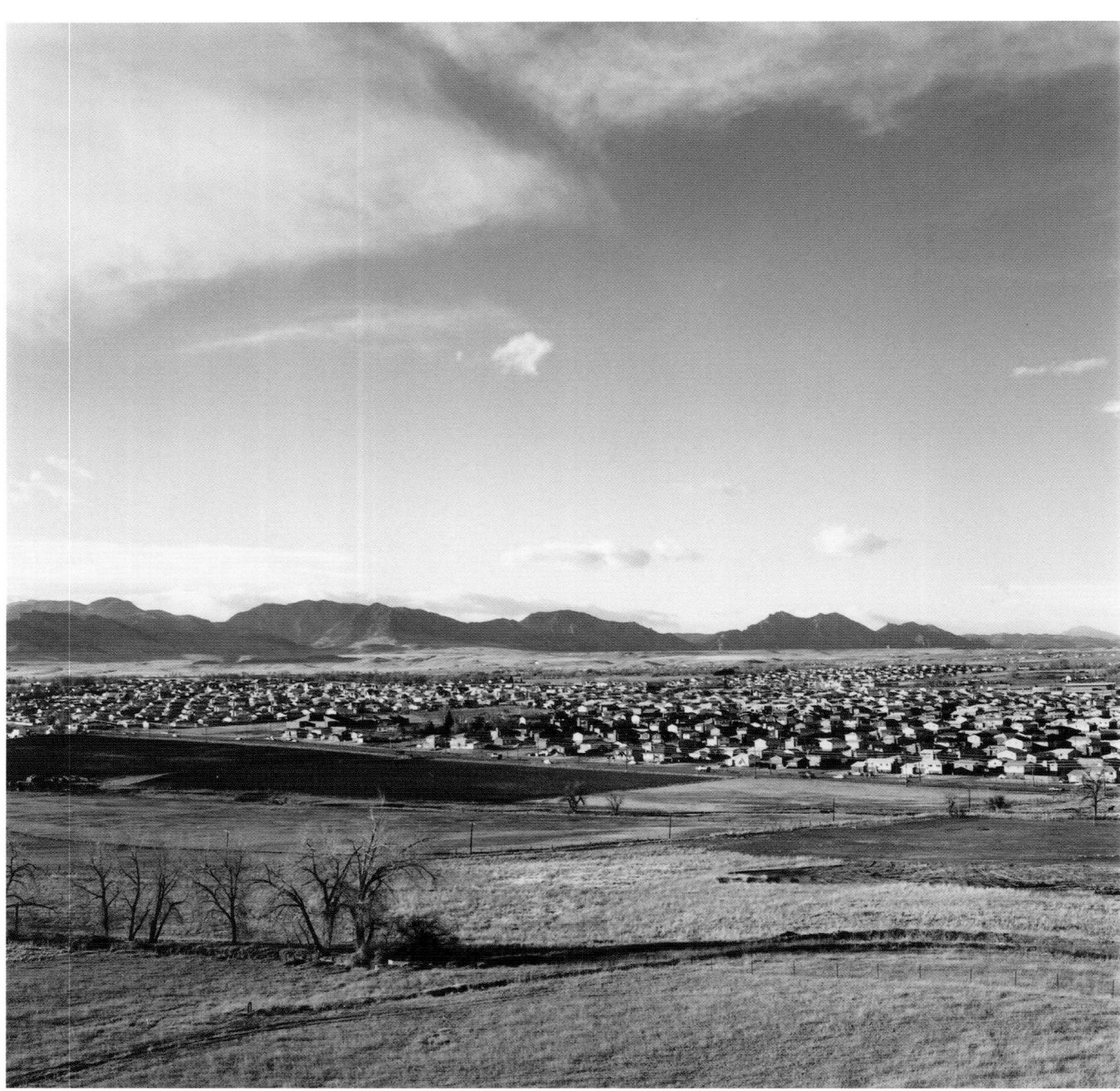

ROBERT ADAMS
American, born 1937

NEW SUBDIVISIONS, ARVADA
1968-1972, gelatin silver print
image: 5 ¾ x 6 in. (14.6 x 15.2 cm)
sheet: 10 x 8 in. (25.4 x 20.3 cm)
Museum purchase, gift of Michael A. Singer
© Robert Adams, Courtesy Fraenkel Gallery,
San Francisco and Matthew Marks Gallery,
New York
2002.13

Robert Adams was born in Orange, New Jersey, and is best known for his photographs of the American West. Both a writer and an artist, he received a bachelor's degree in English from University of Redlands, California and a doctorate in English from the University of Southern California. Adams' work includes images of landscapes in California, Oregon and his home state of Colorado.

In the late 1960s, Robert Adams began recording the suburban sprawl in and around Denver, Colorado, registering the ways the American West had been "civilized." In the tradition of Walker Evans and Robert Frank, he collected 56 of these photos in a book, "The New West," originally published in 1974. With this book, Adams documents the effects of human presence on the landscape, contrasting the mythic Western symbols of freedom and grandeur with the dull and monotonous constructions of suburbia. Adams documents housing tracts, empty lots and endless concrete, bleak and barren environments that contrast starkly with ideas of open and pristine wilderness.

Adams plays with the epic visions of nature created by past artists such as Timothy O'Sullivan and Ansel Adams but infuses them with a modernist aesthetic and a mourning eye on the clash between man and nature. In the tradition of his predecessors, Adams captures the spectacular panorama of Colorado Front Range in the photograph here. It is only with a close look that the photograph reveals the incongruous and massive development of the expanding city. Adams was a key figure in a move towards social landscape photography that emerged in the 1970s. Photographers refused to artificially separate the astounding beauty of nature from the devastating effects of culture. Their efforts were essential to creating a new awareness and respect for the environment.

KO-S

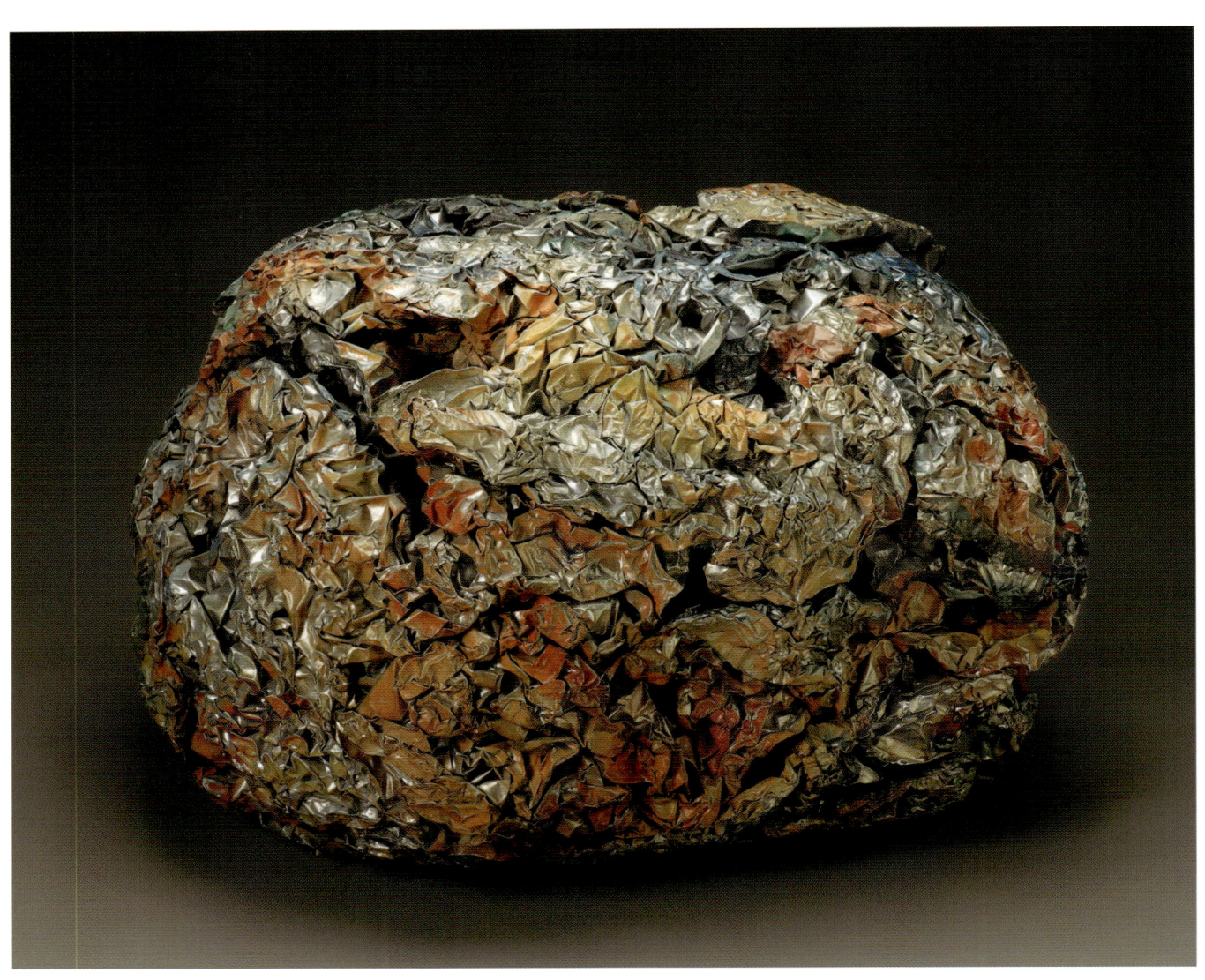

JOHN CHAMBERLAIN
American, born 1927

UNTITLED
1973, aluminum foil, acrylic, lacquer
and polyresin
24 x 40 x 35 ½ in. (61 x 101.6 x 90.2 cm)
Gift of Dr. and Mrs. Robert C. Magoon
in honor of Sam and Bessie Proctor
© 2009 John Chamberlain /
Artists Rights Society (ARS), New York
2003.15

John Chamberlain is a sculptor, painter, printmaker, photographer and filmmaker. He was born in Rochester, Indiana and grew up in Chicago. After serving in the Navy, he returned to study at the Art Institute of Chicago. Influenced by David Smith, he first began constructing flat, welded sculptures. In 1955 Chamberlain studied and taught at Black Mountain College in North Carolina. In 1956 he moved to New York and one year later began to use scrap metal from cars to create sculpture. In 1957 he made *Shortstop*, his first sculpture using automobile parts, which he welded and ran over with his car to create the right texture. Crushed, compressed, painted and welded, Chamberlain's scrap metal sculptures have become his signature medium.

Chamberlain received wide recognition for his work during the early 1960s. In 1961 his work was included in *The Art of Assemblage* at the Museum of Modern Art, and soon after, he began exhibiting worldwide. Chamberlain's car part assemblages are rooted in popular culture and associate the artist with multiple trajectories of postwar art. Initially Chamberlain was deeply influenced by Abstract Expressionism, incorporating elements of chance and spontaneity in his work. His use of detritus and readymade materials associated him with artists such as Robert Rauschenberg, who bridged Abstract Expressionism and Pop art. Still, Chamberlain's interest in process and materials were aligned with the foundational concepts of Minimalism.

Chamberlain's car sculptures were enameled, sprayed and airbrushed in bold and brilliant colors. He also experimented with materials such as galvanized steel, industrial rubber, polyurethane foam, crumpled Plexiglas and crushed metal. The Harn sculpture is part of a series of industrial-weight aluminum foil sculptures that Chamberlain created in the 1970s. Chamberlain would staple two sheets of heavy foil and crinkle them up into a boulder-sized ball. He highlighted the wrinkles and crevasses by spraying them with lacquer and polyester resin. Later Chamberlain returned to his use of car parts, but he has never forfeited his experimental approach.

KO-S

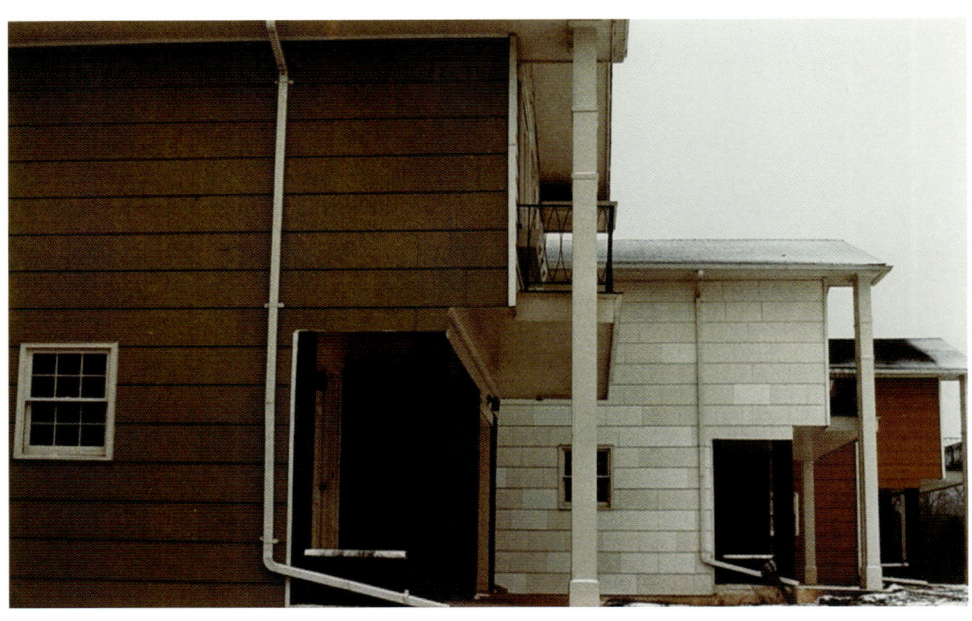

Dan Graham
American, born 1942

Housing Project,
Staten Island
1974, chromogenic development print
image and sheet: 8 ½ x 14 in. (21.6 x 35.6 cm)
Museum purchase, gift of Michael A. Singer
2002.16

Dan Graham is an artist, art critic and theorist known for his critical interrogation of cultural ideology and systems. His work encompasses photography, film, video, performance, installation and sculptural/architectural designs. He has also brought his analysis to architecture, rock music and the media. Graham began his career when he opened the John Daniels Art Gallery in the early 1960s and came into contact with Minimalist artists such as Sol LeWitt, Donald Judd, Dan Flavin and Robert Smithson. It was during that time that Graham began to challenge the museum and gallery structure and entrenched notions of high art. Soon he began to pursue methods of working outside of the conventional art system.

Housing Project, Staten Island is related to his seminal series *Homes for America*, which Graham began in 1965. Aware of the dependence of the art world on publicity, information and money, Graham became interested in the art object's relationship to mass-media representation and dissemination. In an effort to circumvent the system, he decided to directly tie his work to the display and circulation of a magazine with his own work functioning as a kind of advertisement for itself. *Homes for America* was published in *Arts Magazine* in 1967, integrating his deadpan photographs of housing developments with his cultural and architectural criticism of mass produced housing.

In the late 1970s Graham turned to performance and video and began exploring the perception of space and time, the consciousness of body, and issues of interacting with the media. Later he began to concentrate on architecture, working on several series of architectural models and mirrored pavilion pieces that dealt with the subjective experience of the spectator.

KO-S

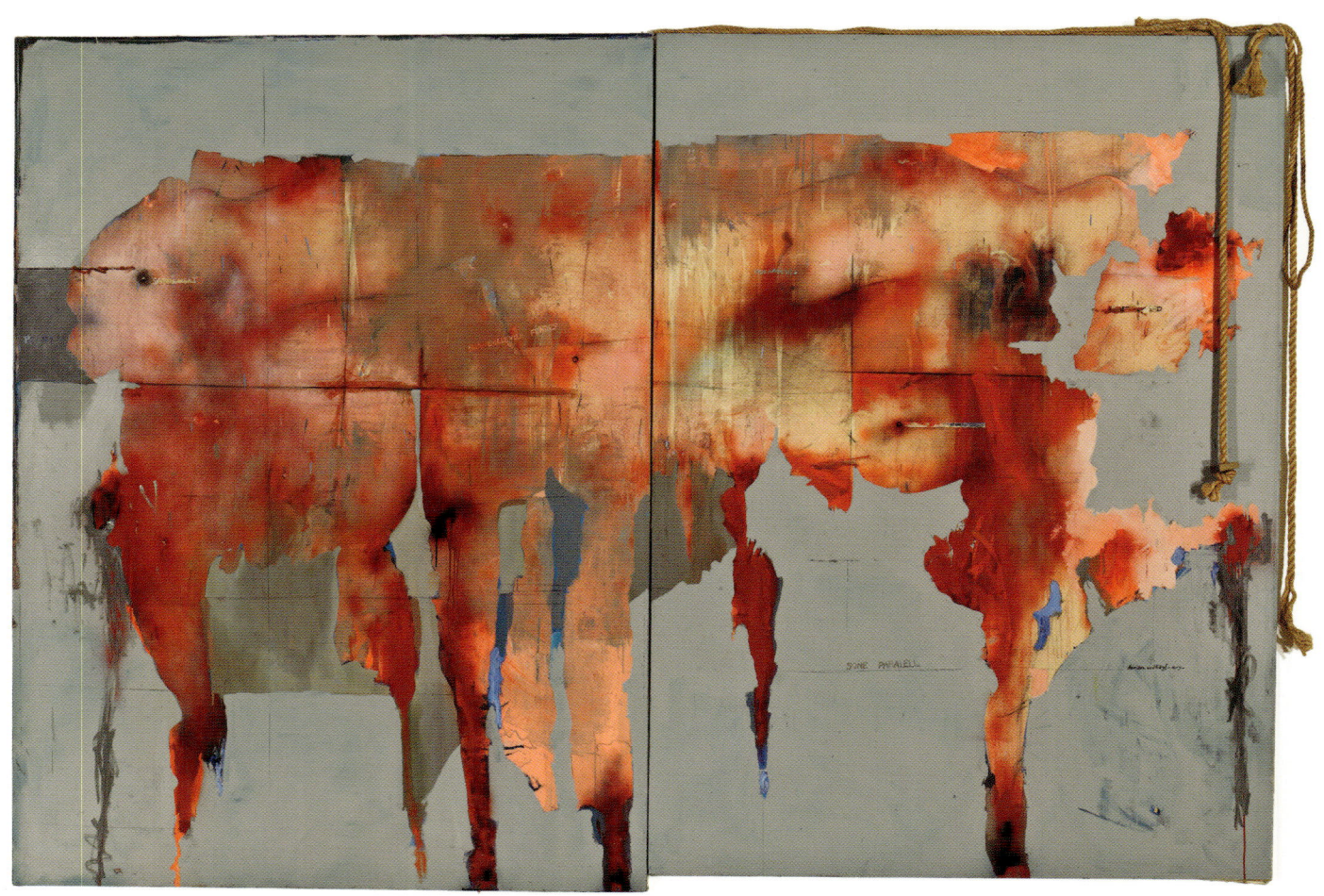

Hiram Williams
American, 1917-2003

Some Parallel
1975, oil on canvas
diptych, 97 x 143 in. (246.4 x 363.2 cm)
Gift of Hiram and Avonell Williams
PA-78-8

Hiram Williams was a painter whose abstract work incorporated overlapping elements of figuration, landscape and still life. Williams grew up as a minister's son in Muncy, Pennsylvania and studied briefly at the Art Students League in New York City. He was drafted in 1942 and served in General George Patton's Third Army in Germany. On returning home, he earned degrees at Penn State. Later he took teaching positions at the University of Texas and the University of Florida, where he retired as Distinguished Service Professor Emeritus in 1982.

Williams' artistic practice took root in Abstract Expressionism, embracing its loosely and freely painted style and emphasis on individual subjective expression. Along with other artists of the time, Williams was profoundly affected by the horror and brutality of World War II. The Holocaust and Hiroshima had shaken faith in government, science and humanity. As a response, artists and intellectuals often adopted an existential perspective that advocated individual authenticity, freedom and intuition as the antidote to an absurd, empty and alien world. Williams had a bleak outlook on life that was nonetheless enlivened by his commitment to art and a sardonic sense of humor.

Williams' figurative, landscape and still-life images blend together in innovative forms. His *Chorus Line* and *Audience Series* merge the abstracted shapes of nude and headless figures into nearly mountainous shapes with horizon lines looking like torso lines. Whether figure or landscape, the images often appear to be partially bruised, wounded, nailed or torn. *Some Parallel* is a large, richly textured painting, part body and part map of the United States. A subtle grid suggests latitude and longitude lines, while some bodies of water and land are identified. Peninsulas suggest legs and the occasional nipple marks a city. In places, the body/map is bloodied, blackened and punctured with nails. A rope hangs, noose-like, off one side. Created in 1975, one year after the end of the Vietnam War, the work gives testimony to a conflicted and troubled time in American history.

KO-S

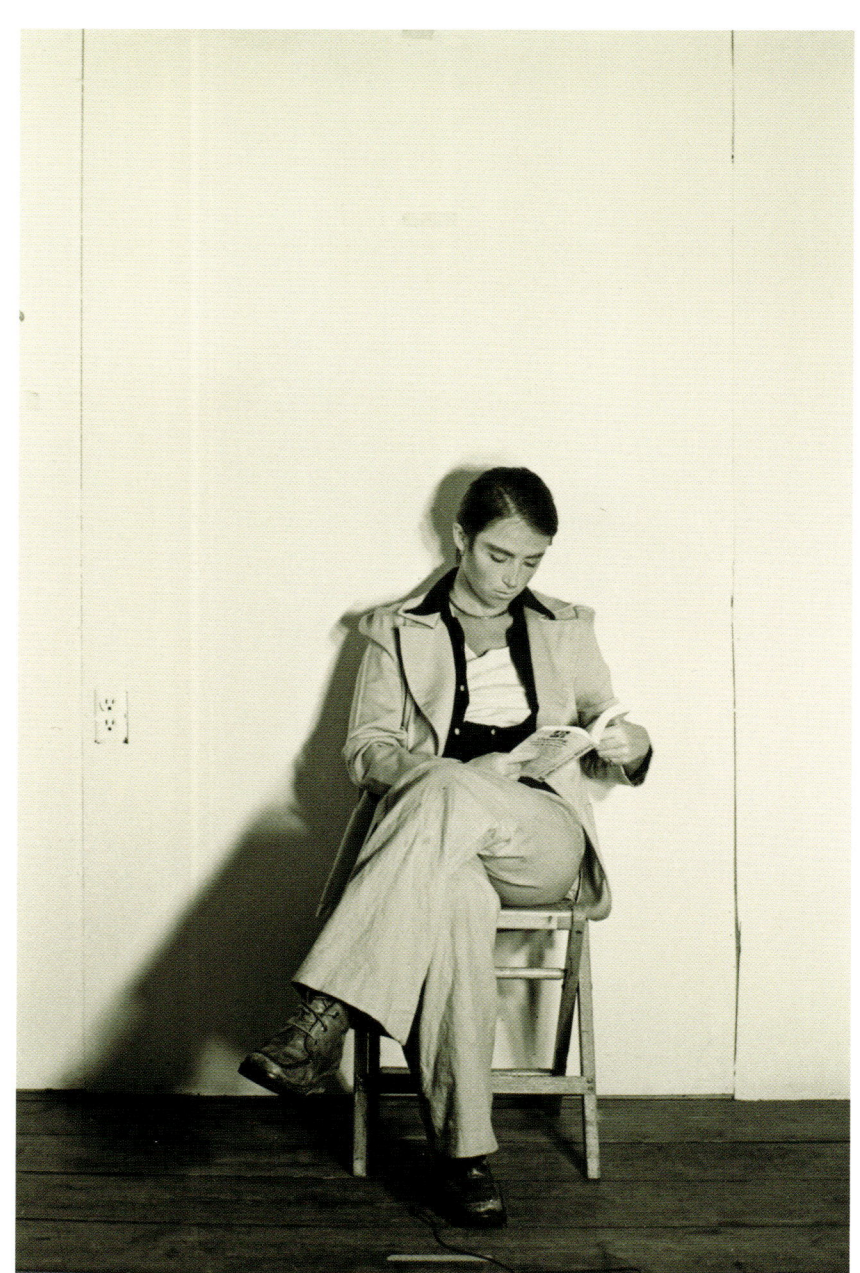

CINDY SHERMAN
American, born 1954

UNTITLED (#373)
1976/2000, black and white photograph
image: 7 7/16 x 5 in. (18.9 x 12.7 cm)
sheet: 10 x 8 in. (25.4 x 20.3 cm)
Museum purchase, funds provided by
the Caroline Julier and James G. Richardson
Acquisition Fund
Image permission courtesy of the
Artist and Metro Pictures
2002.8

Cindy Sherman was born in Glen Ridge, New Jersey. She studied art at the State University College, Buffalo, New York, moving to New York City in 1977, where she launched her groundbreaking series, *Untitled Film Stills*. This series of photographs garnered widespread attention as a challenge to the prevailing modernist concepts of originality, authenticity and the authority of the individual male artist. Sherman's work countered these notions with ideas about constructed identity, the influence of mass media and feminist critique.

Untitled Film Stills is comprised of 69 small black-and-white photographs in which the artist poses as various types of actresses typical of European films and B-movies. For each imaginary character, she altered her hair, makeup and costume to illustrate identity as the product of performance. Through these photographs, Sherman underscored the role of media and popular culture in shaping, reframing and restaging cultural identity and stereotypes. The ideas first developed in the *Untitled Film Stills* continued to inform future work, including series on the centerfold, fashion photography, historical portrait painting, soft-core porn, housewives and the subject of the abject.

Untitled Film Stills was long considered to be the start of Sherman's prolific career. However, in 2000 she printed and publicly released two previous series created in 1976 just after she graduated from school. Represented here is one image from the *Bus Riders* series, fifteen black-and-white photographs depicting people she observed while riding the bus. With just a wall behind her and minimal props, Sherman personally re-enacts these generic types across gender and race using makeup and costumes. Unlike her later photos which used settings and more elaborate props to fill in the "scene," this series focuses more on character and performance. Clearly visible at the bottom of the frame, the camera's shutter release cable underscores the artifice of the image.

KO-S

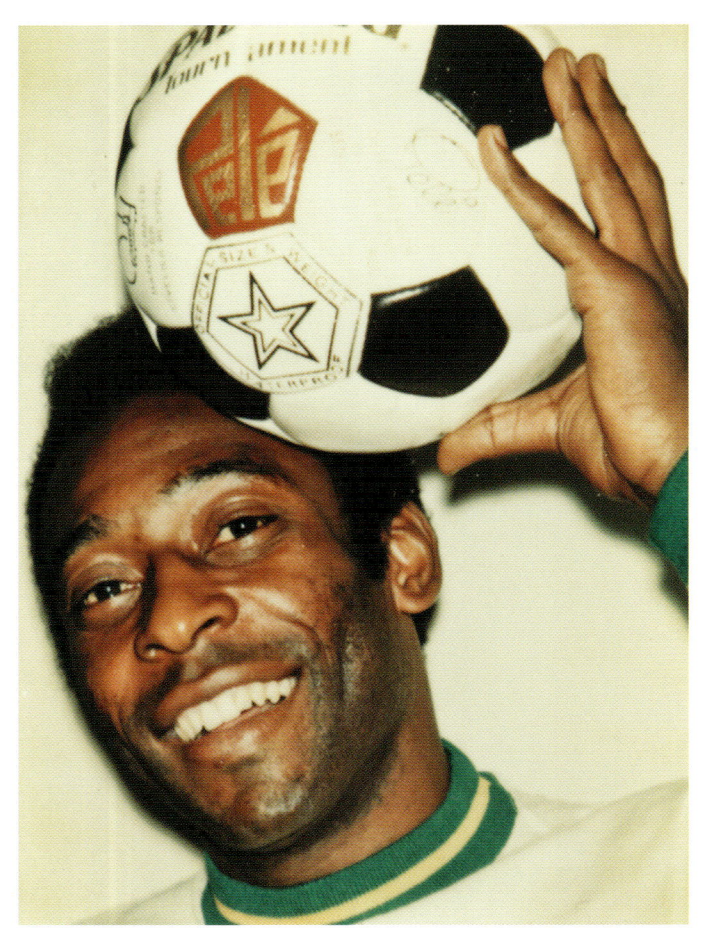

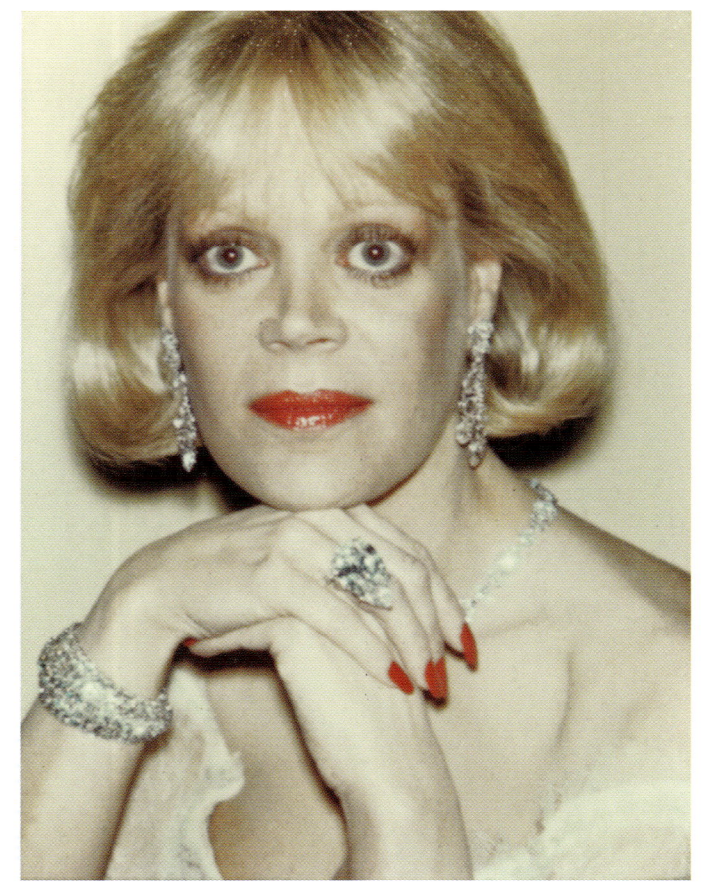

Andy Warhol
American, 1928-1987

Pelé
1977, Polacolor Type 108
sheet: 4 ¼ x 3 ⅜ in. (10.8 x 8.6 cm)
image: 3 ¾ x 2 ⅞ in. (9.5 x 7.3 cm)
Gift of the Andy Warhol Foundation
for the Visual Arts
© The Andy Warhol Foundation for
the Visual Arts, Inc.
2008.28.59

Candy Spelling
1985, Polacolor ER
image: 3 ¾ x 2 ⅞ in. (9.5 x 7.3 cm)
sheet: 4 ¼ x 3 ⅜ in. (10.8 x 8.6 cm)
Gift of the Andy Warhol Foundation
for the Visual Arts
© The Andy Warhol Foundation for
the Visual Arts, Inc.
2008.28.13

The Harn Museum is a fortunate recipient of a generous gift of 150 photographic works from the Andy Warhol Estate. The majority are snapshot-sized Polaroid instant print portraits, plus 50 black-and-white prints, mainly paparazzi-style images of celebrities and strangers caught in off-guard moments. These two Polaroids of Pelé and Candy Spelling suggest the richness and complexity offered by even Warhol's most casual and seemingly simple creations.

Throughout the 1970s, Warhol often used his Polaroid Big Shot photos as sources for ubiquitous screen print paintings of celebrities and wannabe celebrities, continuing and amplifying the iconic transformations begun with his *Marilyn* and *Jackie* series of the 1960s. But Warhol made these Polaroid snapshots in huge quantities, and it is not known if any of the photographs donated to the Harn were ever used by him or even looked at before being stored away, possibly in one of his cardboard boxes of accumulated materials he dated and appropriately called "Time Capsules."

Warhol's self-professed role as artist was to be a mirror and a detached machine in his production. It is thus appropriate to consider the questions raised by these photographs—and his other works—rather than look to them for answers or his personal conclusions. When these snapshots were made in the 1970s, Pelé's name and face were internationally known, especially beyond the United States, as one of the greatest soccer stars of all time. Candy Spelling's face might have been known to the Hollywood and New York art and entertainment celebrity circles Warhol cultivated, but for a broader audience, her name, not face, would be an essential clue to her connection to the powerful TV producer Aaron Spelling. What name and face recognition is now retained decades later in the new millennium? To what degree is the significance of these works dependent on the ebbs and flows of the celebrity of the subjects as decades pass? Are they (and we) all destined to the leveling of time that brings them back to the status of the numerous unidentified subjects in the Warhol collection? Ironically, it may be Warhol the artist-observer, like the artists Rubens, Rembrandt and Goya, who is more remembered than his subjects.

TS

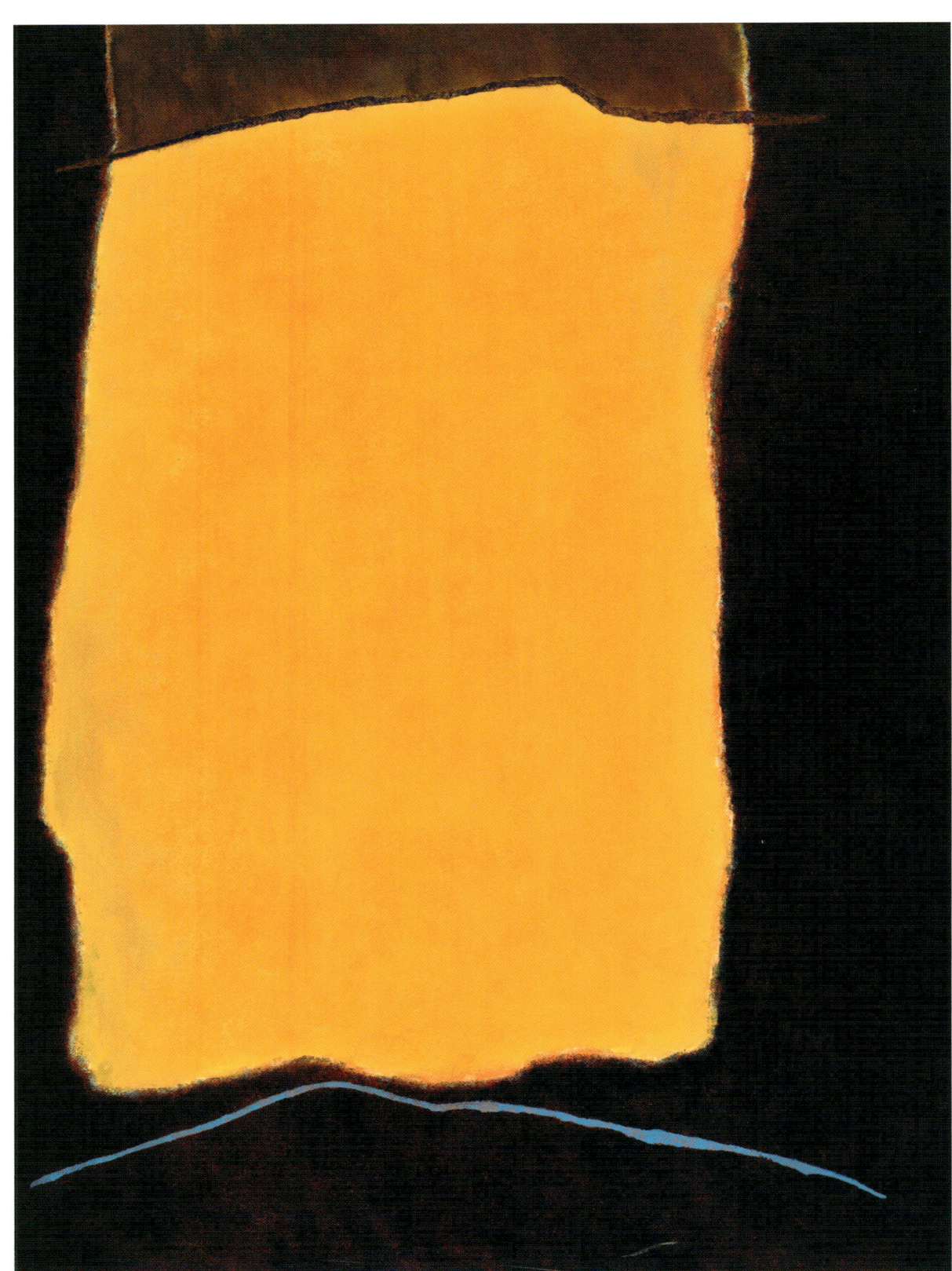

Theodoros Stamos
American, 1922-1997

Infinity Field
(from the Lefkada Series)
1977, acrylic on canvas
66 x 50 in. (167.6 x 127 cm)
Gift of Dr. and Mrs. Robert C. Magoon
in honor of Sam and Bessie Proctor
1996.37

Born to Greek immigrant parents, Theodoros Stamos was an Abstract Expressionist painter who first studied sculpture at the American Artists' School in New York City. By 1939 he turned to painting and opened up a frame shop, where he met several luminaries of the art world. Stamos had his first show with Betty Parsons in 1943; and seven years later, he became one of the youngest members of the "Irascibles," a core group of New York School artists, including Barnett Newman, Mark Rothko, Jackson Pollock and Clyfford Still. Stamos' early work alluded to calligraphy, mythology and biomorphic forms. Like the work of other abstract painters, Stamos' paintings were inspired by intuition and spontaneity.

Stamos bridged the two generations of Abstract Expressionist artists and emerged as a leader in the second generation of Color Field artists. Usually he favored muted colors and organic shapes layered in paintings that seem to radiate a light from within. These characteristics are evident in paintings created in the 1970s, when Stamos began to divide his time between New York and the Greek Island of Léfkas, the birthplace of his father. On the island, he launched a series of paintings called the *Infinity Fields—Lefkada Series*, which included the work in the Harn collection.

Typically paintings in the *Lefkada Series* represented geometric compositions, setting loosely rectangular shapes against a contrasting color. The paintings reference the landscape, seascape and mythology of the island. Of particular interest to Stamos was the sense of light and atmosphere. In this work, a glowing golden color suggests the radiance and warmth of the sun, which in turn is set against the dark, rich and earthy colors that surround it. A thin blue line suggests the sinuous curves of distant hills.

KO-S

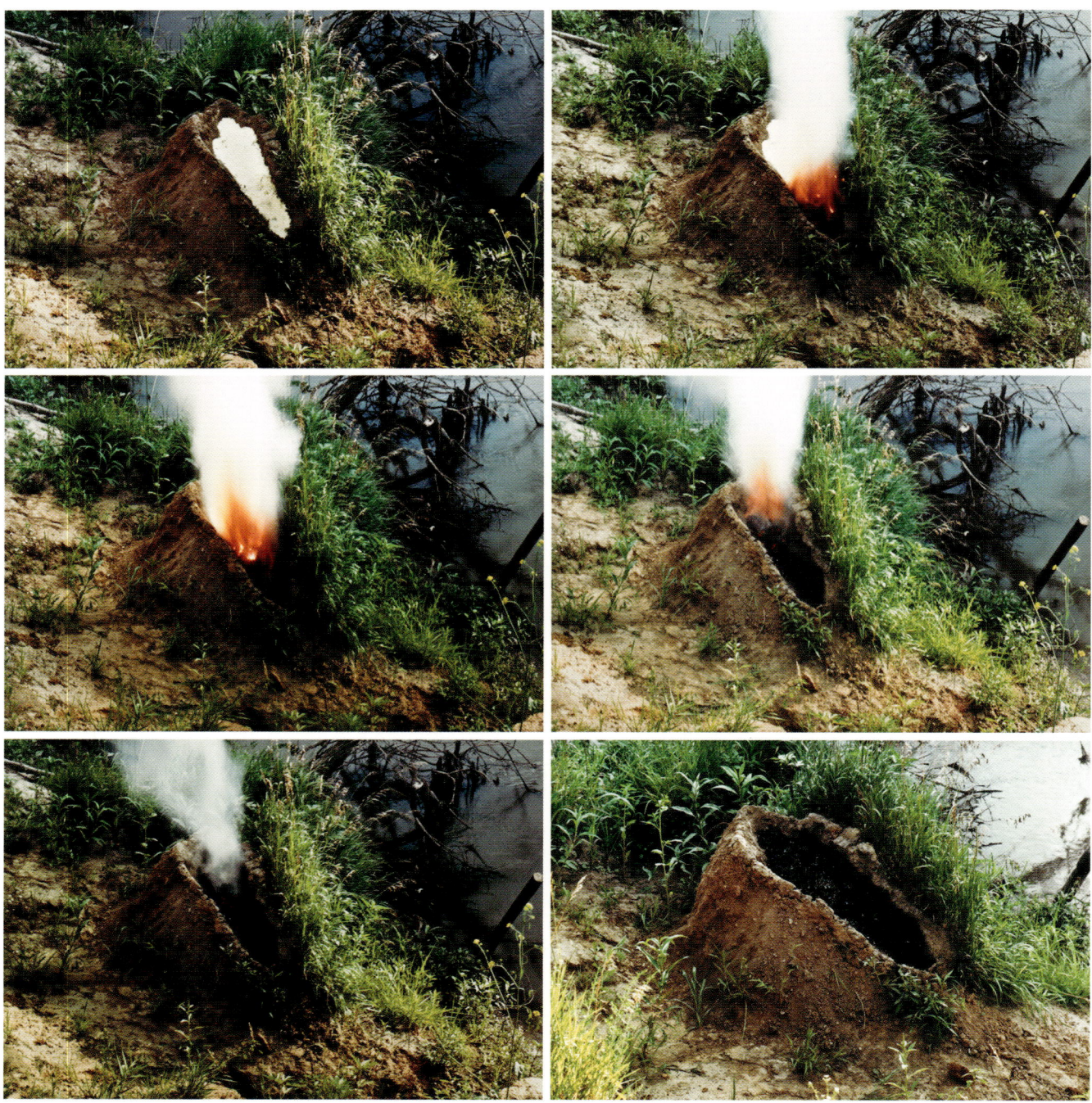

Ana Mendieta
American, born Cuba, 1948-1985

Volcan Series, No. 2
1979, set of 6 color photographs
each sheet: 13 ¼ x 20 in. (33.7 x 50.8 cm)
Museum purchase, funds provided by the
Caroline Julier and James G. Richardson
Acquisition Fund
2002.25

Ana Mendieta was a performance artist, photographer and filmmaker who addressed issues of cultural origin, difference and identity. She rose to prominence in the 1970s and produced an important body of work before her untimely death in 1985. Born to a prominent Cuban family, Mendieta was sent to the United States in 1961. She grew up in Iowa, where she ultimately earned her MFA from the avant-garde Intermedia Program at Iowa State University. In 1978 she moved to New York City.

Mendieta is known for creating and documenting earthworks and ritualistic performances that assert her spiritual and physical connection to nature as well as her feminist challenge to patriarchal ideology. Her primary medium was her body or the outlines of her absent body impressed in earth, grass or trees. Her work reflects her state of exile, the rituals of Afro-Cuban Santería and Abakua societies, and the aesthetic practices of Conceptual and Post-Minimalist artists.

The *Volcan Series* is closely related to Mendieta's well-known *Silueta* (Silhouette) series of 1973-1977, which was originally created in Mexico and also performed elsewhere. Mendieta's body was present or suggested in several ways, including depressions in the ground filled with water, blood or roses; in mounds of earth embellished with flowers; through outlines on beaches and riverbanks; and by narrow cavities scaled to her frame. In *Volcan Series, No. 2*, the molded impressions of her body are filled with gunpowder and set afire leaving traces of ash. Fire evokes the process of consumption and transformation in religious rituals and the forces of fertility, death and destruction. Mendieta's ephemeral performances and sculptures were recorded in documentary photographs and film that extend the dialogue of absence and presence.

KO-S

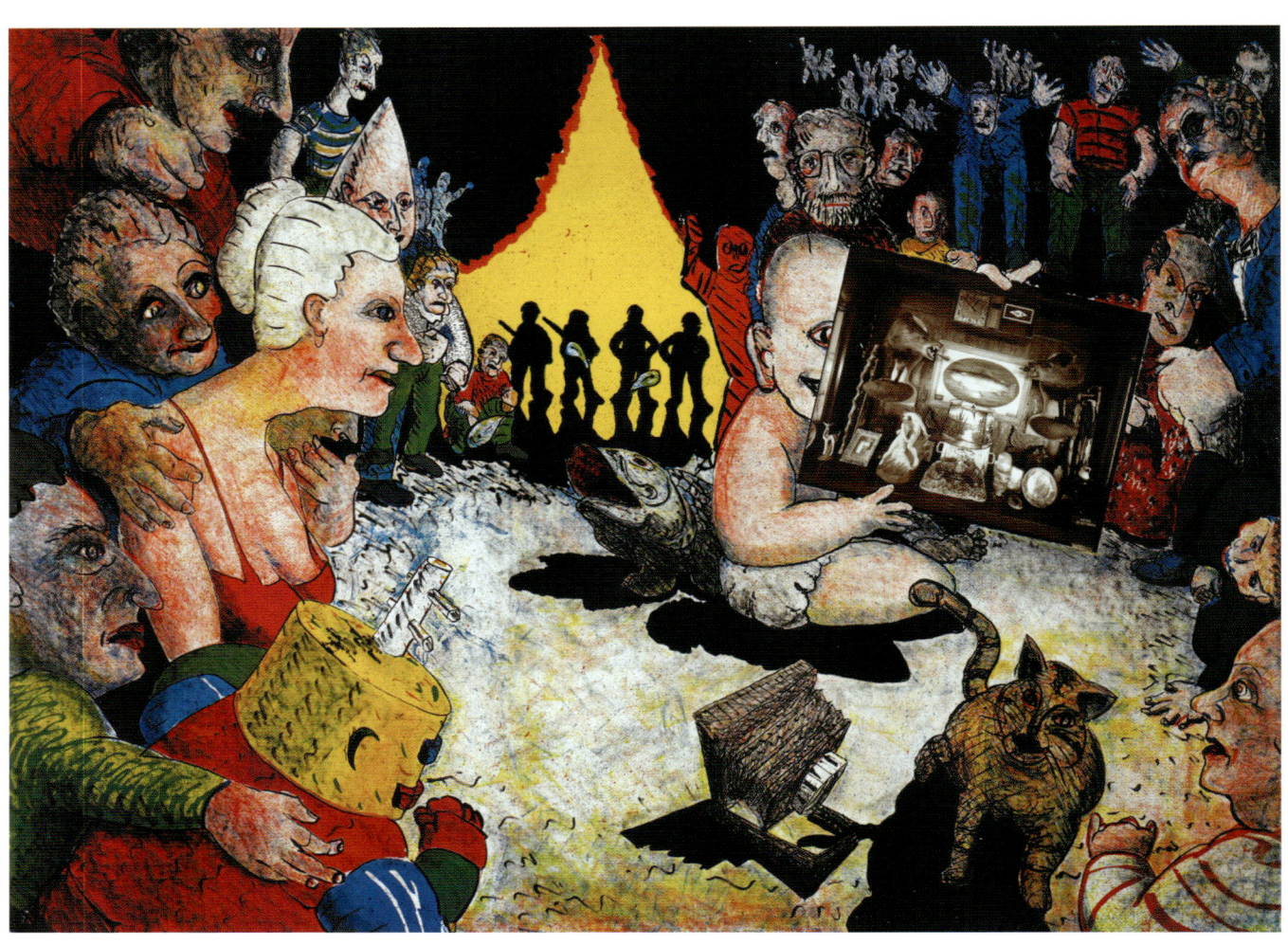

ROBERT FICHTER
American, born 1939

BABY GENE POOL'S
FIRST PHOTOGRAPH

1980s, lithograph with albumen print insert,
Vari Press print
image and sheet: 29 ¾ x 41 ¾ in. (75.6 x 106 cm)
Gift of Robert and Nancy Fichter
Given in honor of my University of Florida
teachers: Ken Kerslake, Jerry Uelsmann and
Jack Nichelson without whose support and
encouragement I would not have continued
to make pictures.
2008.9.12

Robert Fichter's drive toward a multi-media approach to image making was nurtured in his undergraduate studies at the University of Florida (BFA 1963), where he worked especially closely with Jerry Uelsmann (photography), Ken Kerslake (printmaking), and Jack Nichelson (design). Fichter's experimental approach was further encouraged by his subsequent experiences at the University of Indiana (MFA 1966), where he studied under Uelsmann's teacher, Henry Holmes Smith, and Fichter's early museum and teaching jobs at the George Eastman House, UCLA, the School of the Art Institute of Chicago and Florida State University, where he spent most of his teaching career. The broad range of Fichter's work makes it difficult to categorize by medium, style or subject. His imagery ranges from assembled photographic tableaus of ironic objects mimicking Old Master still lifes to cartoon-like drawings with obvious references to popular culture—all executed in a broad range of media from straight photography to Polaroids, using historic photographic processes and just about any printmaking media he could find.

Baby Gene Pool's First Photograph is a terrific demonstration of Robert Fichter's ongoing experimental approach and his refusal to be bound by traditional media categories. His recurring protagonist, Baby Gene Pool, is depicted in this expressive, intensely colored lithographic drawing proudly displaying his "first photograph," an antique albumen print of a sharply rendered still-life scene reminiscent of a 19th-century cabinet of curiosities. "Pretty impressive for a baby," the viewer might be expected to respond. This print's references to the differences between photography and other printmaking processes acknowledges but ridicules art historical boundaries with an ambiguous irony typical of much of Fichter's work. He enjoys breaking down the media borders but also seems to be careful to not take himself—or the art world—too seriously.

TS

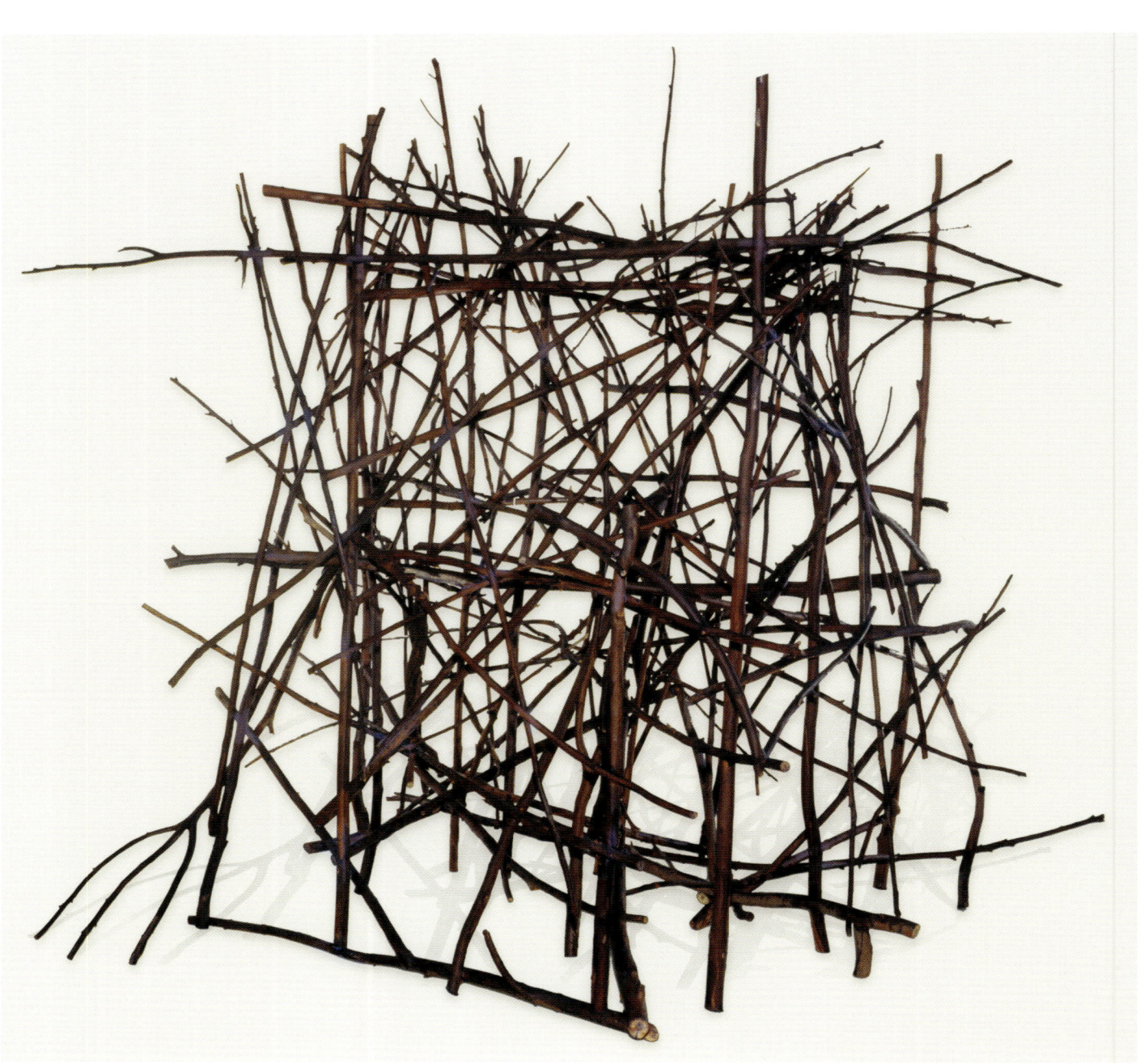

CHARLES ARNOLDI
American, born 1946

UNTITLED
1980, painted tree branches
92 x 93 x 90 in. (233.7 x 236.2 x 228.6 cm)
Gift of Martin Z. Margulies
© Charles Arnoldi Studio
2004.18.2

Sculptor and painter Charles Arnoldi was born in Dayton, Ohio. At the age of eighteen, he left for Los Angeles, where he studied at the Choinard Art Institute and won the Los Angeles County Museum of Art talent award in 1969. Frustrated with formal training, he began to work independently. Arnoldi quickly rose to prominence in the 1970s with his free-standing sculptures, wall reliefs, and later, his brightly-colored abstract paintings. Throughout his work, Arnoldi combined elements of both painting and sculpture, fusing his interests in materiality, color, illusion and painterly expression.

Arnoldi began working with sticks and branches by positioning them against the wall to explore their linear possibilities. Assimilating the sticks in sculptural form, he deliberately exploited the ambiguity between two- and three-dimensional space. Shadows cast by the sculpture on the surrounding floor and walls provide another elusive dimension abated by light. Arnoldi's stick sculptures, such as this work, defy the depth and weight associated with traditional sculptures. Instead, they explore the interplay of negative and positive space and between materiality and immateriality.

Arnoldi's stick sculptures have been likened to drawing in space and to the linear quality associated with Abstract Expressionist painter Jackson Pollock's drip paintings. Arnoldi also drew on elemental strategies of Minimalism. Like other Minimalists, he rejected representation, illusionism and crafts-manship. However, by using objects taken from the natural world, he made a break with Minimalism's more austere character and use of industrial materials.

The tips of the pictured sculpture are colored in a blue indigo, forecasting the artist's future work with intense color. In his later work, Arnoldi used color abundantly and expressively on canvases and his wood relief work.

KO-S

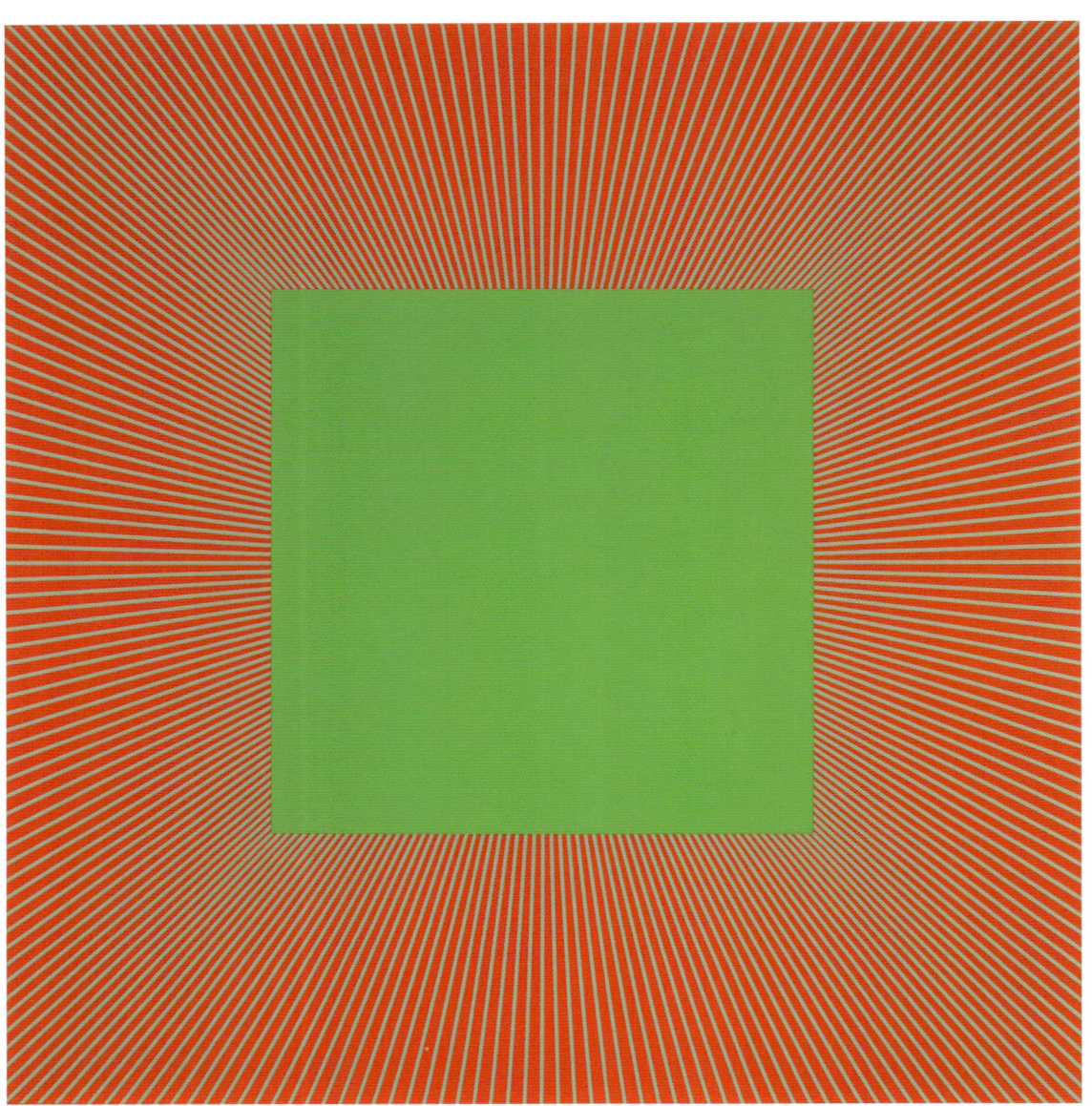

Richard Anuszkiewicz
American, born 1930

Green Square
1981, acrylic on board
24 x 24 in. (61 x 61 cm)
Gift of Budd and Julia Bishop
Art © Richard Anuszkiewicz/
Licensed by VAGA, New York, NY
2008.43

Born in Pennsylvania, Richard Anuszkiewicz is a painter, printmaker and sculptor known for his hard-edged geometric style and experiments with color perception. Anuszkiewicz studied at the Yale School of Fine Art under Josef Albers, a recognized Bauhaus master and color theorist. From Albers, Anuszkiewicz absorbed the lessons of Constructivism, perceptual psychology and color. In 1957 he moved to New York, achieving prominence and success with his inclusion in the Whitney Museum exhibition *Geometric Abstraction* in 1962 and the groundbreaking exhibition *The Responsive Eye* at the Museum of Modern Art in 1965. By that time, Anuszkiewicz was considered a founder of the Optical Art movement and its foremost exponent.

Op art, an abbreviation of "Optical art," is a form of pure abstraction based on perceptual psychology, an objective and scientific approach relating visual phenomenon to the structural patterns of the mind. In his work, Anuszkiewicz plays with the notion of optical illusion, which pits objective knowledge against sensory perceptions, unsettling the viewer's grasp on truth and reality. Anuszkiewicz creates a palpable sense of motion in the flat surface of his paintings through the juxtaposition of complementary colors. Laid out in bold geometric forms and precisely drawn lines, *Green Square* is an excellent example of this method. Anuszkiewicz places cadmium red against green, causing the sensation of vibrating colors. In this painting, he creates tension between flatness and volume, figure and ground, and stasis and movement

At times Anuszkiewicz also works in relief to create a hybrid of painting and sculpture. Often this work was created in units that could be arranged in a variety of ways. Inviting the exhibitor to be a collaborator in giving sculptural shape to the piece, he relinquishes the sole authority of the individual artist. In both his painting and sculpture, Anuszkiewicz is keenly interested in the visitor as a participant in the art experience.

KO-S

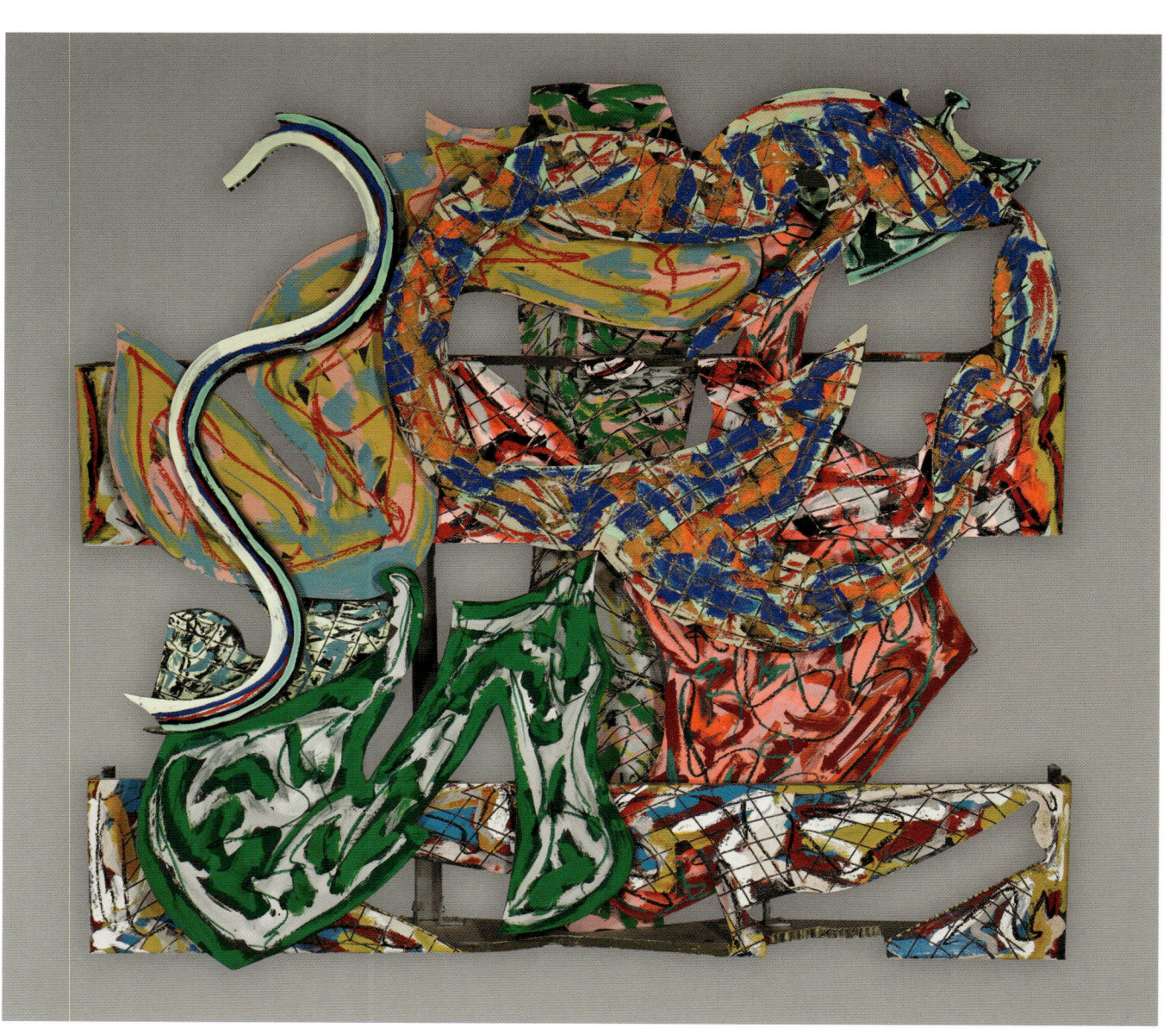

Frank Stella
American, born 1936

Zandvoort (Circuit Series)
1981, mixed media on etched magnesium,
fiberglass and aluminum
70 ¼ x 80 x 13 in. (178.4 x 203.2 x 33 cm)
Gift of Martin Z. Margulies
© 2009 Frank Stella / Artists Rights Society
(ARS), New York
2004.18.1

Frank Stella, a painter, printmaker and sculptor, became a successful artist at a very early age. Stella studied art and art history at Phillips Academy in Andover, Massachusetts, and earned a degree in history at Princeton University. In 1958 Stella moved to New York and began to create his signature stripe paintings. Just a year later, he joined the Leo Castelli Gallery and was included in *Three Young Americans* at the Allen Memorial Art Museum at Oberlin College and in *Sixteen Americans* at the Museum of Modern Art.

Throughout his work, Stella has experimented with new materials, multi-media and hybrid forms. In his earlier Minimalist work, he used industrial paint to create large-scale geometric patterns that ultimately extended the shape of his canvases into non-rectangular forms. Beginning in the 1970s, he began to work with three-dimensional canvases to create what he called "maximalist" painting. He used wood and interlocking planes to create high relief paintings and eventually began using aluminum as a primary support. By the 1980s Stella's work was more ornate in style, in part due to the influence of his residency at the American Academy in Rome, where he was drawn to the illusionist qualities and colors of Baroque painting.

Stella, an enthusiastic aficionado of racing, explored this theme in the Harn piece. *Zandvoort* is part of the series, *Circuits*, begun in 1980, which takes international racing circuits as its inspiration for the 22 works. Each work is named after a city that has hosted the Grand Prix; for instance, *Zandvoort* alludes to a city in the Netherlands. To produce this work, Stella appropriated arabesques and readymade templates employed by marine and railroad draftsmen. The serpentine elements of *Zandvoort* evoke the fast turns of the race track, while the animated painting and vibrant colors of the painting suggest the adrenaline rush of the racing experience itself.

KO-S

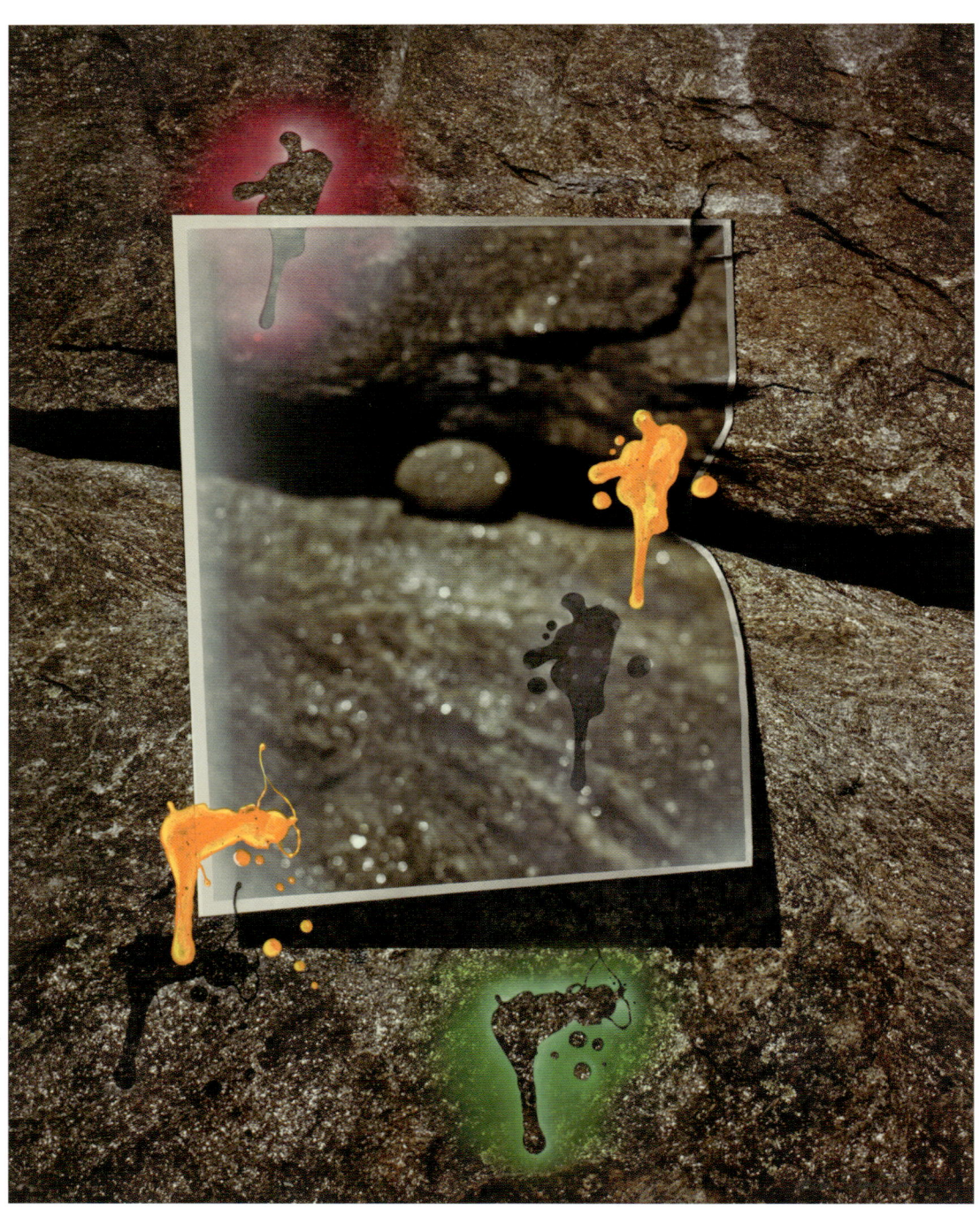

EVON STREETMAN
American, born 1932

HOMAGE TO HENRY
HOLMES SMITH
1983, silver-dye bleach print [Cibachrome]
with acrylic
image: 23 ½ x 19 ⅜ in. (59.7 x 49.2 cm)
Museum purchase with funds provided by
the Melvin and Lorna Rubin Fund
2008.10.1

Evon Streetman has a strong, down-to-earth practical side that is evident in her art, career path, and even her lifelong attachment to fishing and her native Florida environment. While her undergraduate and graduate studies at Florida State University were focused more on painting and the traditional arts, she supported herself in the late 1950s and '60s as a commercial photographer. Her personal work grew into a blending of media and styles that defies easy categorization, but is unified by her central concern for both the beauty of the natural world and the more theoretical aspects of visual intelligence. Her work is emotional and responsive to the beauty of her subjects, but she is also highly deliberate in her pursuit of active "seeing" rather than passive "looking." Her passion for the rewards of perceptive seeing made her an inspiring teacher and imbues her work with playful and profound visual surprises.

Homage to Henry Holmes Smith is a seductive piece filled with witty visual illusions and ironies. On top of the seemingly realistic photograph of a rock wedged in a crevice, Streetman challenges the viewer to decipher the incongruous floating rectangle and splats of paint impossibly suspended in space yet casting even more illogical shadows. The work immediately draws our attention to a variety of issues of perception and representation including scale, surface, space, focus and time.

This homage to Henry Holmes Smith, the noted photography teacher and writer, is especially focused on the deliberate and the accidental, the conscious and the subconscious. Streetman's expressive paint splatters can be compared to Smith's experiments with color and photographic prints made from glass plate "negatives" covered with poured syrup. Like Smith's drip images or even Clifford Still's Abstract Expressionist paintings, Streetman's work contains a powerful suggestion of action and spontaneity, yet is the product of total control and deliberate planning. It is especially appropriate that Streetman would feel an affinity to another teacher who shared her goal of defying traditional boundaries of photography within the arts and inspired students to truly see, not just look.

TS

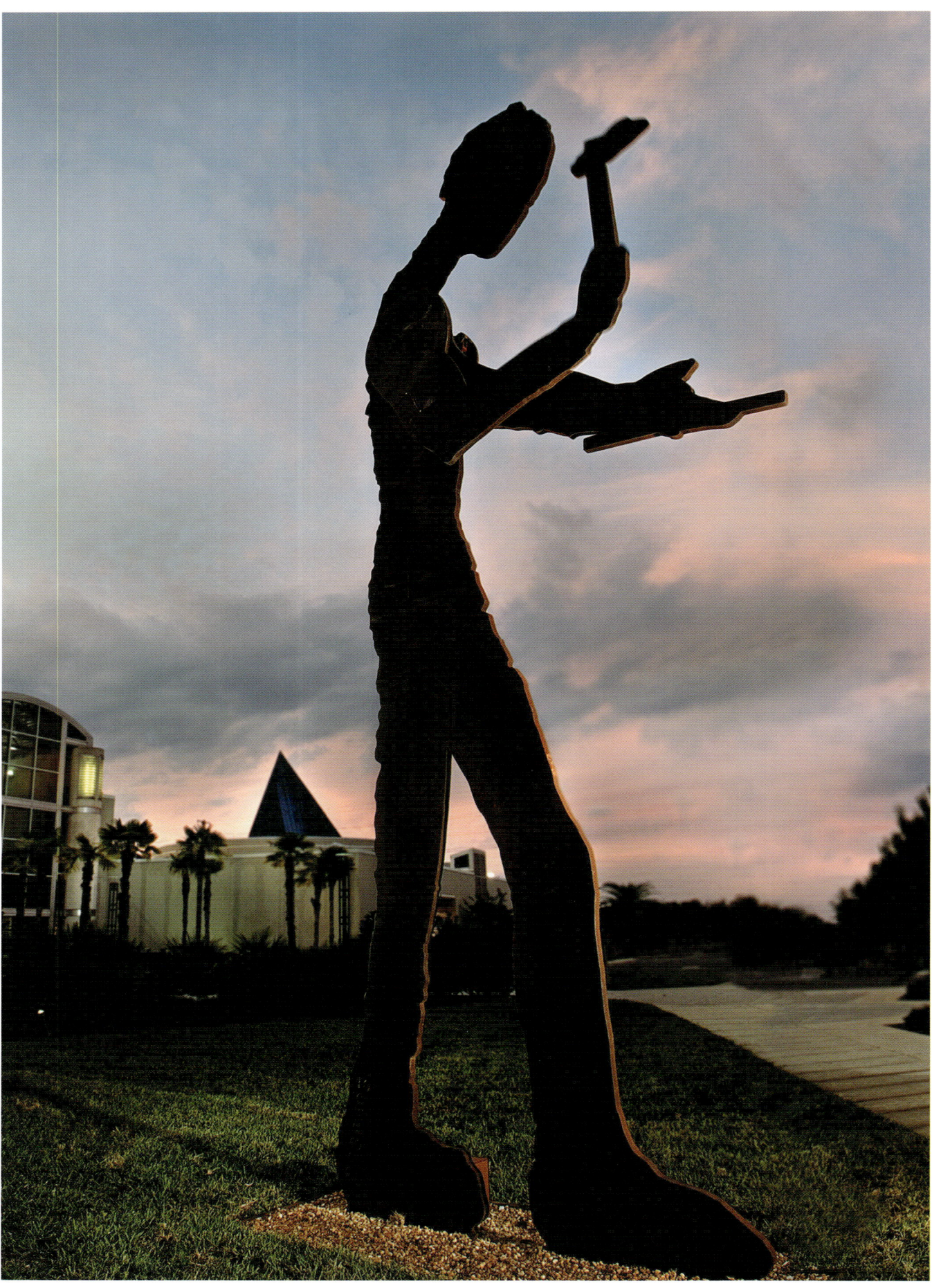

Jonathan Borofsky

American, born 1942

Hammering Man

at 2,938,405

1984, Corten steel
288 x 132 x 24 in. (731.5 x 335.3 x 61 cm)
Gift of the Martin Z. Margulies Foundation, Inc.
Image permission courtesy of the artist
2005.16.1

Jonathan Borofsky is a multifaceted artist who has worked in several media, including painting, sculpture, prints, complex installations, video and light. He received a BFA from Carnegie Mellon University and an MFA from Yale University. He moved to New York City in 1966 and began to record his thoughts, observations and his obsessive counting. By the 1990s Borofsky began to concentrate on large-scale public sculpture. His signature work in this arena is the Hammering Man series. The Harn's sculpture is one of several versions of *Hammering Man* in cities around the world, including Basel, Frankfurt, Los Angeles, Minneapolis, Seattle, Seoul and Washington, DC. The broad dispersal of the work demonstrates its wide appeal and universal relevance.

Hammering Man at 2,938,405 stands 24 feet tall and represents the dynamic silhouetted figure of a man cut from Corten steel. The man holds a hammer which he raises and lowers in the repetitive gesture of a laborer. With this work, Borofsky pays tribute to the universal worker and to those who still work with their hands in a mechanized world. He also honors those who labor at menial tasks. Initially Borofsky intended the figure to represent both genders; thus, the hair gathered at the back of the figure's head lends a feminine aspect, giving the work a more androgynous appearance.

Borofsky's work is often inspired by the world of memories, dreams and free association. However, he exploits these levels of awareness to explore the meaning of daily existence rather than the depths of the subconscious. Mathematics and counting also play a role as a meditative component of the artist's work and as a way to identify each piece. The number 2,938,405 etched on the *Hammering Man* at the Harn Museum represents how far he had counted by the time this work was realized.

KO-S

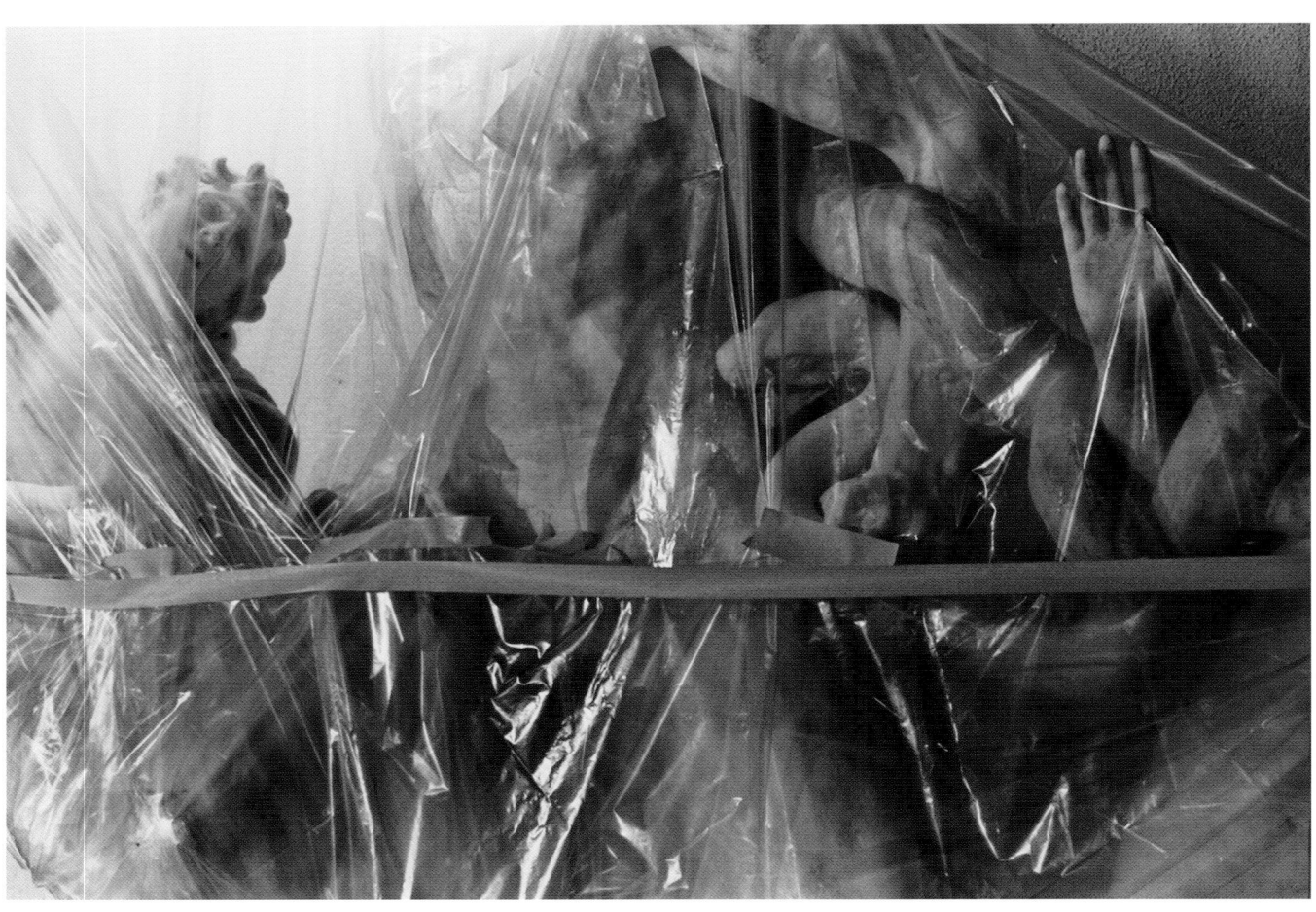

Louise Lawler
American, born 1947

Storage
1984, gelatin silver print
image: 15 ¼ x 23 in. (38.7 x 58.4 cm)
Museum purchase, funds provided by the
Caroline Julier and James G. Richardson
Acquisition Fund
Image permission courtesy of the Artist and
Metro Pictures
2002.19

Louise Lawler was born in Bronxville, New York, and studied at Cornell University, receiving a BFA in 1969. She lives and works in New York City. Lawler is part of a generation of artists who emerged in the 1970s and challenged the grand narrative of modernism with its emphasis on originality, (male) authorship and the aura of the autonomous object. Different strategies to counter this legacy included appropriation, replication, pastiche and feminist critique.

Lawler concentrates on the context and reception of the art object. She is best known for her photographs of art in locations outside of exhibition spaces such as private homes or storage spaces that are unavailable to the general public to view. By highlighting these spaces, Lawler maps the discourse of how art gains value, both material and abstract. Her photographs demystify the art object by presenting it in different contexts, often with subtle humor, reminding the viewer of the process that names, elevates and transforms an object into "art."

The plastic-covered object represented in *Storage* is a Roman copy of the Greek sculpture, *Laocoön and His Sons*. The photograph relates to two seminal essays of art criticism inspired by the original sculpture—*Laocoön: An Essay on the Limits of Painting and Poetry* (1766) by Gotthold Ephaim Lessing and *Towards a Newer Laocoön (Partisan Review*, 1940) by Clement Greenberg. These essays argued for clear distinctions among the arts (poetry and painting) and media (painting and sculpture) and were highly contested by interdisciplinary and multi-media artists working in the 1980s. With *Storage*, Lawler takes the argument further by challenging yet another distinction, in this case, the difference between the art object and the object of everyday life. Here an object considered a masterpiece and the center of art historical debate is humbly wrapped in plastic and placed out of public view. The sculpture is stripped of its museum and cultural context, inviting the viewer to interrogate the notion of value.

KO-S

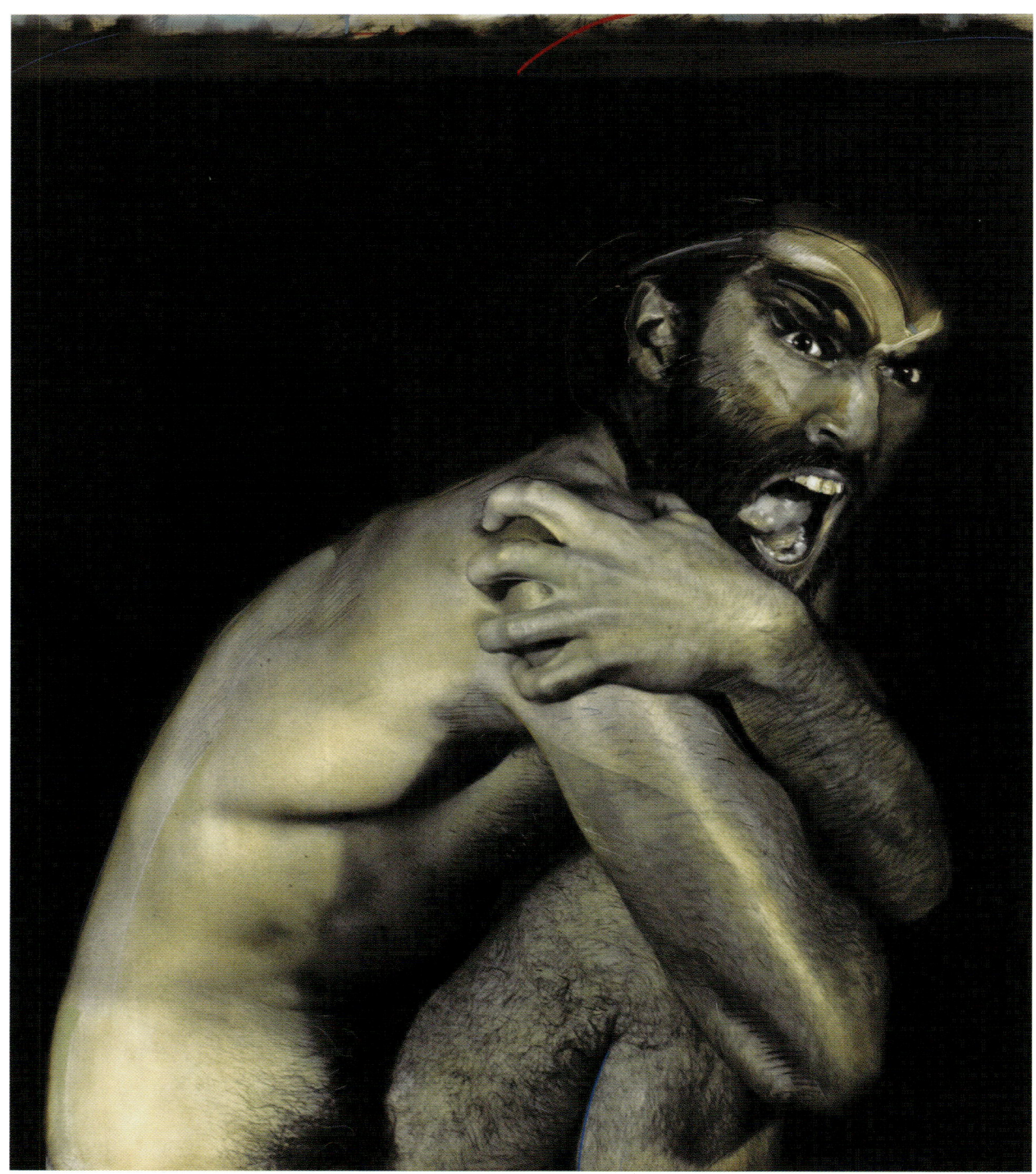

William E. Parker
American, 1932-2009

Der wilde Mann Series/1986: The Temperaments (Fearful I)
1986, gelatin silver print with applied painting and drawing
image: 44 ½ x 39 ½ in. (113 x 100.3 cm)
Gift of William E., Tim Ann and Nevil Parker
2007.26

William E. Parker is perhaps best known as a teacher, editor and writer on photography and the arts with a special interest in the psychological and Jungian interpretation of imagery. The production of art as much as its interpretation has also been central to his life from his BFA (1954) and MFA (1956) studies at the University of Florida through his various professional positions and long tenure as professor at the University of Connecticut (1969 through 1993).

The melding of his critical theory and art production is especially evident in his disturbingly powerful *Der wilde Mann Series/1986: The Temperaments (Fearful I)*. This work is from Parker's extended series, *Der wilde Mann*, all featuring larger-than-life male portrait and figure photographs, heavily reworked with applied painting and drawing. When the full series was shown at Syracuse University in 1988, curator Jeffrey Hoone wrote in the exhibition brochure that "his images evoke the desire to understand fearful taboos and embrace the complexities of the human spirit" (*William E. Parker: Recent Work*). In the same publication, Parker describes this series of portraits as identifying "various aspects of human temperament founded in historical studies on physiognomy and expression as a measure of psychotic identity and types of character."

Parker's interest in exploring the complex symbolism of specific temperaments such as choleric, melancholic and sanguine, among others, may be beyond most modern viewers who have not read Parker's sources and references. However, even viewing an isolated image from the series, its challenging power is palpable. The tension of the pose and clenching hand is accentuated by the expressive energy of the heavy reworking of the image, made even more demanding by its huge scale that demands attention and dwarfs the viewer. Although Parker's imagery is rooted in complex literary theory, he connects with an emotive force that feels beyond words.

TS

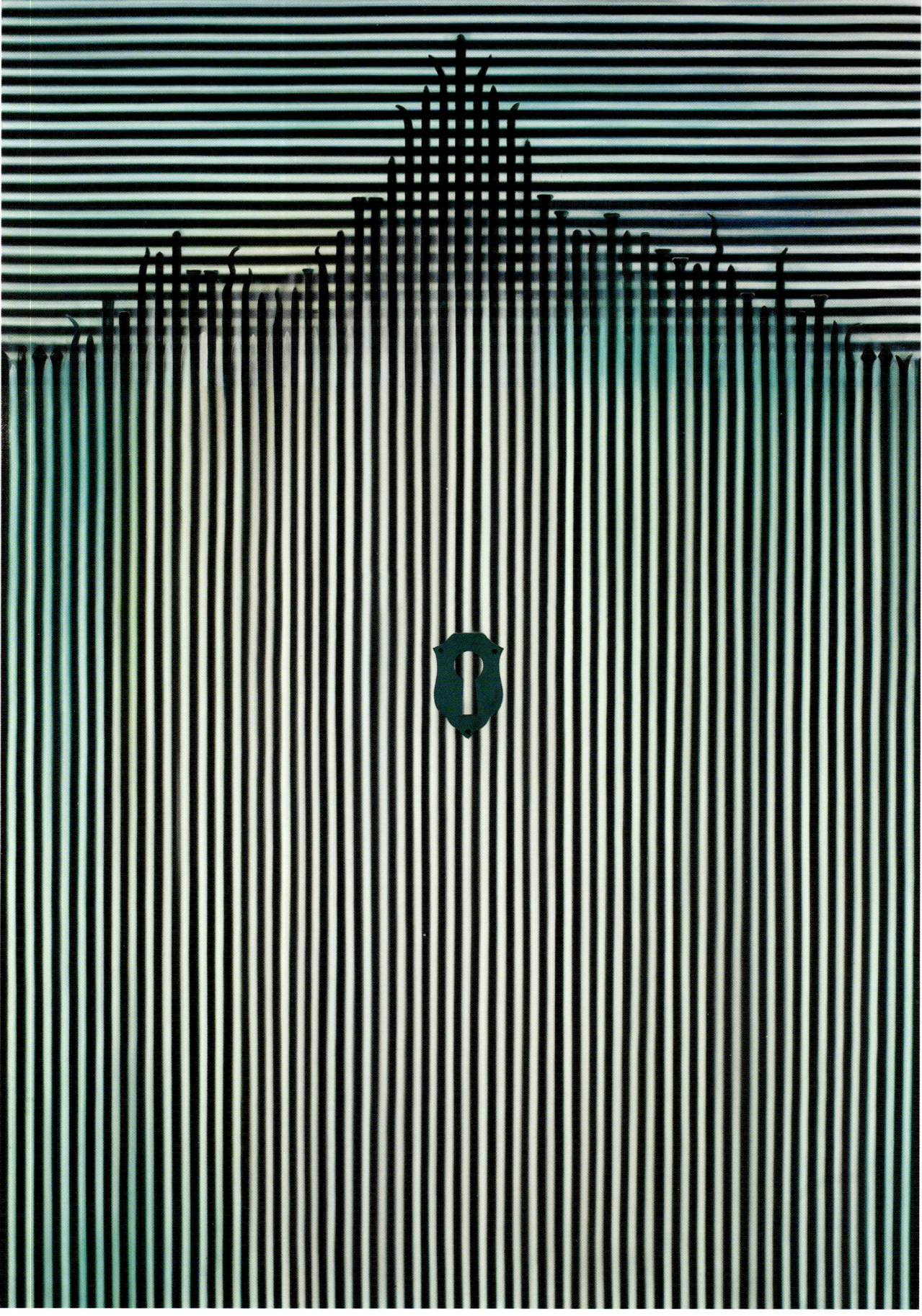

Ross Bleckner
American, born 1949

Gate #2
1986, oil on canvas
120 x 84 in. (304.8 x 213.4 cm)
Gift of Norman and Irma Braman
Ross Bleckner work reproduced
courtesy: Mary Boone Gallery,
New York. (MB G#4014)
2002.37.1

Ross Bleckner rose to prominence as a painter in the 1980s as part of the Neo-Expressionist movement in the United States, Germany and Italy. He began his training under Sol LeWitt and Chuck Close at New York University and later studied at the California Institute of Art (CalArts). Along with fellow graduates and painters David Salle and Eric Fischl, Bleckner rejected the strategies of Conceptual art and antipathy to painting taught at CalArts in favor of a more psychoanalytic approach to art. During his prolific career, he has focused on symbolic imagery and issues of memory, desire and loss.

Bleckner's *Gate #2* is part of a series of stripe paintings first shown at the Mary Boone Gallery in 1981. These paintings celebrate and critique the short-lived Op art movement as exemplified in the work of artist Bridget Riley. For Bleckner, Riley's hypnotic and optically dazzling paintings represented an apex of modernist geometric abstraction. They also embodied the utopian and positivist spirit of modernism with its uncritical faith in science and technology. Bleckner and other postmodern artists rejected this faith as empty and obsolete. During the time of AIDS and fear of nuclear proliferation and annihilation, science and technology appeared to have delivered a poison without providing a cure.

Similar to Op art, Bleckner's work engages the participation of the viewer's corporeality and emotional and sensory response to movement and light, but Bleckner goes further by using light as a conveyor of symbolic and spiritual meaning. In *Gate #2*, light appears to emanate from within the painting and to push through the bars of institutional or personal confinement. The light moves and flickers, creating, in his words, a "momentary schizophrenia where there is a perceptual rupture." The emphasis on the eye and optical illusion as the gateway to light underscores the uncertainty and ambiguity of transcendental meaning.

KO-S

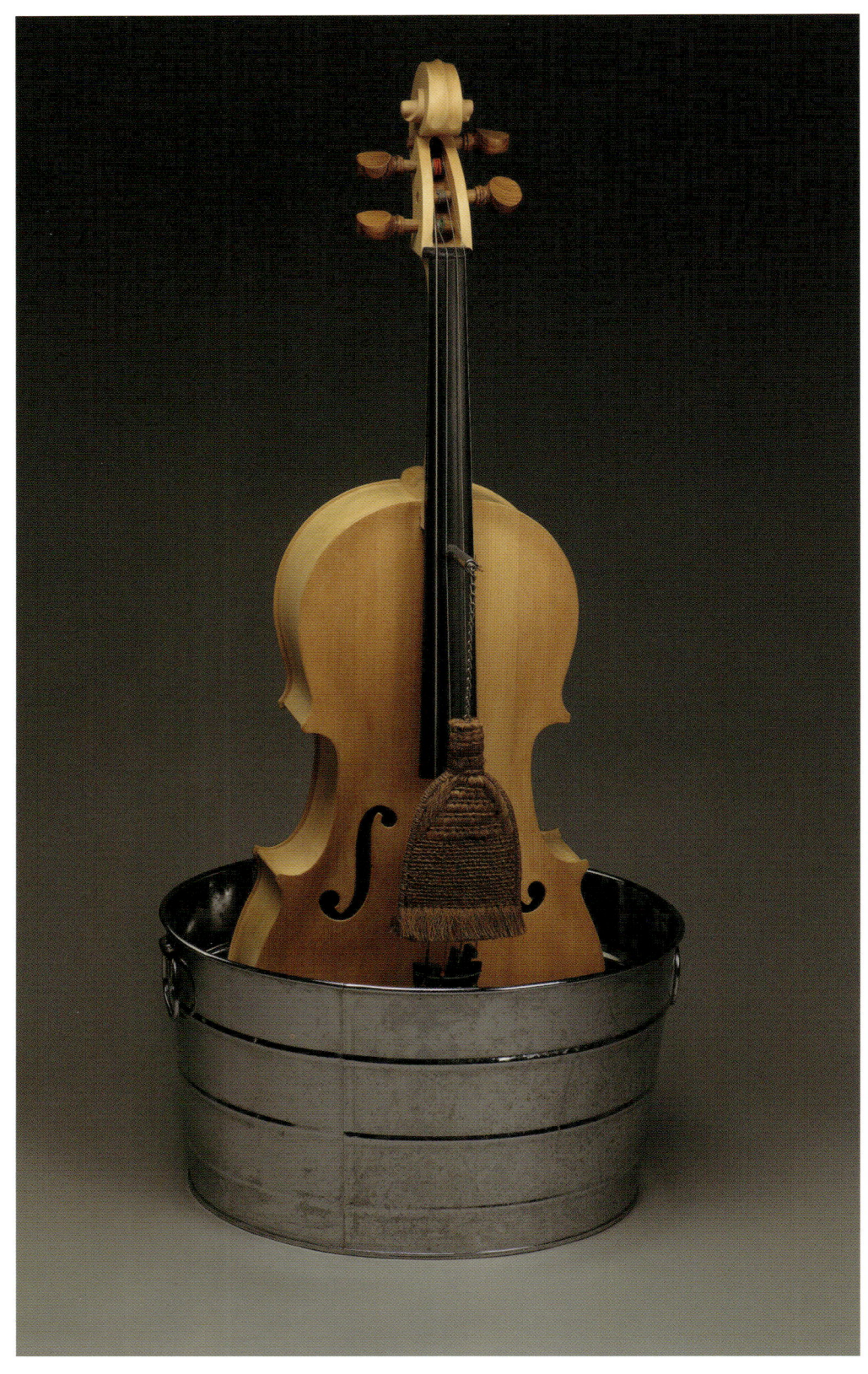

Robert Rauschenberg
American, 1925-2008

Tibetan Garden Song
1986, chrome wash bucket, wood, fiber and oil
43 x 18 ¼ x 18 ¼ in. (109.2 x 46.4 x 46.4 cm)
Gift of Dr. and Mrs. Robert C. Magoon,
in honor of Sam and Bessie Proctor
Art © Estate of Robert Rauschenberg/
Licensed by VAGA, New York, NY
2005.26

An eminent figure in postwar American art, Robert Rauschenberg worked in painting, sculpture, printmaking, performance and photography. Rauschenberg was born in Texas and studied at the Kansas City Art Institute and School of Design. He also trained briefly in Paris and then with Josef Albers at Black Mountain College in North Carolina. There he met composer John Cage and dancer Merce Cunningham, both avant-garde artists who became important collaborators in his future multi-media work.

Rauschenberg is best known for blurring the distinctions between art forms and for his use of found objects, unconventional materials and collage to create paintings he called "combines." Considered by many to provide an important bridge between Abstract Expressionism and Pop art, these works established Rauschenberg's international standing and influence. Rauschenberg proceeded to work with transfer drawing and silkscreen, while also branching off into performance, sculpture and installation work. Throughout his prolific career, Rauschenberg sought to, in his words, "operate in the gap between art and life."

In 1969 Rauschenberg moved to Florida, where he initiated many new projects. *Tibetan Garden Song* was produced in conjunction with the Rauschenberg Overseas Culture Interchange (ROCI), a project created in the 1980s to promote world peace through artistic exchange. The endeavor took the form of a six-year traveling exhibition, where Rauschenberg created the works in host countries in Asia, Eastern Europe and the Americas. Rauschenberg would assimilate images, objects and techniques, creating objects that he also donated to each country. *Tibetan Garden Song* is an enigmatic assemblage that incorporates Rauschenberg's signature fusion of materials, media and form with an interest in everyday objects. Here, the tools of high art, the Chinese cello and scroll maker's brush, are placed in intriguing juxtaposition with an ordinary wash tub, an object of mundane labor.

KO-S

STEPHEN ANTONAKOS
American, born Greece, 1926

ANCIENT ATHENS
1988, neon, gold leaf on wood
64 x 48 in. (162.6 x 121.9 cm)
Museum purchase, gift of Michael A. Singer
Courtesy of the artist
Photography by Greg Heins, Boston
1998.2

Steliainos (Stephen) Antonakos is known for sculptural and architectural forms that combine geometric abstraction with the subtlety and range of neon light. Antonakos grew up and studied in New York City; however, he was born in Agios Nikolaos (Saint Nicholas), a mountain village in Laconia, Greece. Initially a painter, Antonakos turned to more sculptural forms after a return visit to Greece in 1956. He began by creating a hybrid form of painting and sculpture, incorporating found objects that made direct references to everyday life. By 1960 Antonakos had developed a process to adhere neon lights to his unstretched canvases, creating architectural spaces defined and illuminated by neon and called "Rooms." In 1985 he began to create gold-leaf panels illuminated from behind by the glow of neon, creating works that both reflect and emanate light.

Antonakos' work draws inspiration from the abstract and geometric traditions of early 20th-century artists such as Kasimir Malevich and Piet Mondrian. Also influential in his work is Minimalism's emphasis on reductive geometric forms, industrial materials and viewer perception. However, the tenor of Antonakos' work goes beyond the cool and intellectual approach of Minimalism. Like Abstract Expressionist artists, Antonakos was also interested in the inner and subjective dimensions of art and life.

While Antonakos is a secular artist, he is deeply moved by the power of light to intensify the individual and subjective spiritual experience. For him, neon light has a special capacity to create this effect. His inspiration comes in part from the landscape of his ancestral home in Greece. More importantly, Antonakos is deeply affected by the Byzantine icons of the Greek Orthodox Church. In his work, light serves as a symbol of transcendence over time and space and also divine communication. The title of this piece, *Ancient Athens*, also suggests a tribute to a civilization that valued individual initiative and creativity.

KO-S

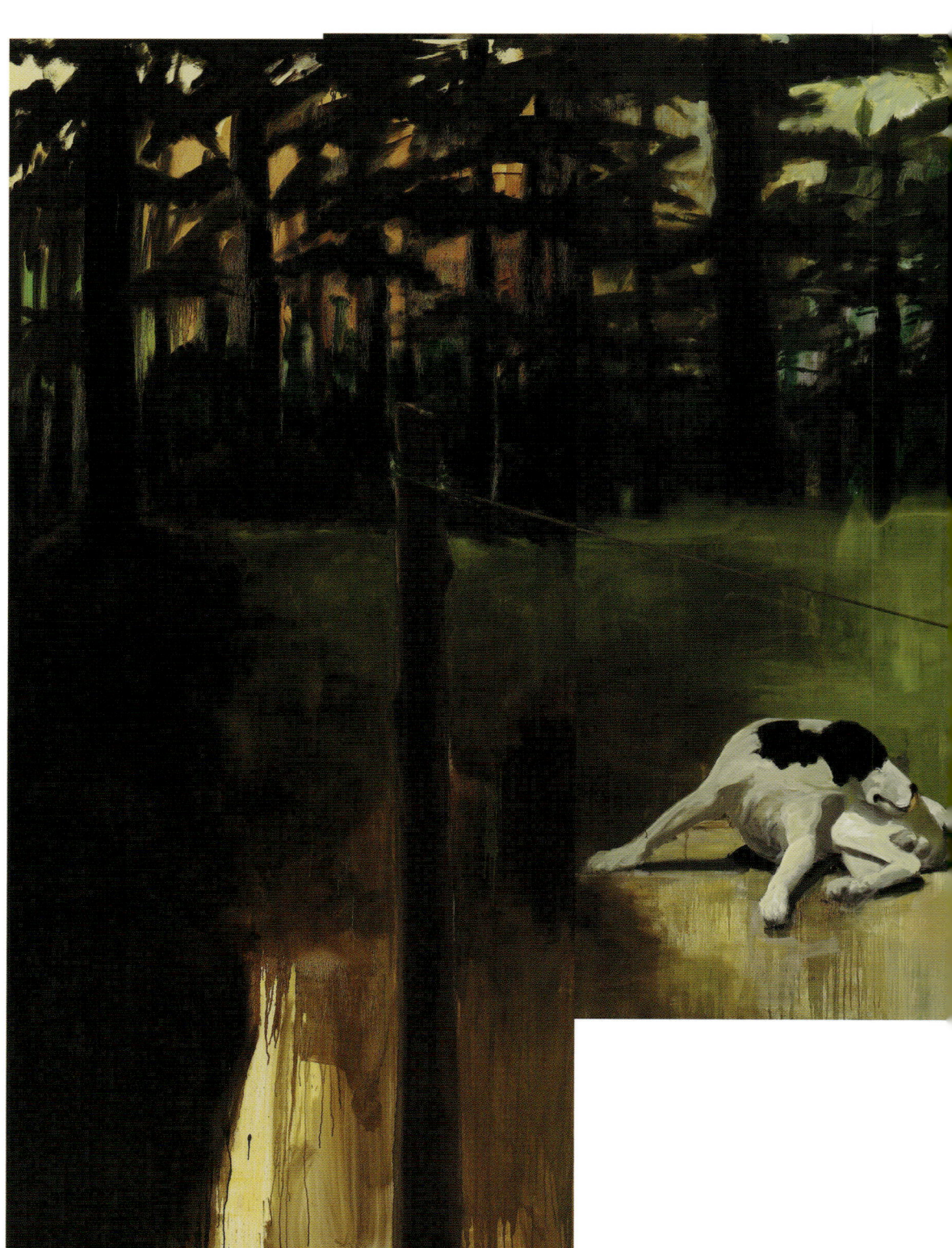

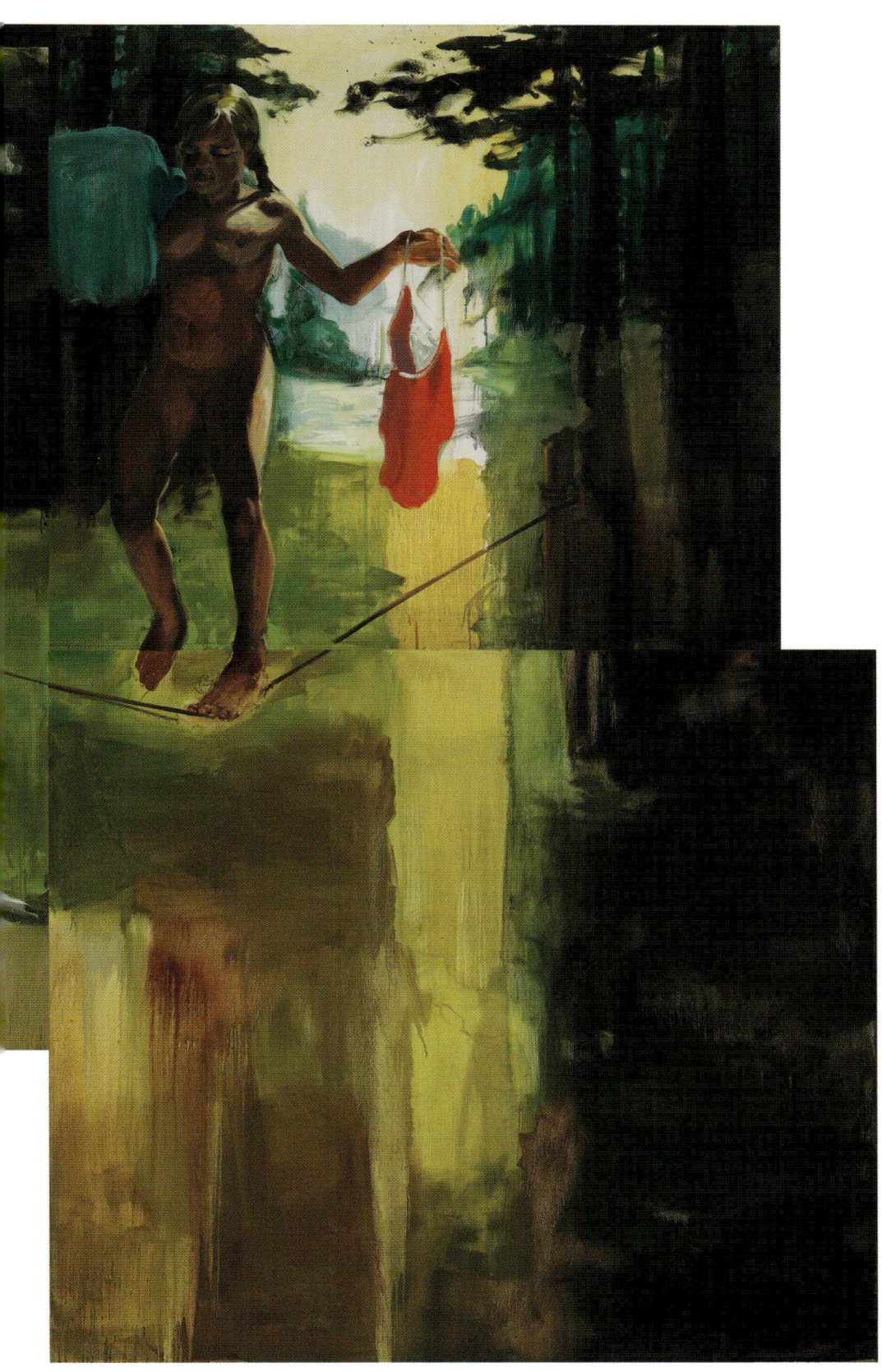

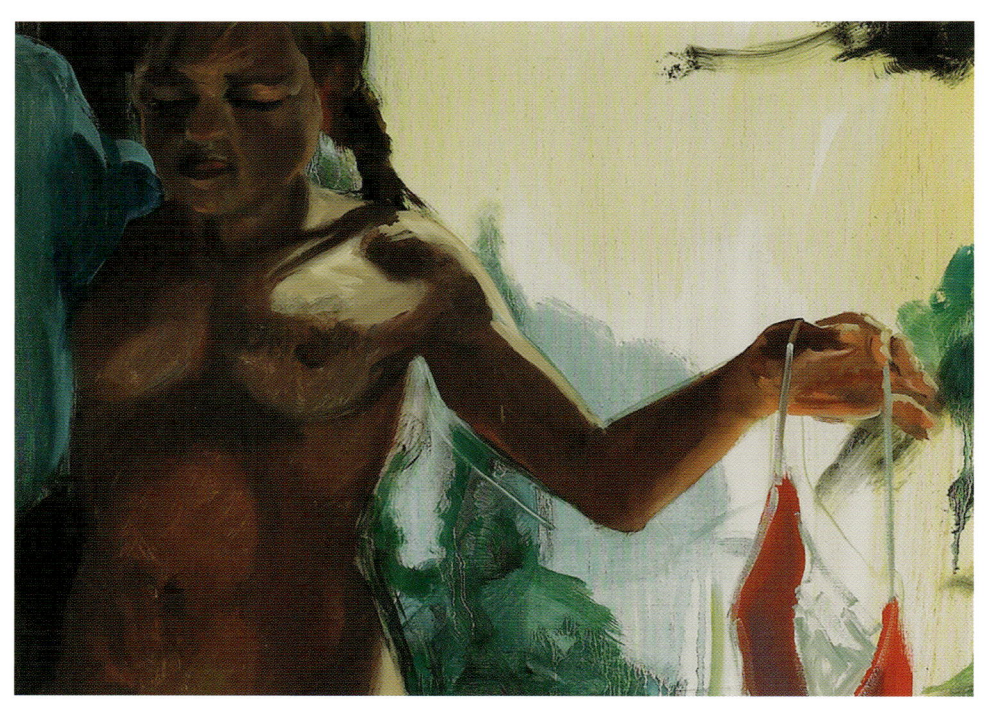

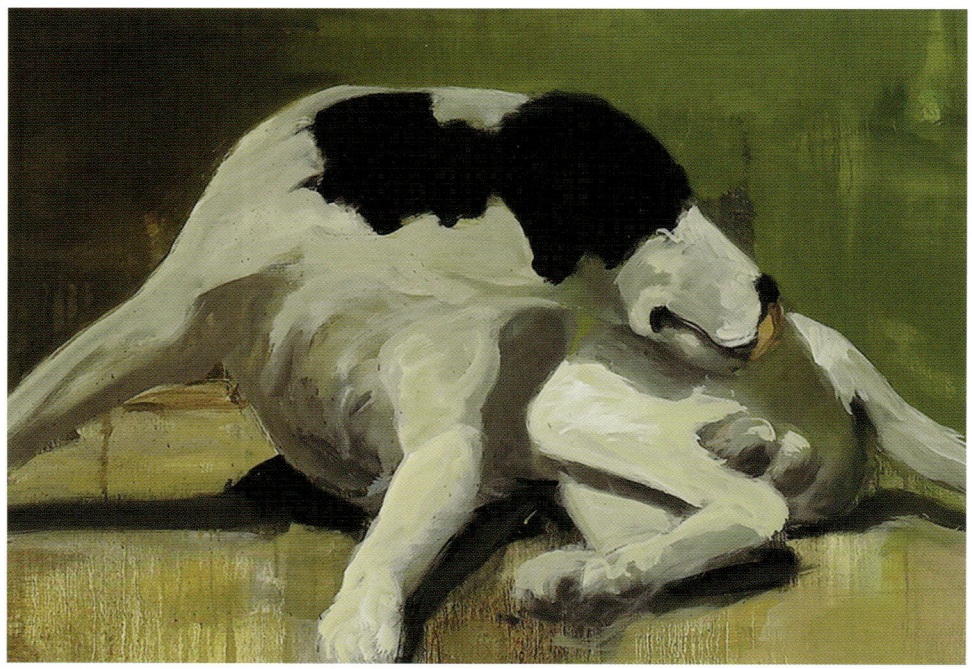

ERIC FISCHL
American, born 1948

THE START OF A FAIRY TALE
1988, oil on canvas, 4 panels
114 x 166 ½ in. (289.6 x 422.9 cm)
Gift of Norman and Irma Braman
© Eric Fischl
2002.37.2

previous spread: full work
left: details

Eric Fischl is a figurative artist whose work includes paintings, drawings, prints and sculpture. Born in New York City in 1948, Fischl grew up in Long Island. He studied at the California Institute of Arts in Valencia, California, in 1972 and later taught at Nova Scotia College of Art and Design. Fischl moved to New York City in 1978 and soon became recognized as one of the leading artists in the Neo-Expressionist movement of the 1980s, which signaled the resurgence of painting and a new interest in individual subjectivity. At the time, he gained considerable notoriety for his paintings of intimate, tense and sexually charged images of middle-class suburban life. His work evokes a sense of emptiness and loneliness in common suburban rituals. In the 1990s, Fischl began to turn to sculpture, and today he continues to paint and push the boundaries of his work.

Eric Fischl's early paintings are well known for intensely psychological, ambiguous and dreamlike scenes. Fischl works with a wide gestural brush stroke and muted colors. Some of his works, such as *The Start of a Fairy Tale*, are painted using overlapping panels that allude to separate memories converging in a single image. In this painting, a nude and nubile girl balances on a rope, red bathing suit in hand. Surrounded by a verdant landscape of trees and rays of sunlight, the girl is closely watched by a dog, a frequent figure in Fischl's paintings. The title and the girl's red bathing suit suggest the story of Red Riding Hood prior to her encounter with the wolf. Fischl's painting is a compelling reflection on the ephemeral and fragile nature of innocence.

KO-S

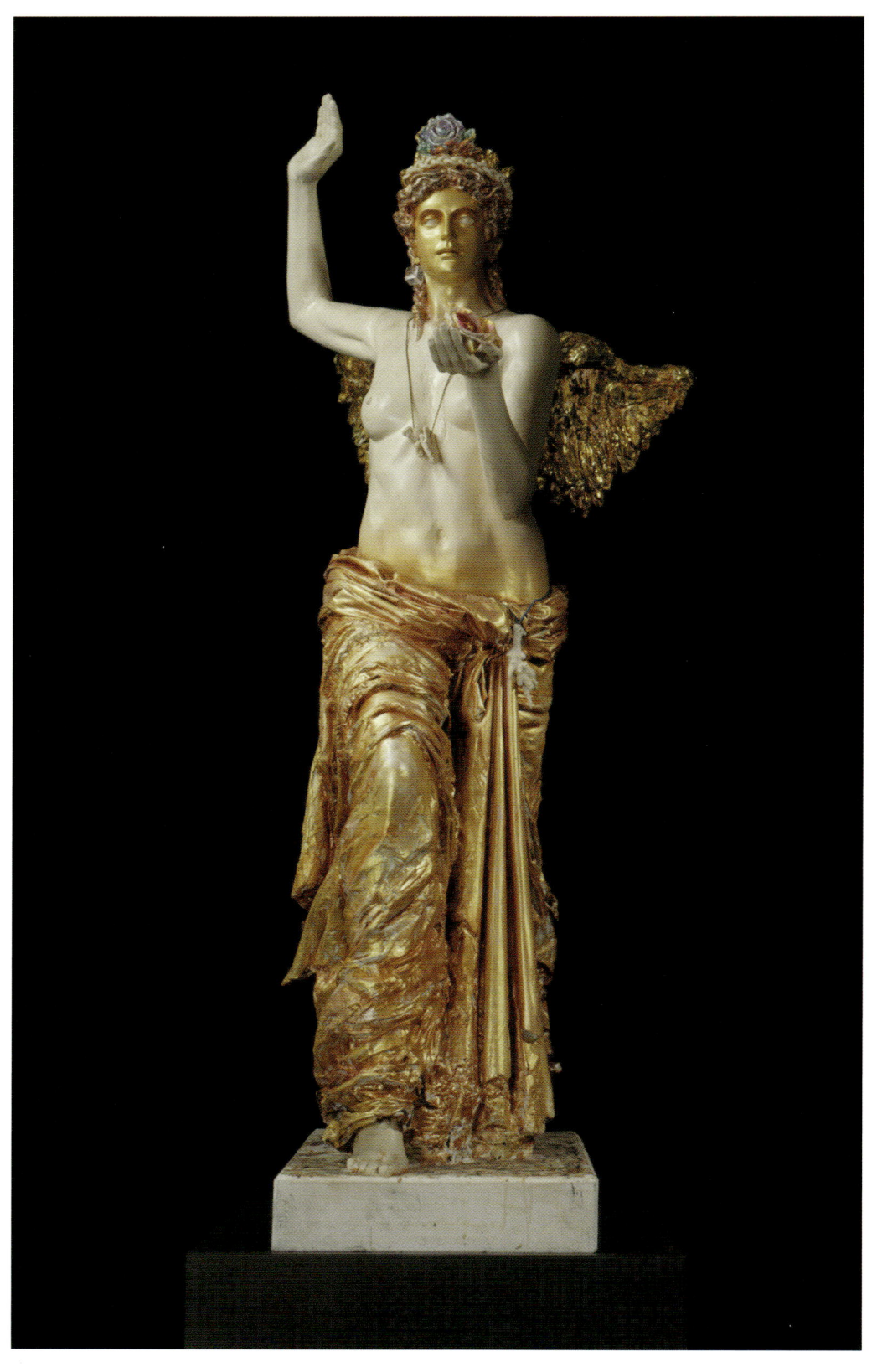

AUDREY FLACK
American, born 1931

ISLANDIA, GODDESS OF THE HEALING WATERS
1988, polychrome and gilded plaster
66 ½ x 26 x 38 in. (168.9 x 66 x 96.5 cm)
Museum purchase, funds provided by
members of the Cofrin family
1991.5

Painter and sculptor Audrey Flack was born in New York City and studied at Cooper Union, Yale University and New York University. Flack began as a figurative and still life painter before concentrating on photographic realism. Her early paintings mimic fashion photography and show the traits of Pop art and the influence of a burgeoning feminist movement. In the 1980s, Flack turned to sculpture and became known for her powerful and celebratory goddess figures. Later she worked on large-scale projects commissioned for public spaces and urban environments.

Flack's work is inspired by the ancient cultures of the Mediterranean and the Americas, and the 19th-century neoclassical sculpture of Europe. Also influential are the philosophical and classical ideals of democracy and equality, especially as they extend to women. Drawing on figurative traditions of the past, Flack creates contemporary images of womanhood— powerful, heroic and mythical in nature. A departure from the subversive irony and critique of other postmodern approaches, Flack's work is more embedded in allegorical narrative and spiritual concerns.

Islandia, Goddess of the Healing Waters is part of a series of goddess figures created by Flack. Like its classical antecedents, the figure incorporates human scale, harmonious proportions, mythical content and the use of bright colors. "Islandia" alludes to the spiritual and elemental beauty of the artist's home of Long Island, referencing both the land and its ancient Native American people. The shells and coral in the goddess' hand and around her neck are the emblems of healing power, while her arms reach out in an offer of reconciliation and regeneration. Gilded and winged like the classical figure of Victory, she is the vision of power and restored hope.

KO-S

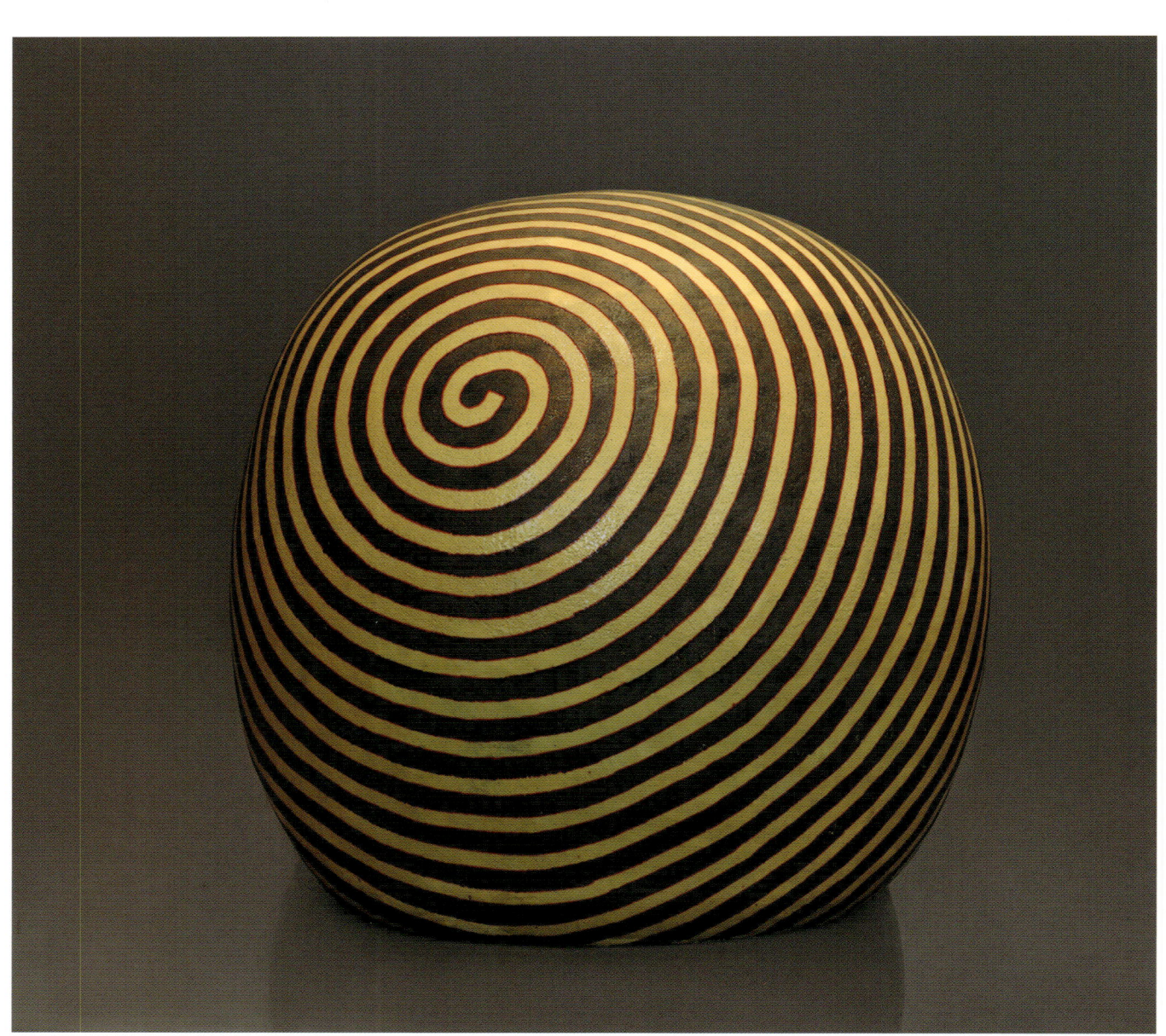

Jun Kaneko
American, born Japan, 1942

Dango
1989, ceramic
36 x 48 x 36 in. (91.4 x 121.9 x 91.4 cm)
Gift of the Martin Z. Margulies Foundation, Inc.
Image permission courtesy of the artist
2004.18.3

Jun Kaneko is a painter and sculptor born in Nagoya, Japan. He moved to Los Angeles in 1963, where he studied painting at the Chouinard Institute of Art. Kaneko lived in the home of ceramic collector Fred Marer and was introduced to the work of John Mason, Peter Voulkos, Jerry Rothman and Ken Price, all revolutionary and master artists in the field of ceramics. From that time on, Kaneko dedicated himself to ceramic sculpture. Later his work also embraced painting, glass, theater design, installations and architectural projects.

Kaneko's ceramic sculptures combine a traditional and Japanese sensitivity to the nuances of form and color with a contemporary and radical approach to scale. He is best known for his series of rounded, hollow and often monumental forms called *dangos* (a Japanese term for steamed, sweet dumplings). Kaneko's dangos can measure up to thirteen feet tall and weigh up to 5,000 pounds. The creation of Kaneko's dangos, head figures and variations of oval and triangular shapes requires formidable technical capabilities. Kaneko builds these works by hand, using the slab technique, usually working on groups of six to ten at one time. Each work takes months to dry before firing. Some of Kaneko's work is created upside down. With thick layers of clay, he forms walls that, once sufficiently dry, support additional layers on top. Passing the test of drying and firing, each piece of glazed stoneware has surfaces that are painted with playful and loosely geometric, abstract decoration.

While scale is a key component for Kaneko, his works still maintain a sense of intimacy. Whether a work is large or small, he seeks the proper size and painterly abstraction for each individual form. Also essential to Kaneko is the manner in which his forms engage and activate the surrounding space. Breaking with the ceramic tradition of delicacy, Kaneko pushes the limits of his medium to create dynamic and bold new forms.

KO-S

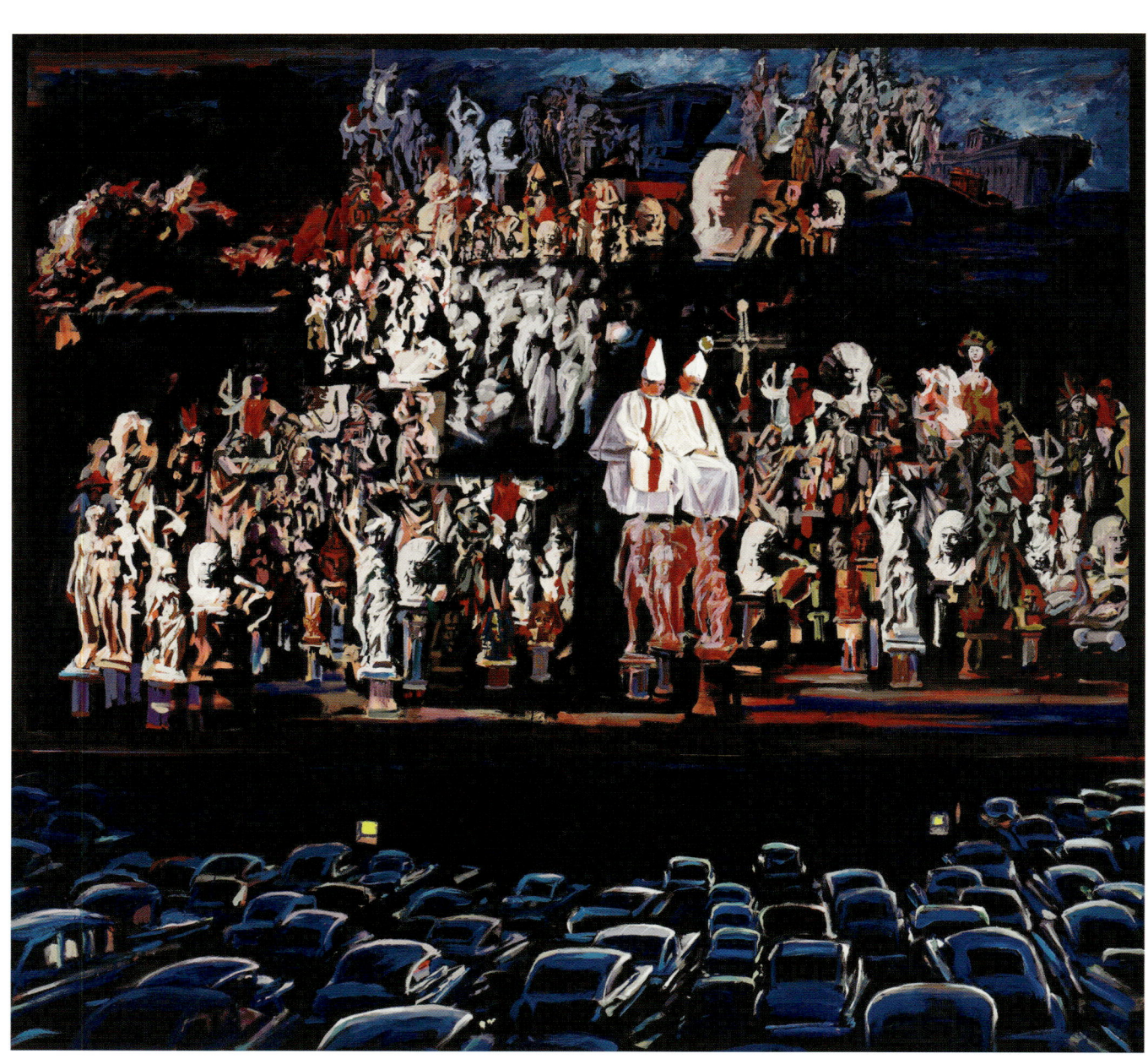

Arnold Mesches
American, born 1923

Anomie 1951;
The Big Picture
1990-1991, acrylic on canvas
79 ¼ x 88 ½ in. (201.3 x 224.8 cm)
Gift of the Frederick Weisman Company
Image permission courtesy of the artist
1992.4.1

Arnold Mesches is a painter best known for his large-scale figurative canvases created with exuberant brushwork, vivid color and collage. His work is characterized by sardonic humor and a critical eye on the social and political events of his time. Mesches was born in the Bronx, New York, in 1923. He has lived and worked in Los Angeles, New York City and Gainesville, Florida, incorporating the culture and landscape of these locations throughout his work.

As a painter and activist, Mesches consistently engages with the panorama of history. Personal and political perspectives are expressed in allegories of grand and tragic events that often fuse with spectacle—the carnival, the amusement park, the masquerade or mass media. The various subjects of his work include the concentration camps of World War II, the experiences of his Jewish immigrant family, the trial and executions of Julius and Ethel Rosenberg, surveillance activities during the McCarthy era, and extremism in contemporary culture and politics.

Anomie 1951; The Big Picture is the twelfth painting in a series entitled *Anomie*, a term that refers to the conditions of chaos, moral decay and alienation that pervade a society on the verge of collapse. *Anomie 1951* refers to the infamous Hollywood blacklisting during the inquisitions by Senator Joseph McCarthy and the House Committee on Un-American Activities. It is also a response to anti-communist hysteria, loyalty oaths, enlarged military budgets and the emerging Cold War of the period. The painting is teeming with familiar cultural icons including military, ecclesiastical and Native American figures. Flattened in the shallow depth of a movie screen, the figures may be the ephemeral products of our imagination. Hidden in the dark recesses of cars, the audience takes in the spectacle in passive repose, implicating viewers of the film and the painting as consumers and passive witnesses of a dark time.

KO-S

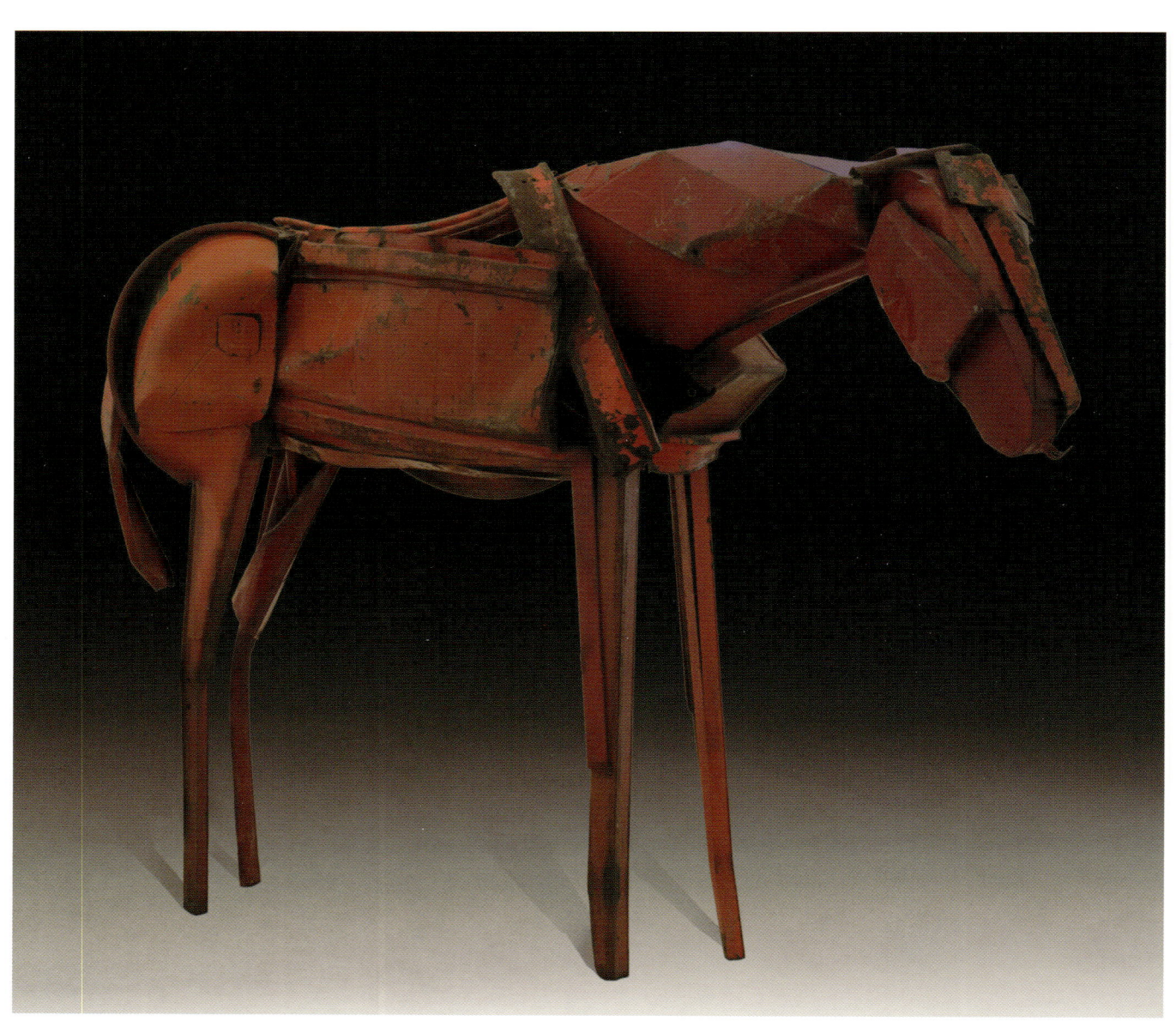

Deborah Butterfield
American, born 1949

Rory
1992, painted steel
79 x 137 x 28 in. (200.7 x 348 x 71.1 cm)
Museum purchase, gift of the
Caroline Julier and James G. Richardson
Acquisition Fund and S.F.I.
Art © Deborah Butterfield /
Licensed by VAGA, New York, NY
1998.4

Deborah Butterfield is best known for her sculptures of horses in a wide range of materials. Born in California, she completed her studies at the University of California, Davis under the guidance of figurative sculptor Manuel Neri. Currently she lives and teaches in Montana. Butterfield began creating large-scale sculptures of standing and reclining horses in the early 1970s. A feminist and an anti-war advocate during the Vietnam War, Butterfield chose to portray mares instead of stallions, which she associated with war-horses. While she grew away from this particular focus, the horse remained at the center of her aesthetic explorations.

The horse serves as a metaphoric self-portrait for Butterfield. Simultaneously, the horse draws on historic and deeply embedded associations with strength, beauty and spirituality. Butterfield initially used plaster over a steel armature in realistic renditions of horses, and then gravitated toward more abstract and fragmented forms using natural materials such as mud, clay and sticks. She later experimented with welded steel, junk metal and discarded industrial materials to create sculptures such as *Rory*.

Rory is made of weathered junk steel, apparently parts of a truck or tractor, which has been aggressively hammered, welded and cut to create a new form. The use of industrial materials transcends the dichotomies of the organic and the inorganic as well as the material and immaterial. The steel transmits the resilience and fortitude of the animal, the sense of power further enhanced by *Rory*'s larger-than-life size. Interestingly, the exposed inner structure of the figure conveys vulnerability. A small pouch may suggest an organ or a pregnancy. Still, the overall structure provides a protective and sheltering shield.

Butterfield continues to produce a compelling body of work related to horses, experimenting with new methods and materials. Butterfield's horses communicate both a visceral immediacy and a ghostly transience that underscores the artist's interest in presence, absence, concrete reality and poetic sensibility.

KO-S

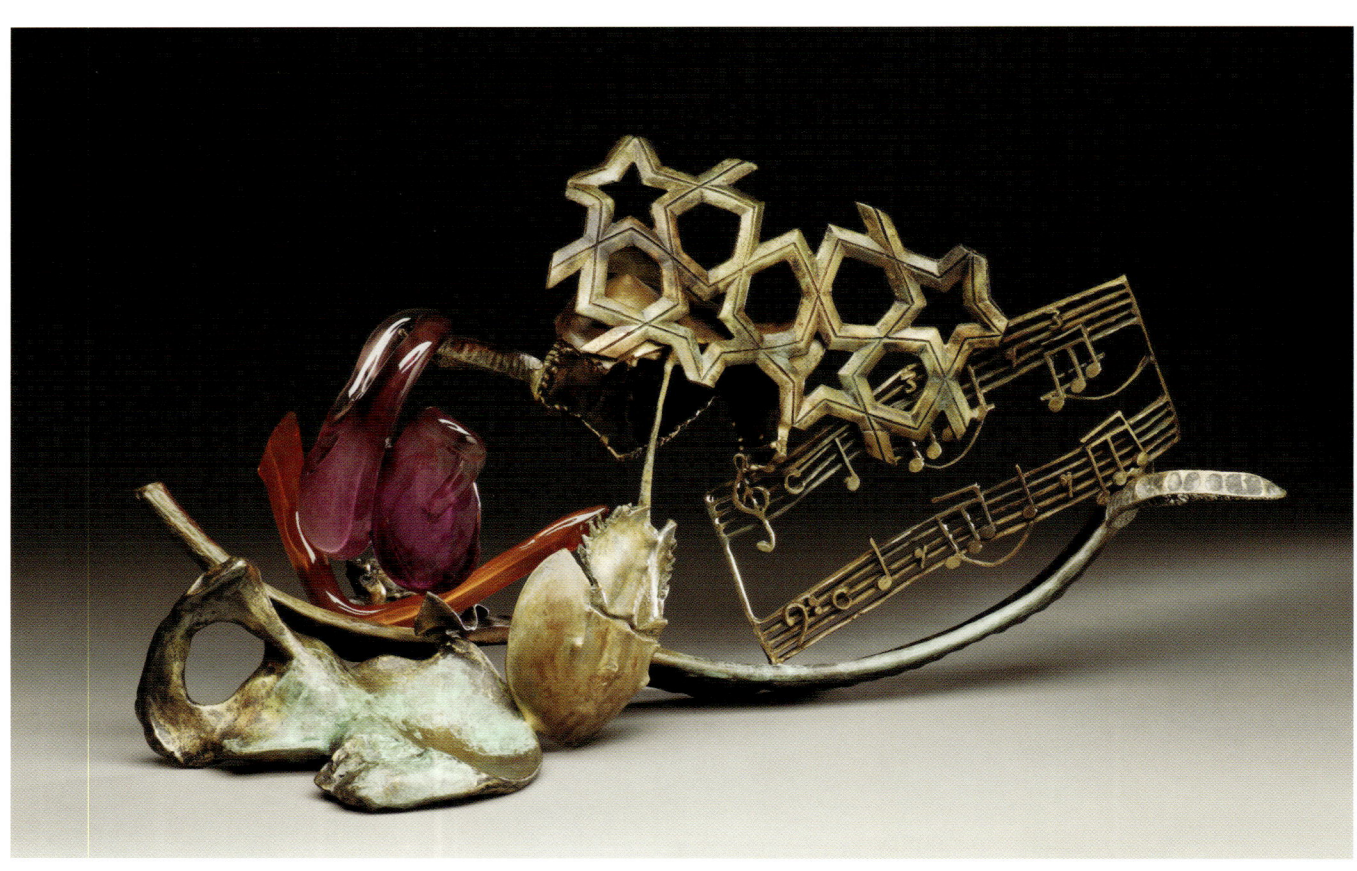

Nancy Graves
American, 1940-1995

II-06-94
1994, bronze with patina and glass
12 ½ x 23 ½ x 9 in. (31.8 x 59.7 x 22.9 cm)
Gift of Mary Ann P. Cofrin
Art © The Nancy Graves Foundation/
Licensed by VAGA, New York, NY
2003.16.1

Nancy Graves was a pioneering American artist whose work encompasses multiple media, including drawings, paintings, installations, sculpture and film. Influenced in childhood by her father's workplace at the Berkshire Museum, she developed a strong interest in art, science, history and cultural studies. Graves majored in English at Vassar College and received her BFA and MFA at Yale School of Art and Architecture. She studied briefly in Paris and moved to New York City in 1966. There her mentors in painting included Jack Tworkov, Al Held, and Alex Katz. Graves is distinguished by being the first woman artist to have a solo retrospective at the Whitney Museum of Art.

Graves' figurative and abstract work draws directly from the arts and sciences. In the arts she found compelling inspiration in historical precedents from Egyptian and Classical antiquity to the Renaissance and Asian cultures. Her scientific interests included paleontology, anatomy and the psychology of perception. Prior to 1970 she concentrated primarily on the conceptual, cultural and anatomic significance of the camel. Later she turned to more painting and filmmaking. In the late 1970s, Graves once again took up sculpture, casting small-scale bronzes that were both expressive and richly colored. Using direct casting, enameling and collage of found objects, she created open and playful forms that seem to defy gravity. Her vibrant and polychromed patinas were created by experiments in manipulating chemical processes.

Graves' work, *II-06-94*, brings together a variety of materials and references including paleontology, botany and anatomy along with a brilliant wit and sense of whimsy. A horseshoe crab offers a glimpse of the origins of life on earth, while the fragments of human bone and teeth recall ancient histories. The bones with their connotation of death are paradoxically juxtaposed with bright colors, stars and musical notes. These remarkable pairings represent the various dimensions of land, air and sea, suggesting the symbiotic nature of apparent opposites such as plant and animal, organic and inorganic, natural and man-made, and archaic and new.

KO-S

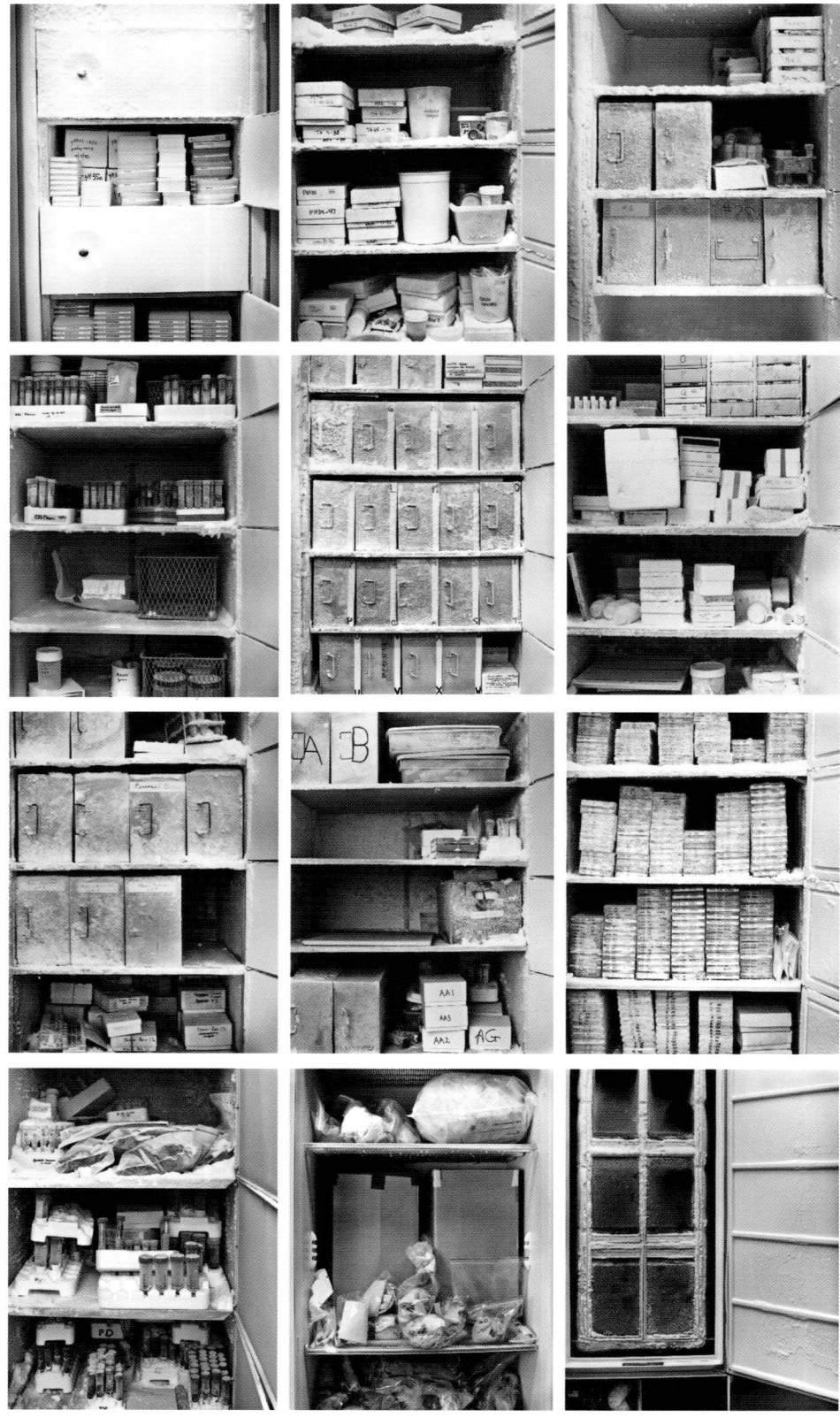

CATHERINE WAGNER
American, born 1953

-86 DEGREE FREEZERS (TWELVE AREAS OF CONCERN AND CRISIS)
1995, 12 gelatin silver prints
installed: 71 x 59 in. (180.3 x 149.9 cm)
each image: 21 ¾ x 16 ½ in. (55.2 x 41.9 cm)
each sheet: 24 x 20 in. (61 x 50.8 cm)
Gift of Martin Z. Margulies
Image permission courtesy of the artist
2005.16.27

Catherine Wagner is a photographer whose work reflects on objects of science and the impact of science on contemporary society. Wagner received her bachelor's and master's degrees from San Francisco State College and teaches at Mills College. Created with formal precision, her black-and-white gelatin silver prints are both objective and abstract. Since the 1980s, Wagner has been interested in the constructed environment, including architecture, urban scenes and institutional settings such as Disneyland, art museums and science labs. While her photographs are devoid of human presence, they frequently suggest the trace of human activity.

Wagner finds an affinity in the conceptual and philosophical investigations and the creative work undertaken by both artists and scientists. The twelve photographs that constitute *-86 Degree Freezers (Twelve Areas of Concern and Crisis)* show her special interest in the instruments of technology and science. In particular, they reflect her deep involvement with the research of the Human Genome Project. The photographs depict freezers containing archival genetic samples of DNA from people suffering from Alcoholism, Alzheimer's, Bipolar Disorder, Breast Cancer and HIV, among other diseases.

Wagner's work is not intended as a document of scientific practice. Instead she conceives the suture of image and idea as a way to consider and stimulate complex questions about human existence. In Wagner's photograph, the accumulated knowledge represented by the genetic samples is extraordinary. At the same time, she challenges the viewer to question the power and politics that support the research, protection and distribution of this information.

KO-S

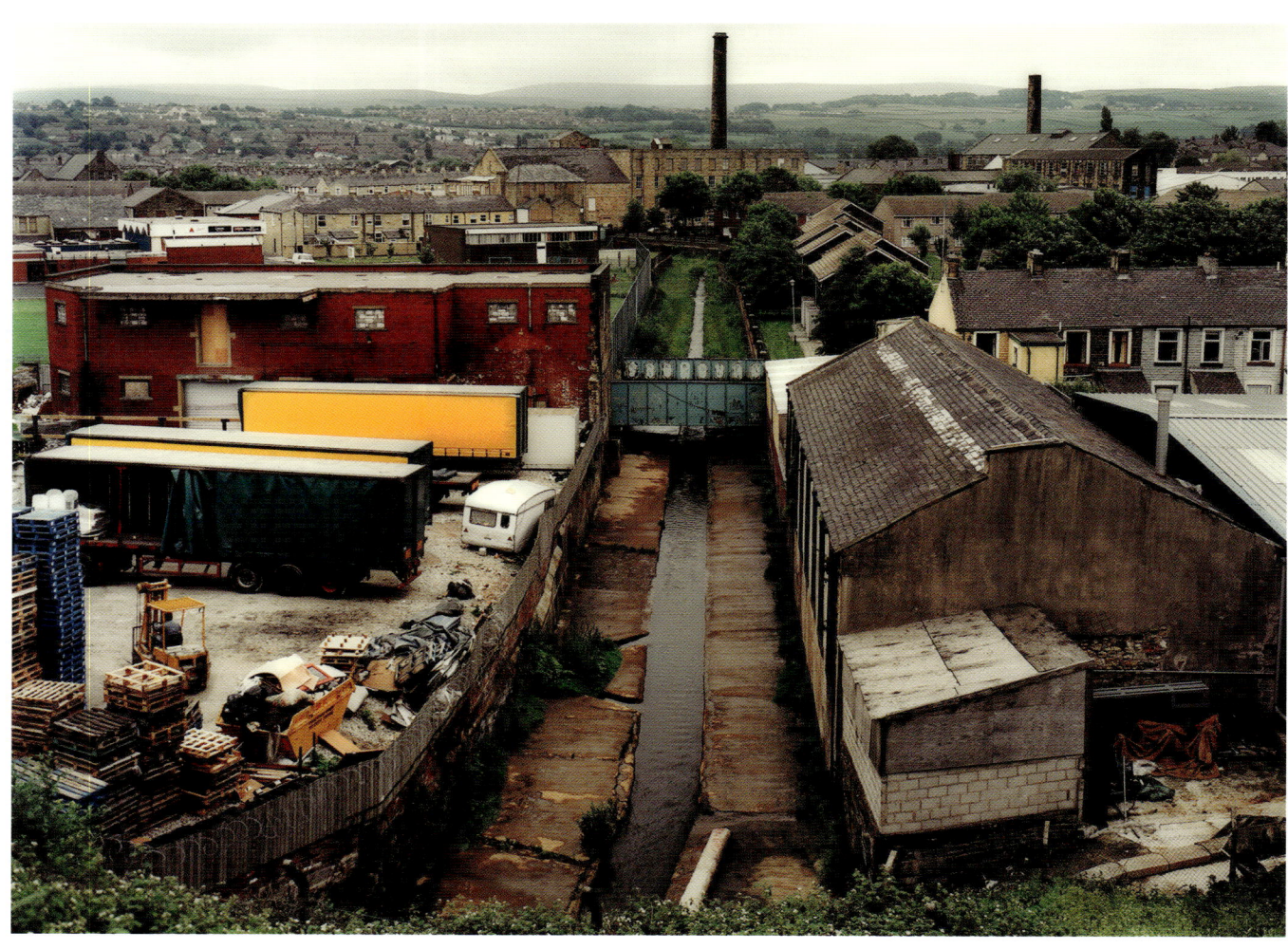

JOSEPH BARTSCHERER
American, born 1954

CANAL 13
1997-1998, chromogenic development print
image: 46 x 64 ½ in. (116.8 x 163.8 cm)
sheet: 60 x 78 ½ in. (152.4 x 199.4 cm)
Gift of Martin Z. Margulies
2005.16.3

Joseph Bartscherer's work explores engineering of the environment. Having received his bachelor's degree from Harvard College and MFA from Nova Scotia College of Art and Design, Bartscherer currently lives and works in New York City. While his landscape photography presents an objective representation of surface appearances, the resonance of his work emerges from the sociological and historical dimensions of his chosen sites.

Canal 13 is part of a series of canal photographs that were commissioned for *Artranspennine 98*, an exhibition of 50 artists who worked in several sites in Northern England in 1998. For two years, Bartscherer researched and created images of the landscape around the Leeds & Liverpool Canal, once a main artery during the industrial revolution of the 19th century. In this series, the canals create links between geographical sites, historical time periods, and between ways of looking at the past and the present. Bartscherer effectively exploits the multiple meanings of "canal" beyond what is directly visible.

Canal 13 shows a modest waterway dissecting the landscape and the picture plane. A relatively narrow canal begins off-image and ends rather abruptly without indicating its direction. It is constrained by cement walkways and surrounded by a wasteland of industrial chaos. There is an incongruous touch of green and a hint of verdant landscape in the distance. Details proliferate, including eroded cliffs, a bank of flowers and the effects of industrial pursuits. The photograph provides an image of a work and living space that has accumulated and transformed over time. Linear perspective leads the eye, yet its interruption suggests both seeing and the limits of seeing.

KO-S

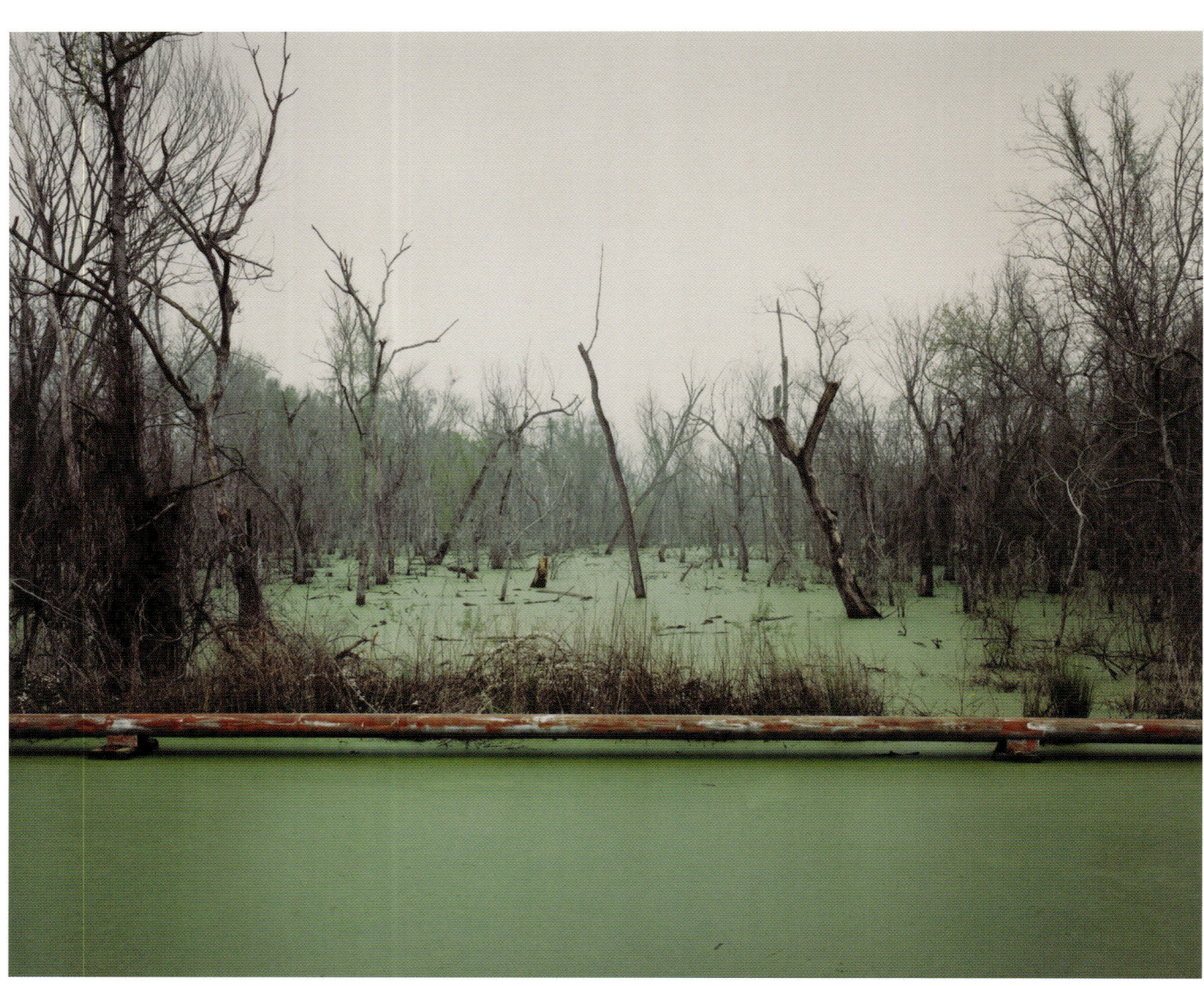

RICHARD MISRACH
American, born 1949

SWAMP AND PIPELINE, CANCER ALLEY, LOUISIANA
1998, chromogenic development print [Fuji Crystal Archive]
image: 38 ½ x 48 ³⁄₁₆ in. (97.8 x 122.4 cm)
Museum purchase, gift of
Dr. and Mrs. David A. Cofrin
© Richard Misrach, courtesy Fraenkel Gallery, San Francisco, Marc Selwyn Fine Art, Los Angeles and Pace/MacGill Gallery, New York
2001.2

Richard Misrach focuses on photography as a way to interrogate and illuminate the complex relationship between humankind and nature. He is best known for *Desert Cantos*, a series of photographs that record the environmental devastation of the American West; however, his profound concern for the environment informs the entire body of his work.

Misrach received a bachelor's degree in psychology from the University of California before beginning his career as a black-and-white photographer during the early 1970s. By 1978 Misrach began concentrating on color photography with his trilogy of the jungles of Hawaii, the swamps of Louisiana, and the gardens of Los Angeles. Taken two decades later, this photograph captures a view from Louisiana's "Cancer Alley" where oil refineries and more than a hundred heavy industrial facilities line the banks of the Mississippi River and release poison into the air, land, and water at a rate of almost half a billion pounds per year. The surrounding area has extraordinarily high incidents of cancer and asthma. Since the 1930s, oil companies have laid more than 12,000 miles of pipeline through parishes and wetlands, allowing salt water to infiltrate and kill the marshlands. While not identifying himself as an environmental activist with this series, Misrach participated in a larger project to reclaim and restore the Cancer Alley region.

Swamp and Pipeline, Cancer Alley, Louisiana is a beautiful and carefully composed photograph that recalls the eloquence of traditional landscape photography. Yet the pleasing aesthetics of the work are placed in a provocative and stark juxtaposition with its subject matter. While Misrach's work evokes the aesthetic traditions of 18th- and 19th-century landscape painting, his images focus on irony and loss rather than idealized nature.

KO-S

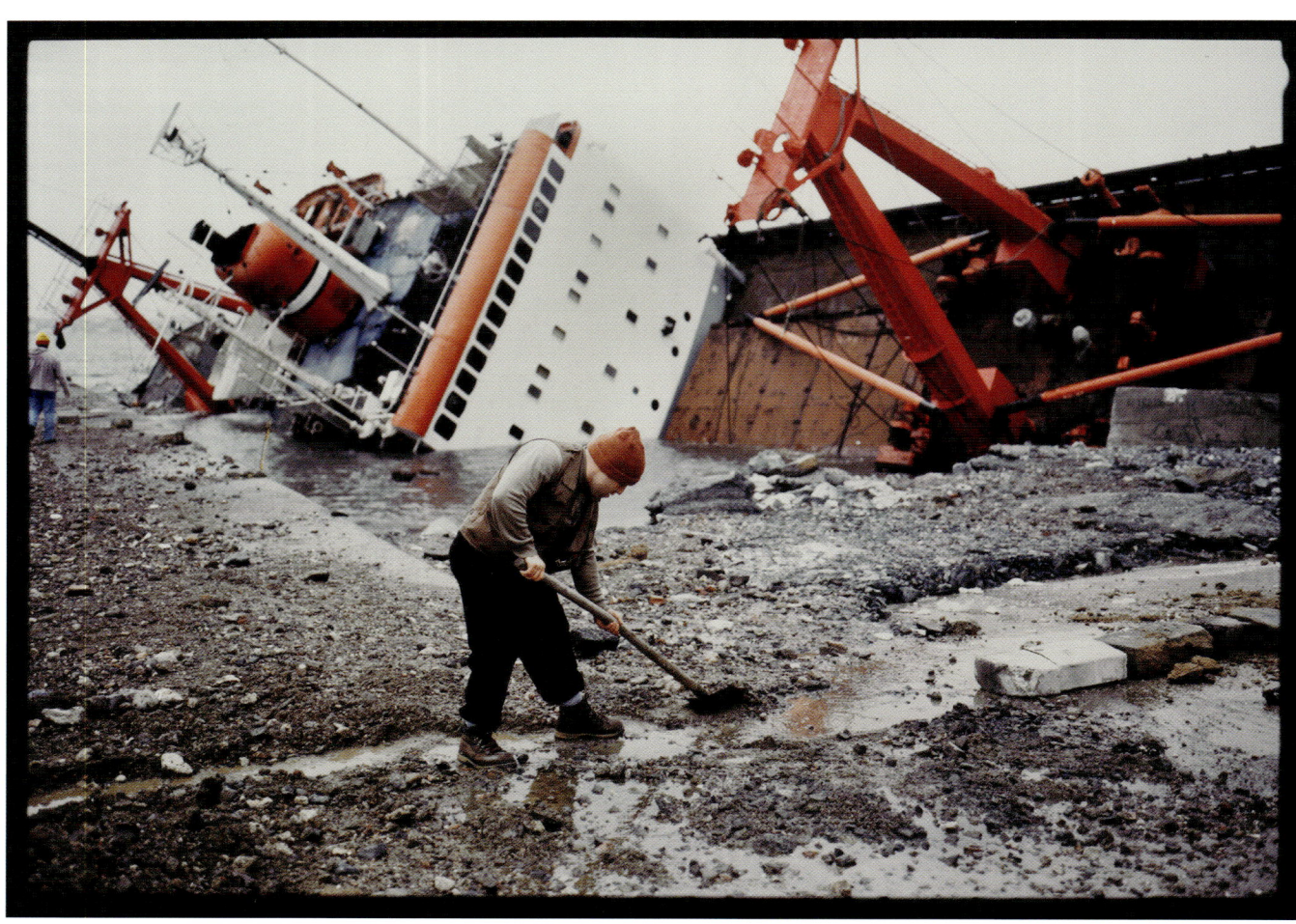

ALLAN SEKULA

American, born 1951

SHIPWRECK AND WORKER, ISTANBUL

1998-2000, silver dye bleach print
(Cibachrome)
image: 34 x 50 in. (86.4 x 127 cm)
sheet: 42 ¾ x 57 ¾ in. (108.6 x 146.7 cm)
Museum purchase, gift of Michael A. Singer
Image permission courtesy of
Christopher Grimes Gallery
2002.14

Allan Sekula is a photographer, filmmaker, historian and theoretician. Early in his career, he turned away from painting to explore the formal and conceptual limits of documentary photography. Sekula has emerged as an advocate of a "critical realism" that calls for an engagement and critical reflection on current socio-economic realities. In particular, he has focused on the world's oceans as a way to map and examine the mechanisms and consequences of globalization.

Shipwreck and Worker, Istanbul was photographed along the Sea of Marmara in Istanbul. It is a product of the artist's travels along the ocean's commercial corridors and to world seaports. In the photograph, a worker shovels debris against the background of a shipwreck, a relic and symbol of the innovation, ambition and the ultimate failures of capitalism. The wreckage of the ship looms in disproportionate scale to mud and stones the worker clears away. Nonetheless, the man persists in his task of cleaning up. Throughout his work, Sekula acknowledges the dignity and respect due to the everyday contributions of working people.

Sekula's work is created in interrelated series, juxtaposing image and text in hybrid combinations that examine history, politics and aesthetics. *Shipwreck and Worker, Istanbul* is part of the series *TITANIC's wake* (1998/2000). The series' title refers to the initial maritime disaster, a metaphor for the technological hubris and excesses of 19th-century industrialism. Also, it refers to the recent film, *Titanic*, shot in Popotla, a Mexican fishing village on the Baja coast that suffered environmental and economic devastation from the Hollywood enterprise. Lastly, "Titanic" refers to capitalism and wreckage left in the path of globalization. "Wake" suggests the trace of a passing ship, a ceremony to mourn, and the notion of awakening from apathy and unawareness.

Shipwreck and Worker, Istanbul was the point of origin for another photo-installation series, *Shipwreck and Workers*, which Sekula featured at the international exhibition *Documenta XII* in Kassel, Germany, 2007.

KO-S

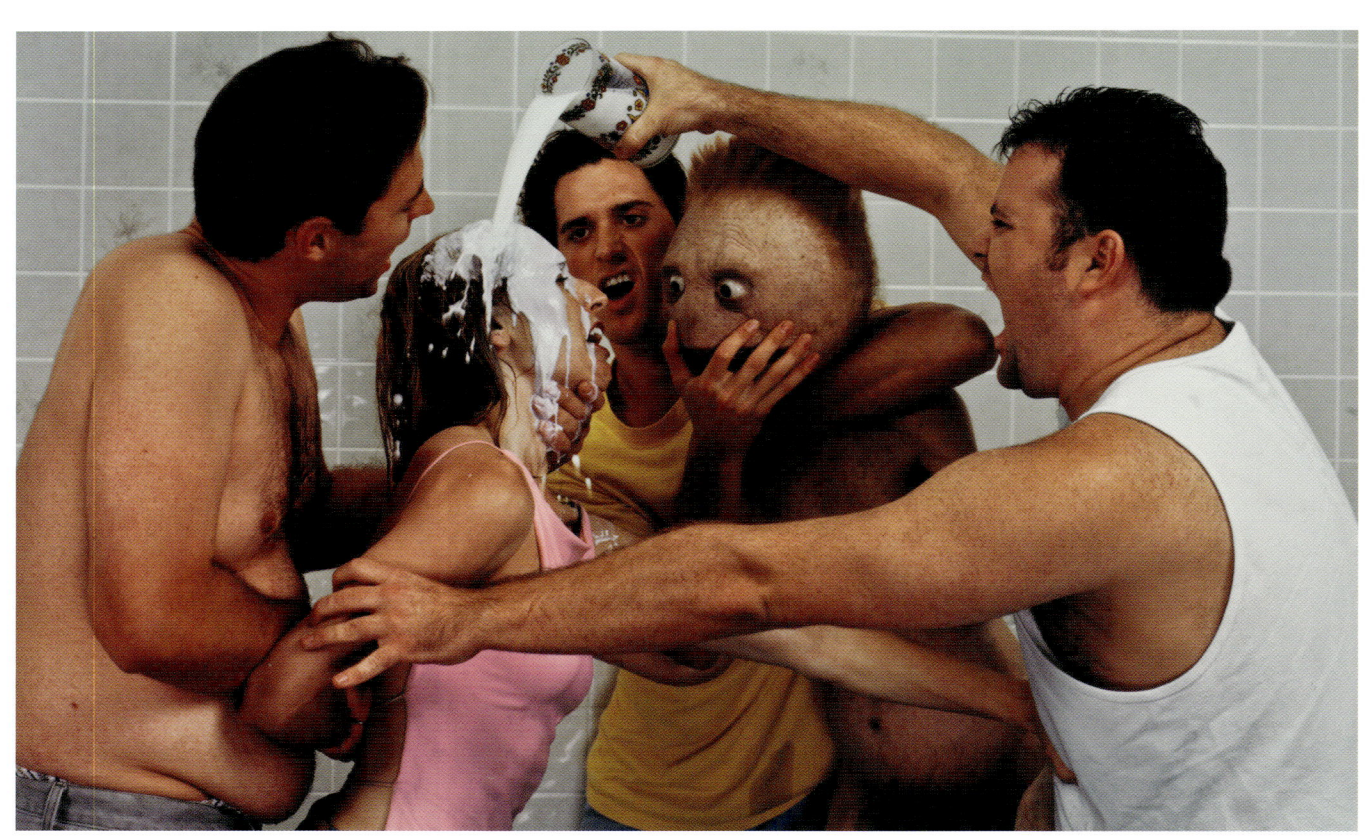

CHARLIE WHITE
American, born 1972

GETTING LINDSAY LINTON
2000, chromogenic development print
image and sheet: 36 ⅛ x 60 ¼ in. (91.8 x 153 cm)
Gift of Martin Z. Margulies
Image permission courtesy of the artist
2005.16.28

Charlie White works primarily as a still photographer but stages each image as though he were shooting a film. His works often have a seemingly casual, even cartoonish spontaneity, yet they are the result of careful staging of his subjects and the construction of complex sets and props, further enhanced with precise digital manipulation of his images and prints. *Getting Lindsay Linton* is from a series of photographs in which White used a life-sized puppet named Joshua. Although Joshua was obviously artifical, White wanted him to be seen as a living, breathing person—a physical embodiment of insecurity. How viewers then respond to this alien, even grotesque figure and the situations Joshua is placed in by White challenge viewers' empathy and reflect their own insecurities.

Audiences have been engaged and repelled, even angered by this work. Nearly life-sized and hung at eye level, the pictorial space of the image merges with that of the viewer in the gallery. White carefully positioned the arm of one of the tormenting men across the front of the group, creating a kind of barrier preventing the viewer from entering and interceding. According to White, the ongoing torture of a shower of milk was meant to suggest impending and escalating violence—rather than the completed action of a physical blow. This creates a tension and an impossible desire to intercede that is more powerful than if he had shown the aftermath of a violent act that would have left the viewer as a voyeur rather than participant-observer.

Although the staging of this work and the artificiality of the puppet figure, Joshua, is obvious, this picture still provokes a strong emotional response in the viewer. Both male and female viewers are appalled by the obvious cruelty of the tormenting of a woman by this circle of brutish young men, yet some empathize with both the victim and the attackers. Curiously the unrealistic figure of Joshua may be the means of creating the contradictory responses. His role as tormentor, passive observer or even another victim remains ambiguous, but like the passive viewers in the gallery, he is automatically implicated by his inaction.

TS

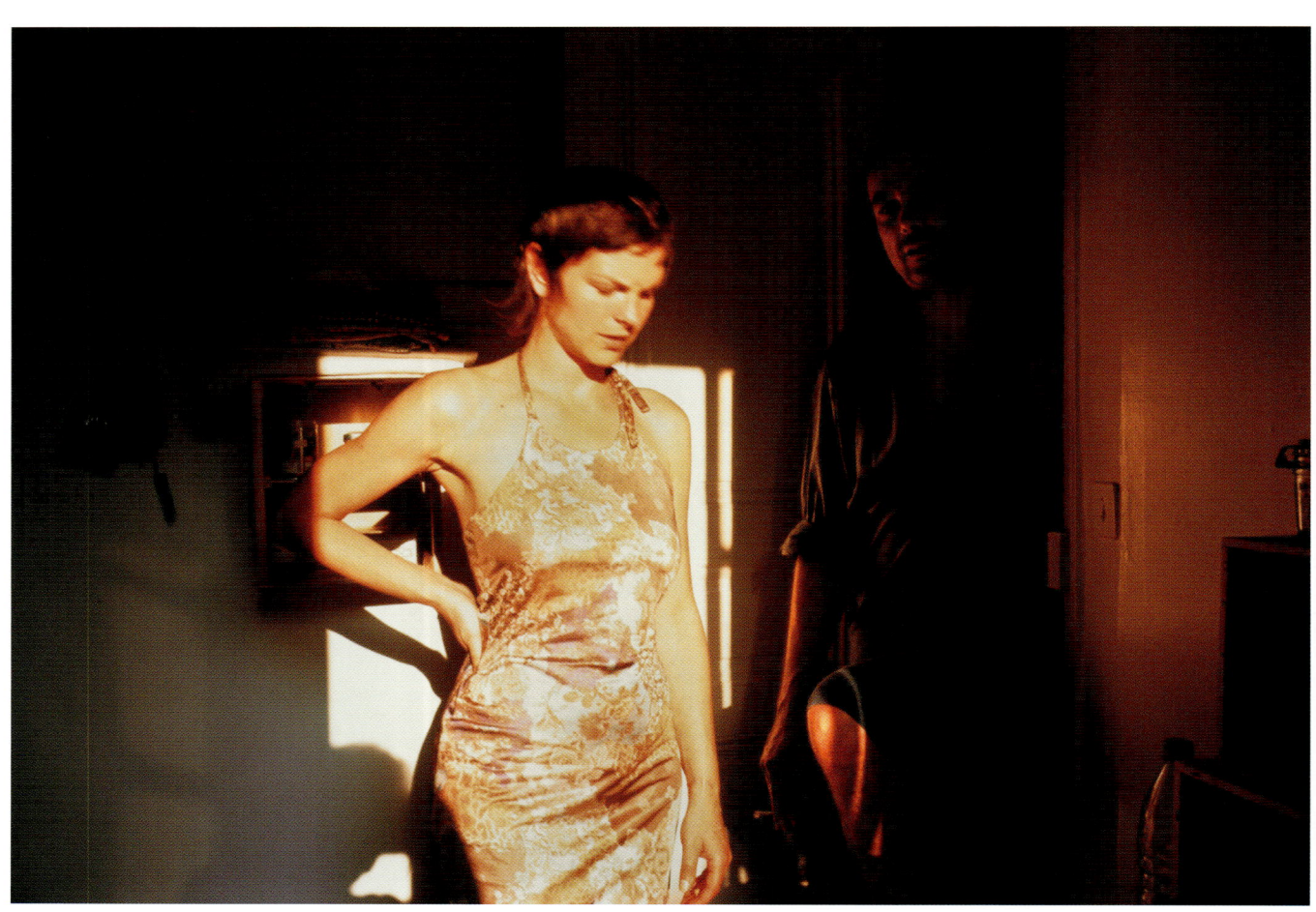

Nan Goldin
American, born 1953

Valerie in the light, Bruno in the dark, Paris
2001, silver dye bleached print [Cibachrome]
image: 25 ⅝ x 38 ½ in. (65.1 x 97.8 cm)
sheet: 26 ¾ x 40 in. (67.9 x 101.6 cm)
Museum purchase, gift of Michael A. Singer
with additional funds provided by the
Caroline Julier and James G. Richardson
Acquisition Fund
© Nan Goldin, Courtesy Matthew Marks
Gallery, New York
2002.9

The snapshot effect of Nan Goldin's photographs invites the viewer into the private world of her family and friends, where she acts as both observer and participant. Goldin's first snapshots were taken as a way to remember the fleeting people, places and events of her life, a practice that continued throughout her professional career.

Goldin's early photographs were in black and white and primarily made use of available light. However, after she began her studies at the Boston School of Fine Arts, she made a transition to color photography and began to use flash. Her photographs have also been presented as slides with accompanying music and have often been noted to have an affinity to film stills.

While capturing ephemeral moments, Goldin's photographs possess a formality and emotional weight that is both profound and compelling. *Valerie in the light, Bruno in the dark, Paris* is part of a series that celebrates physical intimacy and love. This particular body of photographs was taken in the wake of previous work that was dedicated to the passing of her friends lost to AIDS. In *Valerie in the light*, Goldin uses color, light and chiaroscuro for their poignant effects, adding layers of atmosphere and mood. Though appearing natural, Goldin and her circle of friends are highly influenced by film and fashion magazines, not just posing for the camera but assuming these media postures and roles in their daily lives. Their reality is already inflected by this imagery and is then re-imaged by Goldin to reveal both their vulnerabilities and desires.

KO-S

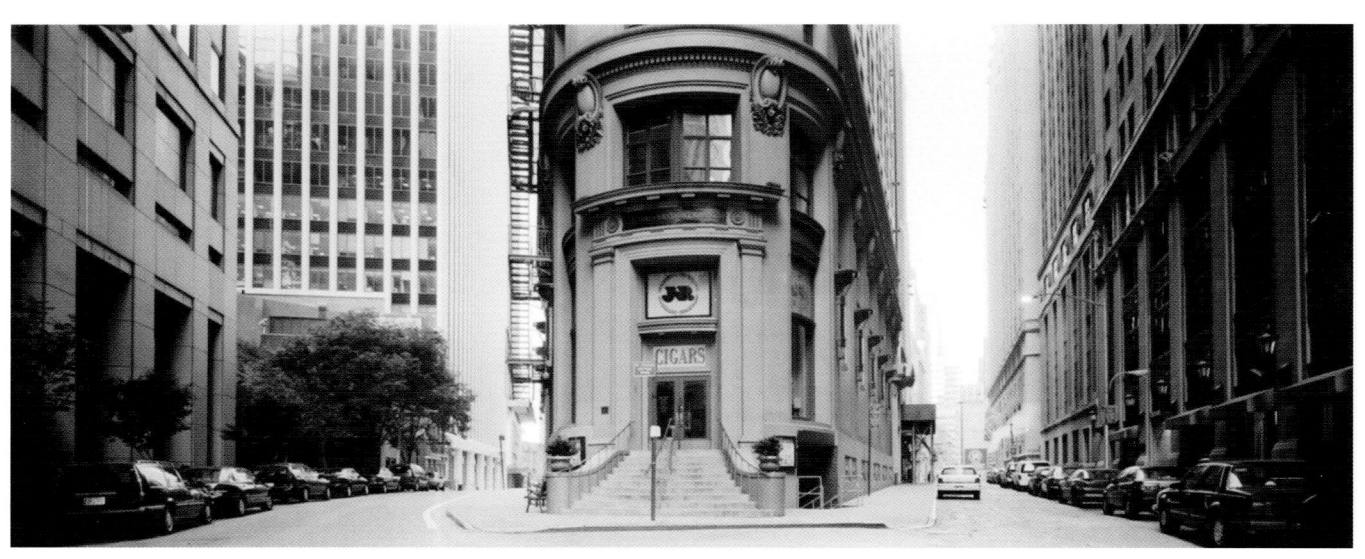

Catherine Opie
American, born 1961

Untitled #11 (Wall Street)
2001, inkjet print (Iris)
image: 16 x 41 in. (40.6 x 104.1 cm)
sheet: 22 x 47 in. (55.9 x 119.4 cm)
Museum purchase, funds provided by the
Caroline Julier and James. G. Richardson
Acquisition Fund
Image permission courtesy Regen Projects,
Los Angeles,
© Catherine Opie.
2002.15

Catherine Opie is a social documentary photographer who focuses on issues of community and identity. Opie began her art career as a street photographer. First training at San Francisco Art Institute, her greatest influences were the work of master photographers such as August Sander, Lewis Hine, Walker Evans and Helen Levitt. Opie continued her studies at the California Institute of the Arts (CalArts), where she studied critical, feminist and conceptual strategies under artists such as Allan Sekula, Connie Hatch and Catherine Lord. Opie combined these influences to document the visual formations of community with subjects ranging from gender stereotypes to urban landscapes and the American Dream.

Opie's work first came to prominence in the early 1970s with the portraits of her intimate friends in the Los Angeles community. After working on various projects, she turned her attention to documenting Los Angeles freeways, mini-malls and high-end residential areas. Opie takes her landscape photographs at dawn when the streets are emptied of human presence. She captures these scenes in a way that emphasizes their iconic qualities, attempting thereby to cast a critical eye on what we normally overlook. These bleak suburban landscapes convey a sense of loss for earlier ideals of urban community.

Opie photographed the *Wall Street* series as panoramas, imposing a horizontal sweep on a vertical city as she transferred her look at the West coast to the East coast. Her photographs of Manhattan's financial district were taken during early weekend mornings, imparting a deserted and uncanny feeling to the usually bustling downtown area. This untitled photograph invites the viewer's scrutiny of the socio-political dimensions that have shaped American financial institutions both nationally and globally in the past and in the present. The Wall Street series was shot one year prior to 9/11 and several years prior to the 2008 economic collapse. As time passes, Opie's photographs continue to elicit new and more layered associations.

KO-S

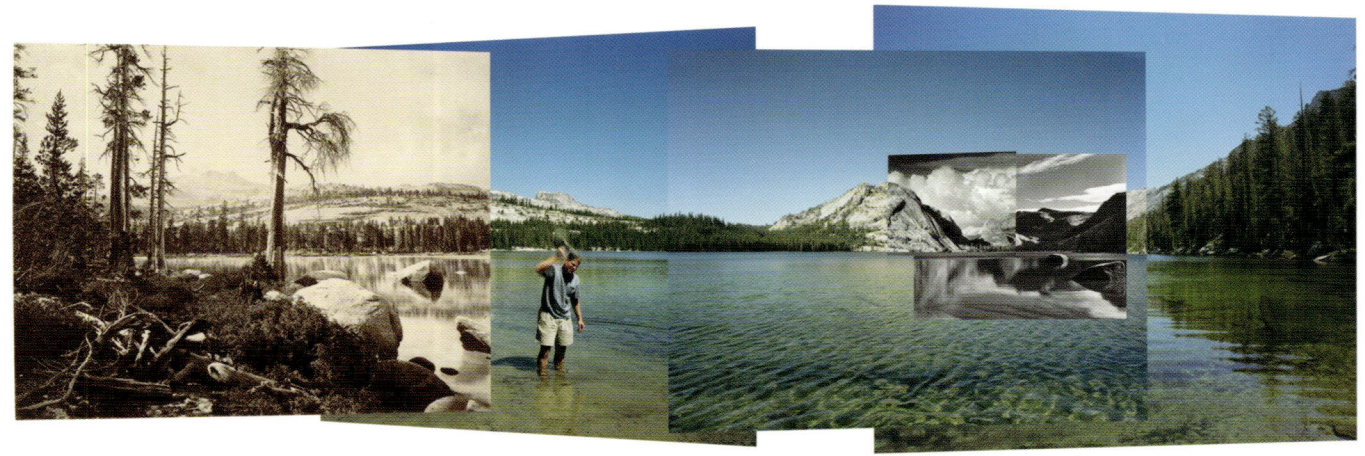

Mark Klett and Byron Wolfe

Americans, born 1952 and 1967

Four views from four times and one shoreline, Lake Tenaya, 2002

Left to right: Eadweard Muybridge, 1872 (Courtesy The Bancroft Library, University of California, Berkeley) Ansel Adams, c. 1942 (Courtesy the Center for Creative Photography, University of Arizona), Edward Weston, 1937 (Courtesy the Center for Creative Photography, University of Arizona), back panels: Swatting high-country mosquitoes
2002, pigment inkjet print
image: 20 x 61 in. (50.8 x 154.9 cm)
sheet: 24 x 66 in. (61 x 167.6 cm)
Museum purchase with funds provided by the David A. Cofrin Acquisition Endowment
Image permission courtesy of Mark Klett and Byron Wolfe
2009.6.2

Mark Klett's undergraduate studies in geology gave him a body of knowledge and respect for scientific methodology that have served him well as a photographer. He gained national attention for his work with a team of photographers and historians working on the Rephotographic Survey Project in the 1970s to re-photograph images made 100 years earlier by the first photographers of the American West, including William Henry Jackson and Timothy H. O'Sullivan. Klett's personal work since this project, continued to focus on the American West with particular attention to the evidence of human activity and inhabitation rather than the idealized wilderness that had attracted Ansel Adams and many earlier landscape photographers.

In his most recent work, Klett's critique of earlier photographers is even more direct and central as evidenced in this panorama made in collaboration with Byron Wolfe, a former student. *Four views from four times and one shoreline, Lake Tenaya, 2002* is a montage of facsimile reproductions of three earlier black-and-white pictures made by Eadweard Muybridge, Ansel Adams and Edward Weston from the same vantage point on the edge of Lake Tenaya in Yosemite. The contrast of these three historic works juxtaposed on top of a composite of contemporary color images made by Klett and Wolfe results in a dramatic, yet subtle study of concepts of time and experience, conservation, photographic history and the active process of picture-making. The earliest photographer, Eadweard Muybridge, selected a vantage point that emulated the grand scale of Albert Bierstadt and other 19th-century painters' depictions of Yosemite. Mid-20th century views by Ansel Adams and Edward Weston used longer telephoto lenses to simplify the composition in more abstract and fragmented ways.

The patchwork of the color back panels by Klett and Wolfe suggests the dynamic realism of the wide-angle experience, yet remains an incomplete surrogate of the natural scene. The contrast between real experience and abstracted picture is made even more evident by the actions of the central figure of Byron Wolfe fighting off pesky mosquitoes—the only human depicted in this series of photographs over four points of time.

TS

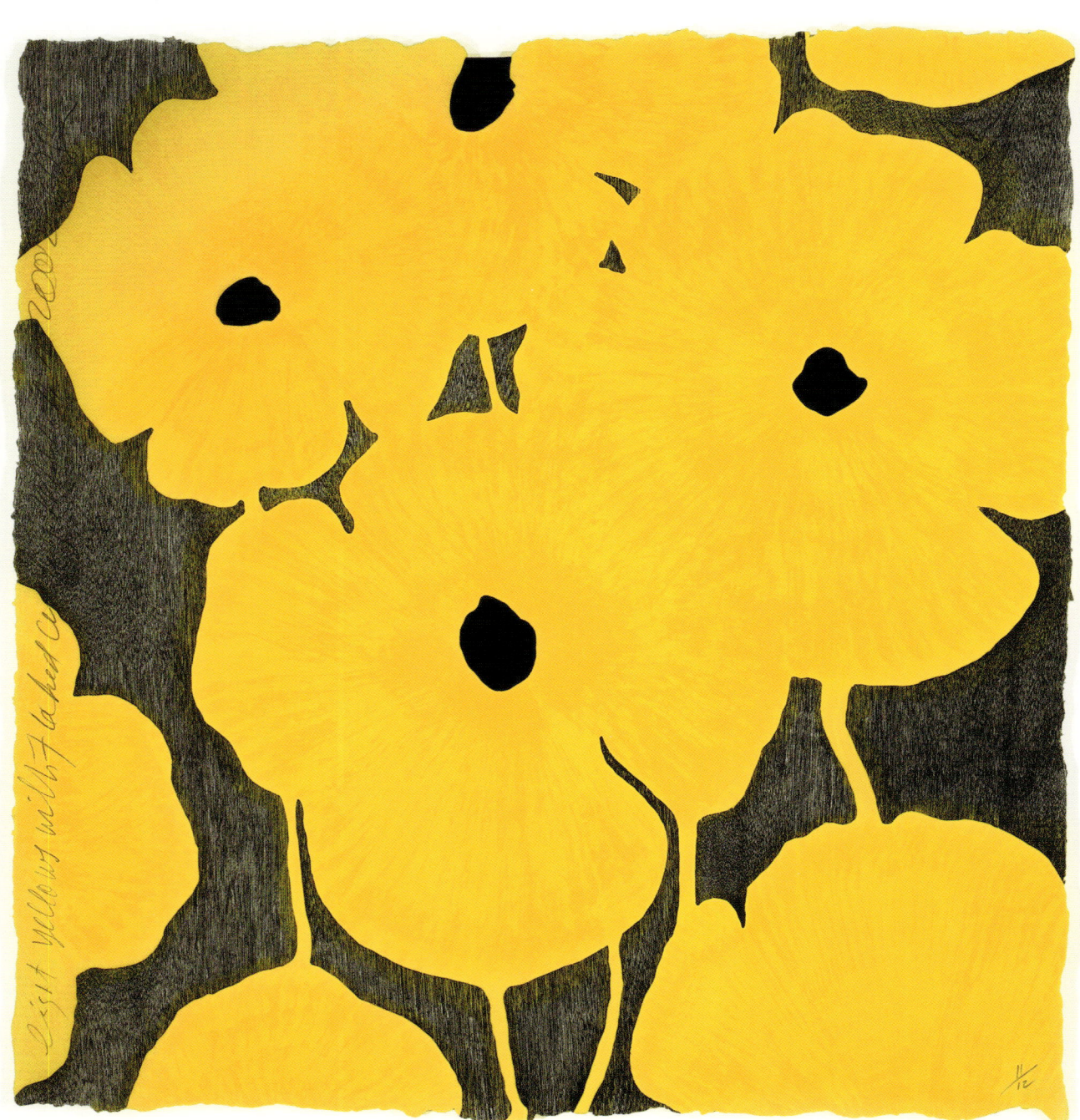

Donald Sultan
American, born 1951

Eight Yellows with
Flocked Centers
March 16 2002

2002, woodcut, lithograph, flocking on
handmade paper
image and sheet: 49 ⅝ x 49 ¼ in. (126 x 125.1 cm)
Museum purchase, funds provided by friends of the
Harn Museum of Art
© Donald Sultan
2004.15.1

Donald Sultan is known for working with unorthodox methods and materials and for provocative inquiry into the relationships among man, nature and technology. A painter, printmaker and sculptor, Sultan was born in North Carolina and studied art and art history at the University of North Carolina, Chapel Hill and the School of the Art Institute of Chicago before moving to New York in 1975. As a beginning artist, Sultan was particularly influenced by the focus on process and materials that was characteristic of Minimalism. He has embraced subjects as wide ranging as environmental pollution, industrial disaster, fruit and flowers.

Eight Yellows with Flocked Centers March 16 2002 is part of a series of large-scale woodcuts depicting poppies, a subject favored in several paintings and drawings by the artist. The poppy prints have a joyous color and shapes that recall Pop art and popular culture. Alternately, some of Sultan's flower and fruit prints have a dark and ambiguous quality suggesting death and decay. Sultan's work captures the exuberant and life-giving aspects of nature as well as its darker, more chaotic forces.

In this work, Sultan enlarges the scale of the flowers to emphasize flat pictorial space and bold forms that contrast with more conventional ideas of flowers as delicate and fragile objects. For Sultan, his flower prints and paintings are as much about formal qualities of form, color, texture and composition as they are about blossoms. While the image produces a powerful impact from a distance, up close the softness of edges, curved lines and patterns provide an intriguing contrast. When viewed closely, the woodcuts in the series are seen to be printed on handmade paper with richly saturated color, the product of an experimental printmaking project in Singapore with the master printer Kenneth Tyler.

KO-S

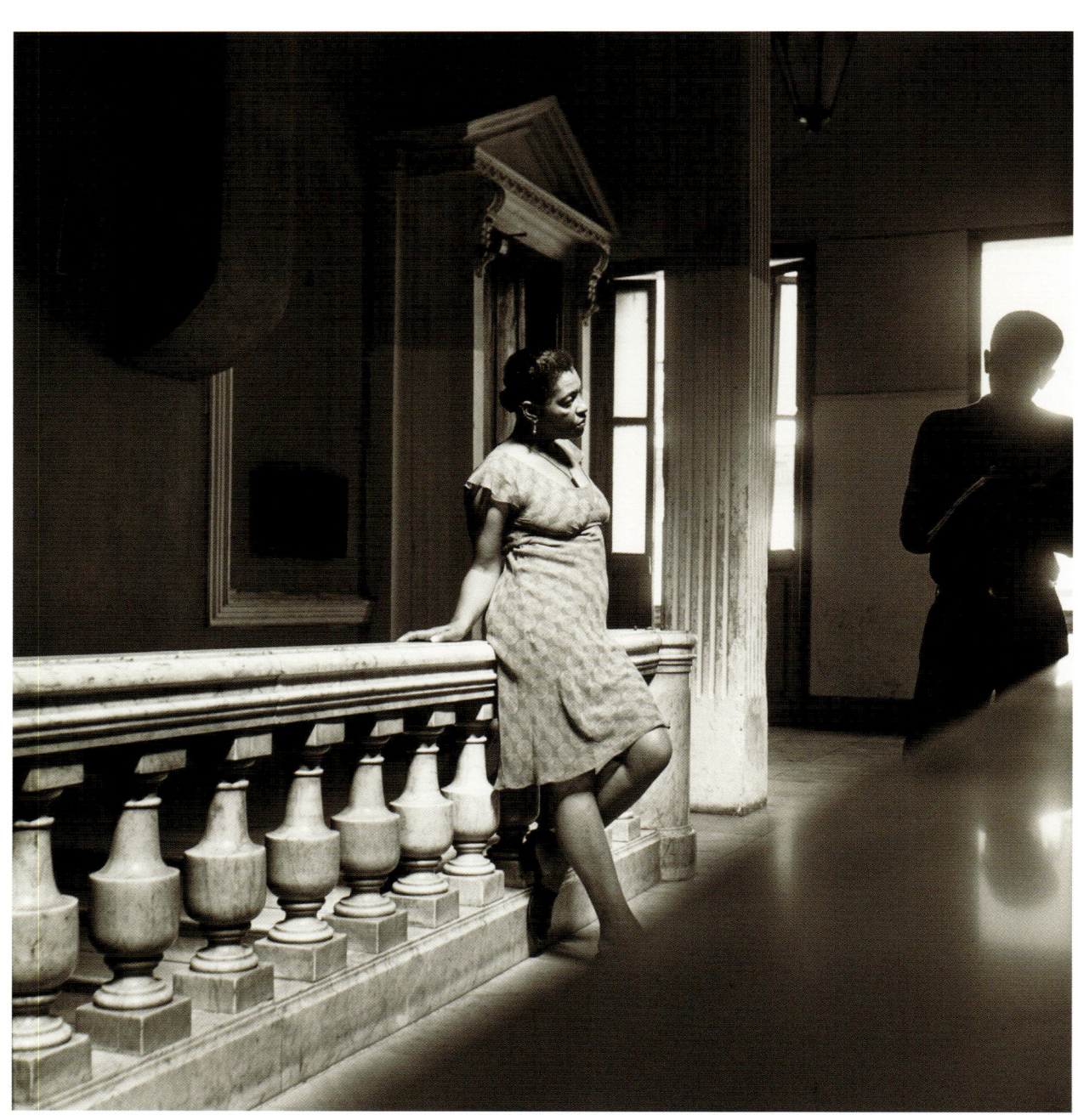

Carrie Mae Weems
American, born 1953

In the Halls of Justice (from the series Dreaming in Cuba)

2002, gelatin silver print
image and sheet: 29 ⅜ x 29 ¼ in. (74.6 x 74.3 cm)
Museum purchase, funds provided by the
Caroline Julier and James G. Richardson Acquisition
Fund and the 2004 Photo Forum Acquisition Fund
Image permission courtesy Artist and Jack Shainman Gallery,
New York
2004.5

Carrie Mae Weems is a photographer and installation artist dedicated to an art of radical social change. Weems was born in Portland, Oregon and studied dance in San Francisco before receiving art degrees from the California Institute of the Arts, Valencia, and the University of California, San Diego. She produced her first collection of photographs in 1983, beginning a career that has been deeply engaged with history and the issues of race, class and gender.

Carrie Mae Weems' *Dreaming in Cuba* series, was commissioned for an exhibition, *Cuba on the Verge*, which was presented at New York City's International Center of Photography in 2003. The exhibition featured the work of Cuban and American artists and writers responding to an acute and transitional period in Cuba during the 1990s. Called the "Special Period," it marked the collapse of the Soviet Union and the loss of Cuba's most important economic support. The subsequent economic hardship contributed to a punishing poverty and increased repression that, nonetheless, underscored the continued resilience and ingenuity of the Cuban people.

Weems' *Dreaming in Cuba* series incorporates her poetry with photographs of sugarcane farmers, abandoned buildings and urban interiors. The men and women in these quasi-documentary photographs assume poses that are mannered in the tradition of 19th-century Realist fiction. In *In the Halls of Justice*, the artist appears not as herself but as a persona. She inserts herself in a milieu, seeking the historical traces and spiritual essence of the site. She serves as a ghost, witness and marker of the forgotten black presence of the past. *In the Halls of Justice* reflects her profound commitment to a just record and recognition of black history.

KO-S

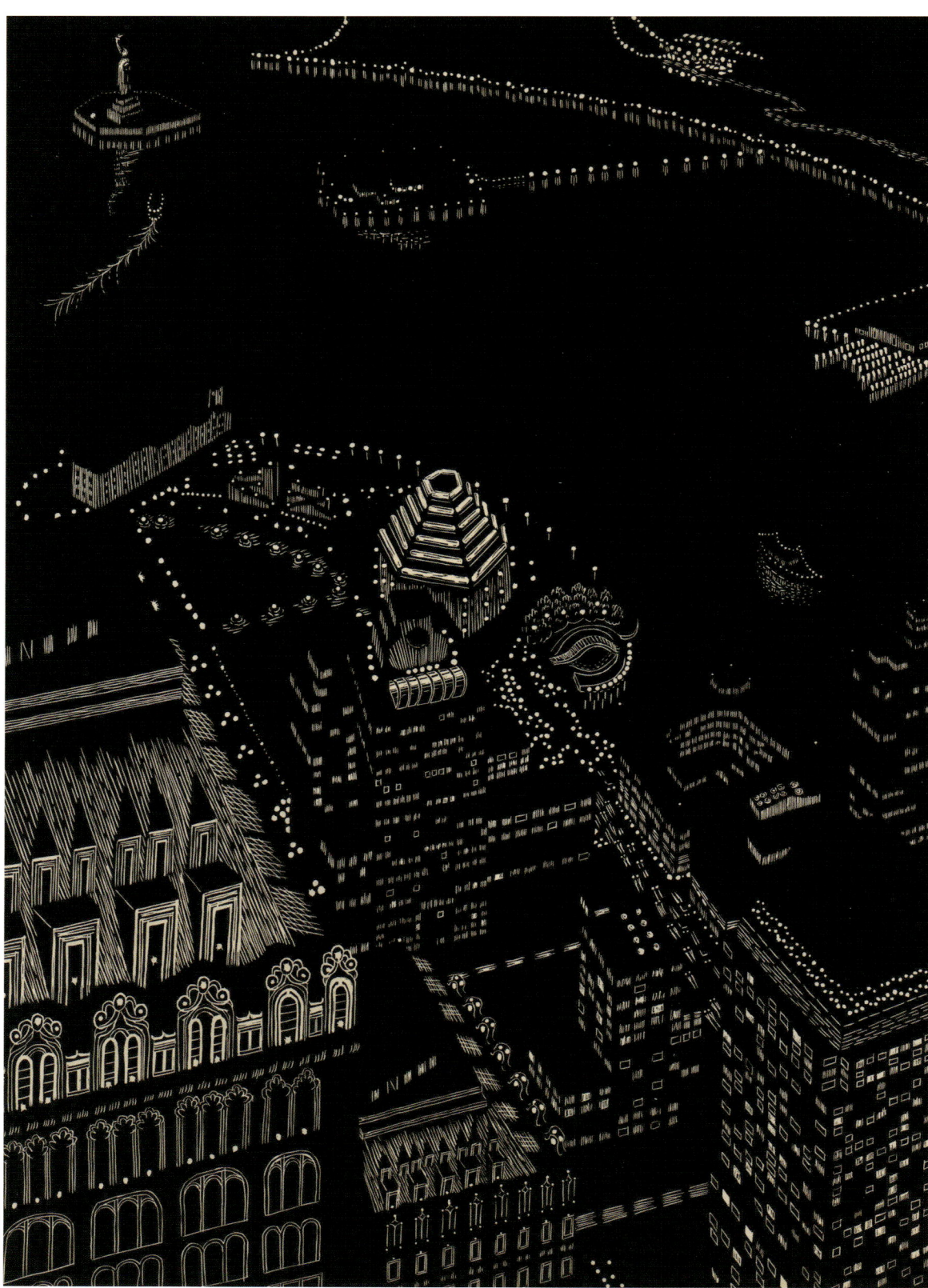

Yvonne Jacquette
American, born 1934

New York Harbor Composite
2003, woodcut on paper
image and sheet: 45 x 32 ⅞ in. (114.3 x 83.5 cm)
Museum purchase, funds provided
by friends of the Harn Museum of Art
2004.15.2

Yvonne Jacquette is a painter and printmaker best known for aerial depictions of urban and rural landscapes. Born in Pittsburgh, Jacquette lived in Connecticut and studied at the Rhode Island School of Design. Later she moved to New York City, where she continues to live and work today. In addition to being an artist, Jacquette is an ardent and dedicated environmentalist. Throughout her work, she carefully explores the tension between natural and manmade environments.

During her early years in New York, Jacquette created paintings and prints with the encouragement and mentorship of her friend Alex Katz. By the 1970s she began to produce her signature work—aerial perspectives taken from various vantage points such as commercial airplanes, private jets, helicopters and tall buildings. The project began as Jacquette was sketching the clouds she saw from airplane windows. As she watched the clouds part, she began to focus on the cities, harbors, farmlands, woodlands and even nuclear power plants below. Soon the intricate patterns of these landscapes made their way into her work.

Jacquette primarily focuses on the American landscape as her subject, although her paintings and prints also feature cities such as Tokyo and Hong Kong. Still, New York City has figured as one of the most important and frequent sites for her work. In 1999 Jacquette worked throughout several nights from the World Trade Center. The resulting drawings led to the production of several seminal woodcuts produced before and after 9/11. *New York Harbor Composite* portrays the dark of the water and sky, while brilliant spots of light articulate the geometry of buildings, towers and the sinuous curves of the waterline. The work is created from an amalgam of perspectives from different floors of the Trade Center buildings. Mixing fiction with reality, Jacquette captures the radiant beauty of the city.

KO-S

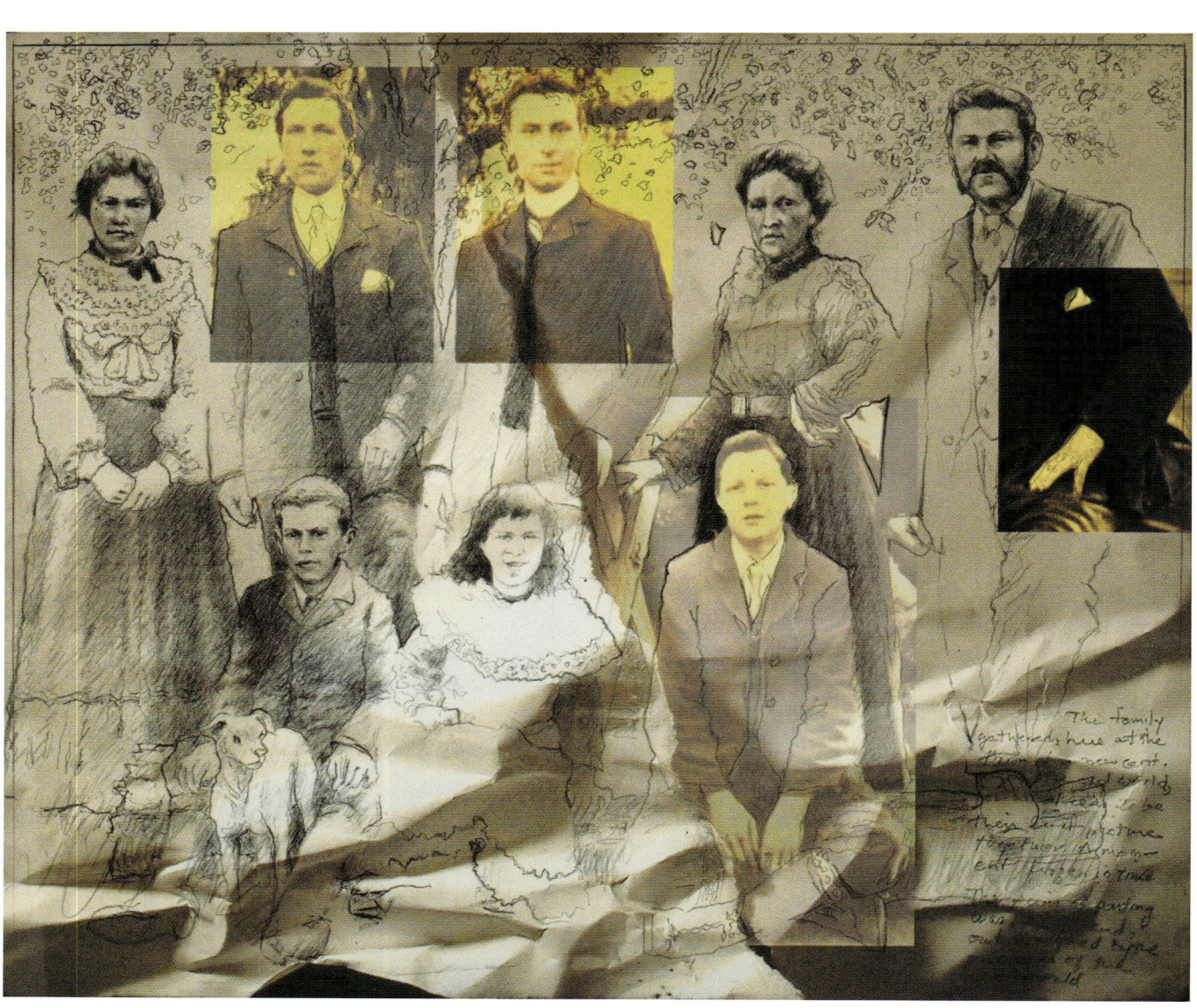

Kenneth A. Kerslake
American, 1930-2007

The Immigrants
2003, waterless lithograph and digital transfer
image: 24 x 29 in. (61 x 73.7 cm)
sheet: 29 ⅜ x 35 ¼ in. (74.6 x 89.5 cm)
Gift of Sarah A. and Kenneth A. Kerslake
2004.38.4

Ken Kerslake is credited as one of the most important catalysts for the resurgence of printmaking in the Southeast after World War II. A painter and printmaker, Kerslake was born in Mount Vernon, New York, and began his formal training in art at the Pratt Institute in New York under the guidance of Philip Guston and Roger Crossgrove. He received his BFA and MFA at the University of Illinois, where he committed to printmaking with the encouragement of his mentor Lee Chesney. Kerslake took a position at the University of Florida in 1958 to establish a print department. In 1996 he retired as a Distinguished Service Professor. He was a leading figure in the Southern Graphic Council and the American Print Alliance.

Kerslake's pioneering work contributed to the American Print Renaissance of the 1960s, which included multi-media artists such as Jasper Johns, Robert Rauschenberg and Andy Warhol, all of whom helped transform printmaking from a minor art to a form of high aesthetic ambition. At the same time, print shops flourished throughout the United States, growing to include the Universal Limited Art Edition (ULAE) in Long Island, Tamarind in Albuquerque, Crown Point Press in San Francisco, Gemini G.E.L. in Los Angeles, and Graphicstudio in Tampa.

Kerslake's work explores everyday life and personal landscapes of dreams, memories and metaphor. His principle media were intaglio, photoetching, monoprints, vitreographs, drawing and painting. He collaborated with other artists and created mixed media work using traditional tools and the computer. *The Immigrants* is based on an old photograph taken of Kerslake's father and his two brothers, immigrants to the United States in the early 20th century. The base black-and-white image was drawn on a ground glass plate (waterless lithograph) while the color and photographic images, including the wrinkled paper, were developed using a computer (Photoshop). Subsequently, this portion of the work was printed on a film coated with water soluble emulsion and transferred to the paper directly over the just-printed lithograph.

KO-S

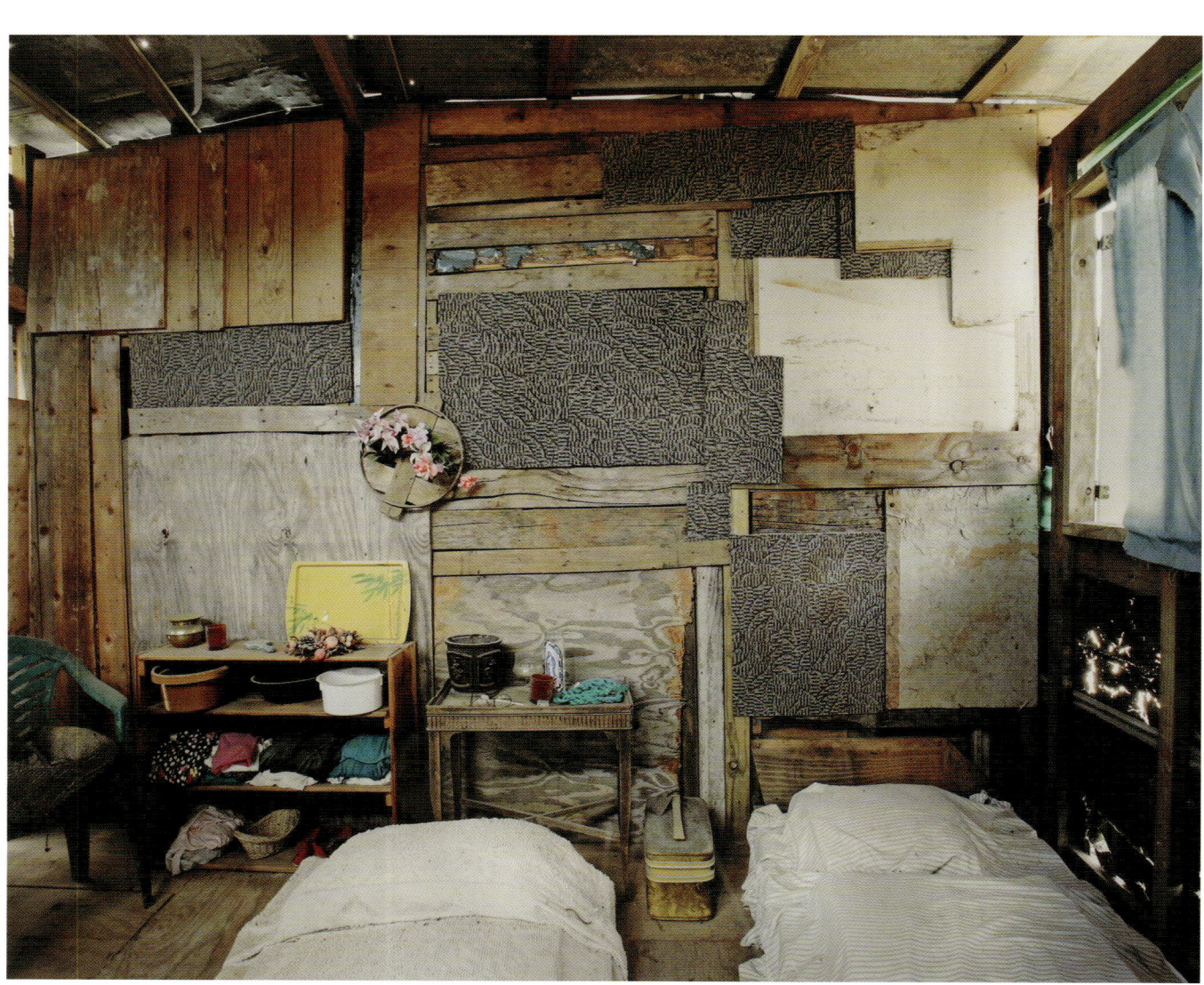

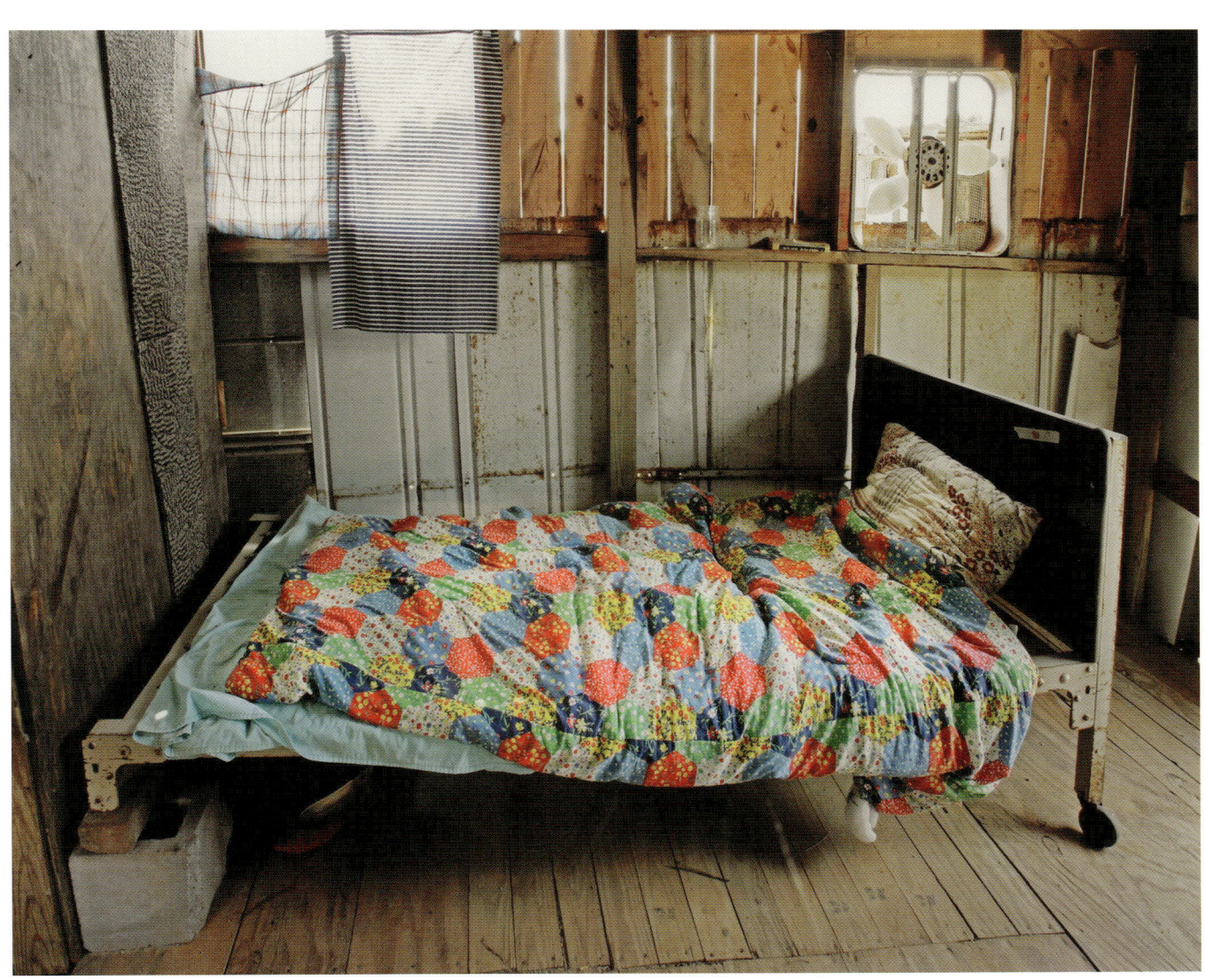

ARTISTS STATEMENT:

The Global Village and Discovery Center in Americus, Georgia is a small "poverty theme park" intended to educate visitors about the living conditions of the world's poorest populations. The Global Village was built in 2003 by the nonprofit organization Habitat for Humanity—an ecumenical Christian ministry dedicated to eliminating substandard housing worldwide. In 1976, Millard and Linda Fuller chose Americus, a city of 18,000 residents in Sumter County, Georgia, for the headquarters of Habitat for Humanity. The organization has been extremely successful at building affordable shelters around the world and is considered a model charity. This success is due in part to the Fullers' vision to educate and reform public opinion through a combination of tourism and volunteerism. Stated Millard: "People like to see what their money is paying for. It's been said that Americans will support anything they can take a picture of."

In the 1930s and 40s, social documentary photographers such as Walker Evans and Dorothea Lange photographed impoverished living conditions as a means of "making real" the situations endured by communities otherwise invisible to the mainstream public. Today, individuals or organizations wishing to draw attention to such conditions have gone to further extremes to try to explain what it might be like to live in poverty. One of the exhibits at the Center is the "Living in Poverty Area," a collage of some of the worst slum dwellings from Latin America, Africa and Asia. Connected by a meandering path, each dwelling represents a different communal function—a school, a store, or a home—and is based on careful research and photographs. The reconstructions refer to specific slums but also involve a combination of objects—both imported and locally available. Because the exhibit is intended as an appeal to a public rather than an exposé; it treads lightly on public sentiments, and mostly places blame for global poverty on regional corruption and mismanagement. Overall, *Global Village* generally avoids a discussion of American responsibility, economic policy, and the historic role of Christian missionaries in the process of Colonialism. Ironically enough, according to the 2000 census, 44% of those under the age of 18 and 20% of those 65 and older are living below the poverty line in Americus, Georgia. Global Village has plans to include an example of poverty housing from America in the near future.

Andrea Robbins and Max Becher

ANDREA ROBBINS
American, born 1963
&
MAX BECHER
German, born 1964

GLOBAL VILLAGE: TWO BEDS
2003-2005, chromogenic print
image: 20 x 24 in. (50.8 x 61 cm)
Gift of Andrea Robbins and Max Becher
Image permission courtesy of Andrea Robbins
and Max Becher
2006.11.1
on previous spread, left page

GLOBAL VILLAGE: BED ON CONCRETE BLOCK
2003-2005, chromogenic print
image: 20 x 24 in. (50.8 x 61 cm)
Gift of Andrea Robbins and Max Becher
Image permission courtesy of Andrea Robbins
and Max Becher
2006.11.2
on previous spread, right page

Since 1984, Andrea Robbins and Max Becher have collaborated on conceptually-based photographic works that examine the interrelationship of memory, history and geography. Robbins, born in Boston, and Becher, born in Dusseldorf, Germany, met at Cooper Union School of Art in New York, where they began working as a team. Photographing in various locations around the world, they address in images and text what they term as "the transportation of place"—how a community assumes the characteristics of another through the overlapping influences of history, colonialism, immigration, tourism and mass communication.

Robbins and Becher record instances of cultural dislocation, such as when Germans adopt the guise of Native Americans, Africans retain the dress of 19th-century Germany, and Hasidic Jews assimilate the life-style of suburban Iowa. They begin their projects with copious research about the social patterns of specific communities with an eye on hidden, overlooked or lost histories. They maintain an objectivity and clarity in their work that allows for the collision of appearance and reality to surface in subtle and uncanny ways. What is familiar appears unfamiliar, and the ironies of situations slowly reveal themselves.

The photographs represented here are part of a series focusing on the Global Village and Discovery Center in Americus, Georgia. The site was constructed by Habitat for Humanity to bring awareness to substandard housing world-wide. Mindful of the photographic history of raising social consciousness, Robbins and Becher give a nod in their work to the aesthetic framing of Depression Era artists such as Walker Evans. Their work also reveals the erasure of human struggle in the Global Village, underscoring the irony of trying to end poverty without actually facing poverty. The text on the facing page is a statement by the artists and is considered part of the work.

KO-S

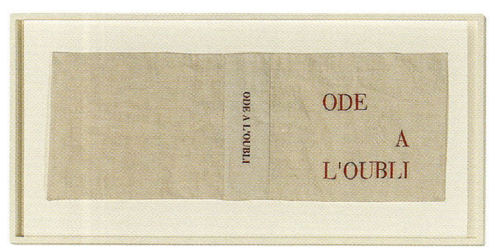

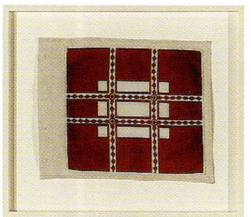 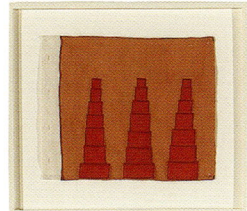 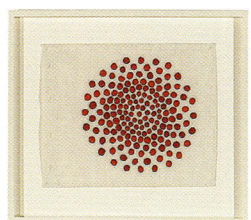 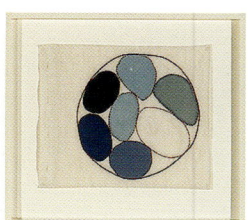

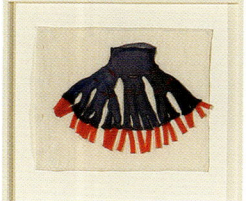 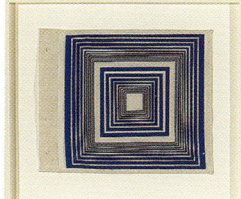 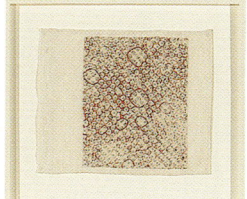 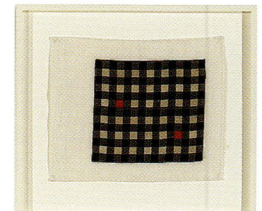

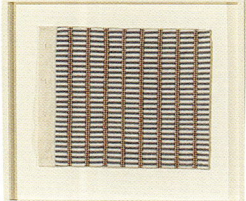

I had a flashback
of something
that never existed

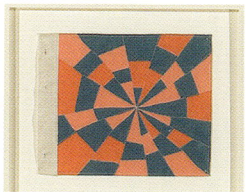 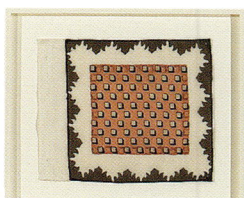

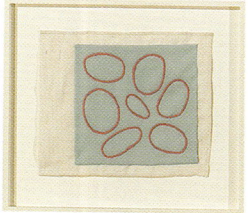 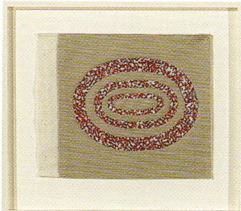 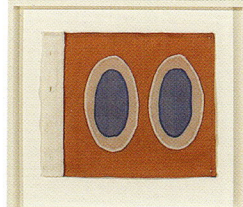

The
return
of
the
repressed

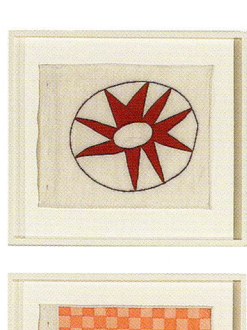
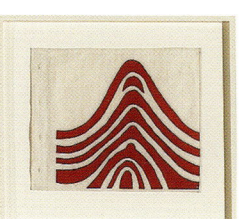
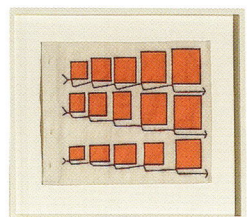
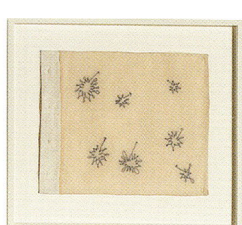
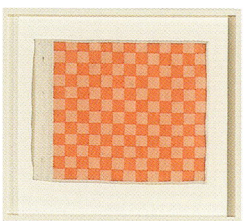
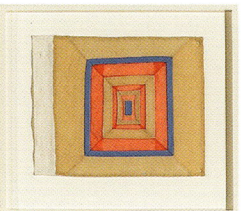
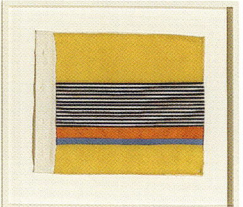
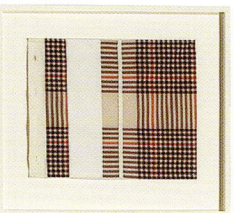
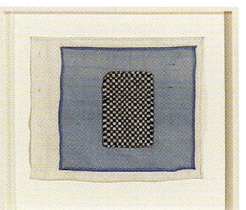
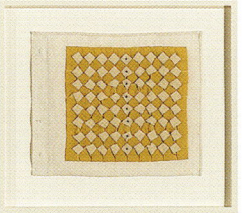
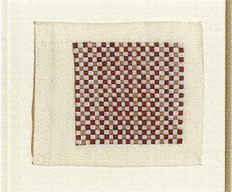
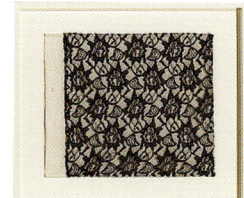
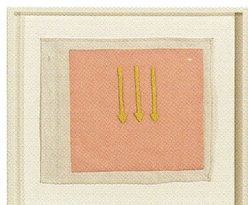
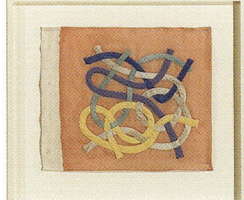
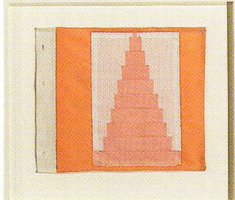
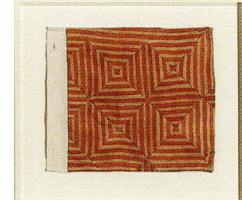
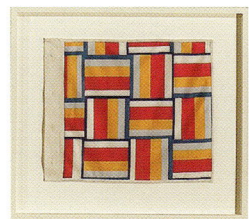
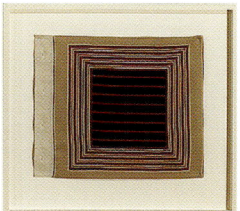

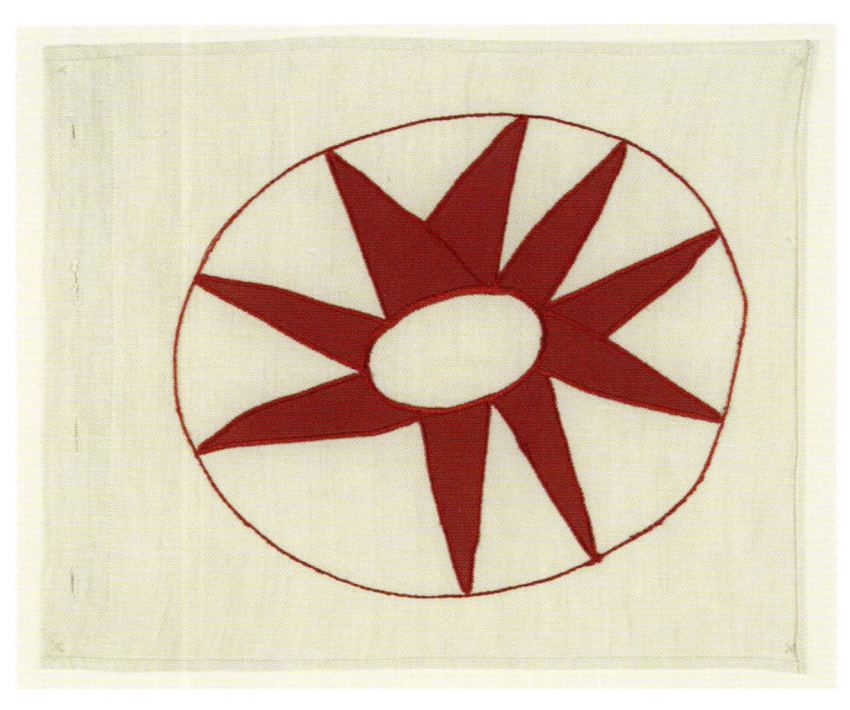
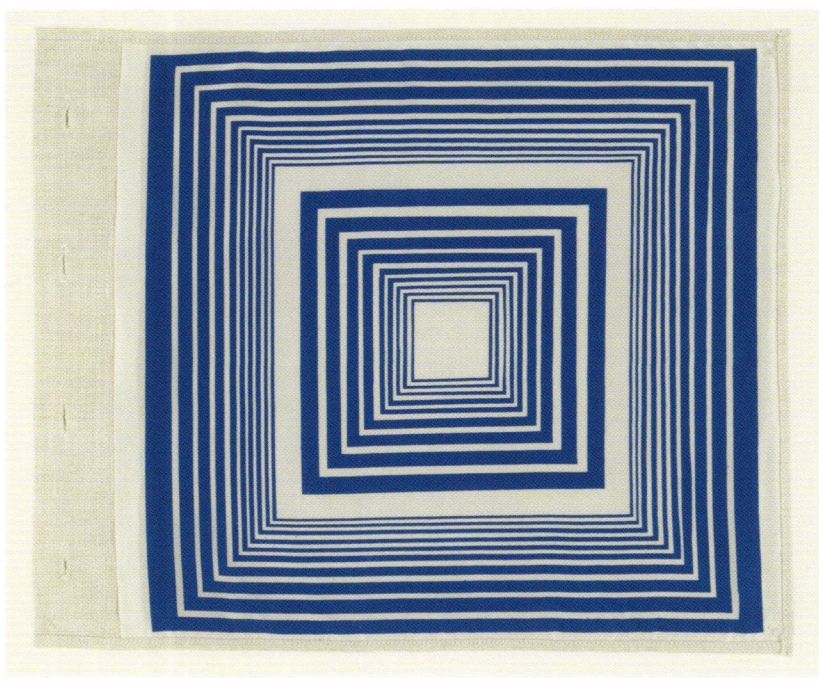

Louise Bourgeois
American, born France, 1911

Ode à l'Oubli
(Ode to Forgetfulness)
2004, hand-made bound book, fabric,
lithographic ink and archival dyes
36 pages, each sheet: 10 ¾ x 13 ¼ in. (27 x 34
cm), edition of 25
Museum purchase, funds provided by
the David A. Cofrin Acquisition Endowment
Art © Louise Bourgeois/Licensed by VAGA,
New York, NY
2004.23

previous spread: full work
left: details

Born in Paris in 1911, Louise Bourgeois forged an independent and eccentric path throughout her career. As a child, she assisted with her family's tapestry restoration business by designing patterns for missing sections. Although Bourgeois studied mathematics at the Sorbonne, by the late 1930s, she had transferred her interests to art. In 1938 she moved to New York City. Over a period of years, Bourgeois developed a strong body of multi-media work characterized by abstract figuration with a symbolic and psychological emphasis. However, it was not until the artist was in her seventies that she received recognition with a retrospective exhibition at the Museum of Modern Art. Since then, Bourgeois has produced some of her most ambitious and extraordinary work and has been lauded as one of the most influential artists of the 20th and 21st centuries.

At an early age, Bourgeois suffered through her father's infidelity and ten-year affair with the family's live-in English tutor. Complicating the experience was her mother's complicity and acceptance of his betrayal. The struggle with her father and the patriarchal society he represented produced rage, fear and guilt that found powerful expression through her work. Bourgeois' creativity is full of wit and anger, showing the influence of Surrealism and a deeply psychological approach to her art.

Ode à l'Oubli (*Ode to Forgetfulness*) is a 36-page fabric book created from garments and odd remnants of cloth saved and sequestered throughout the life of the artist and produced in an edition of 25. Created when Bourgeois was 93, the book signals her recurring interest in the intimate materials of clothing and household linens. The work suggests a return to the artist's origins through a lens of remembering, forgetting and forgiving. Carefully cut, embroidered, quilted and layered, the pages of this book recollect and reconstruct a life deeply considered.

KO-S

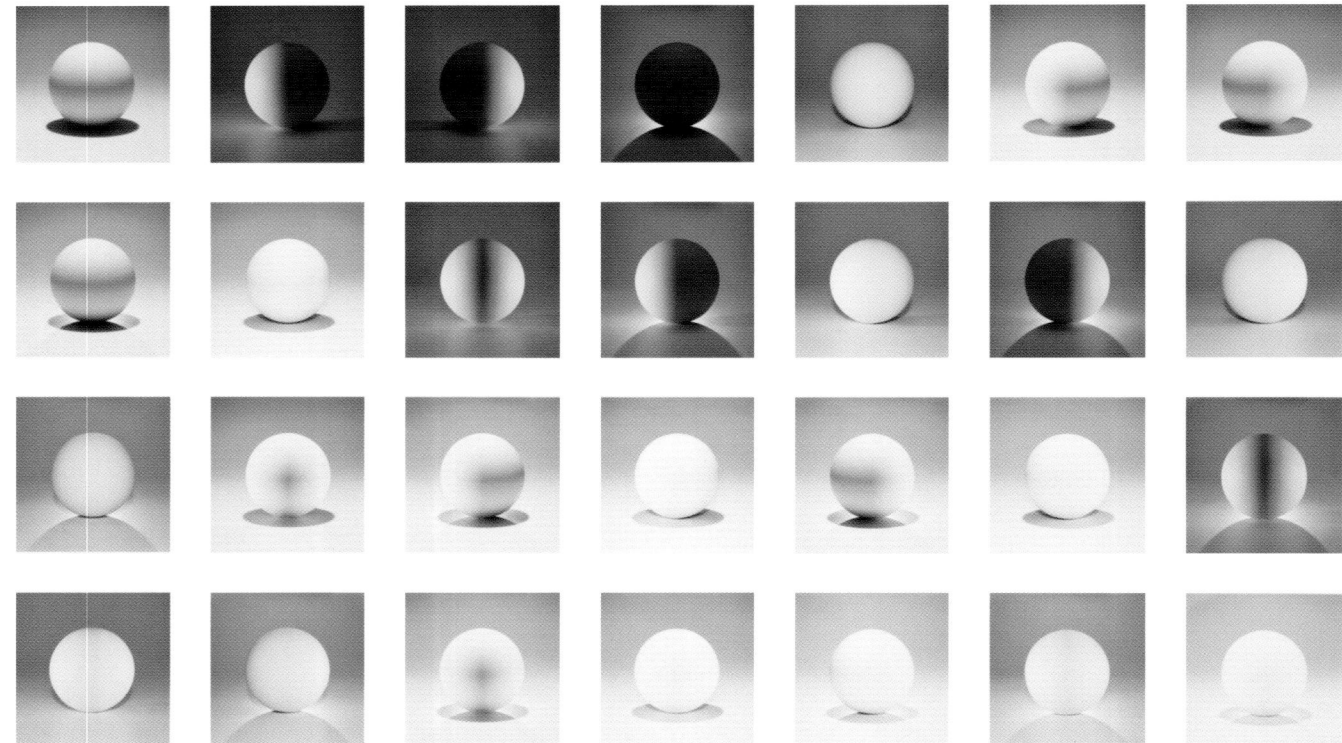

Sol LeWitt
American, 1928-2007

A sphere lit from the top, four sides, and all their combinations
2004, 28 pigment ink jet prints
installed: 90 x 141 ½ in. (203.2 x 359.4 cm)
each image and sheet: 18 x 18 in. (45.7 x 45.7 cm)
Museum purchase, funds provided by the
David A. Cofrin Acquisition Endowment
© 2009 The LeWitt Estate / Artists Rights Society
(ARS), New York
2005.27

Sol LeWitt established a reputation for his Minimalist sculptures, paintings and other works that were rigorous and precise in plan and execution. In contrast to the emotive handwork and even accidental gestures of the Abstract Expressionists and earlier generations of artists, LeWitt's conceptual work was systematic and precisely planned. In his influential notes published in *Artforum* (Summer 1967) he wrote, "When an artist uses a conceptual form of art, it means that all of the planning and decisions are made beforehand and the execution is a perfunctory affair. The idea becomes a machine that makes the art." In many ways LeWitt's sculptures, paintings, drawings and photographs are predetermined by his clearly defined plan, even mathematical formulation, and can long exist as an idea awaiting execution/production. LeWitt's earlier use of photography was mainly as just another, highly mechanical image-making tool, especially in his production of books such as *Autobiography* (1980) in which he created a visual catalogue of photographs of every object in his living and work space in New York City.

This series of 28 images showing the systematic variations of light on a sphere has the characteristic conceptual distance we expect from Sol LeWitt. As was his custom with his paintings and drawings, the pictures were not directly created by LeWitt but by an assistant—in this case Jeremy Ziemann, who followed LeWitt's specific instructions. Yet there is a softness and even a visual humor in the shifting images that transcend mere mathematical formulation and systematic execution. There is a kind of magic in the way the sphere seems stable in one frame, but precariously balanced on the round edge of its shadow in another frame. In some images the shadow even appears as a void, making the sphere appear to float miraculously in an ambiguous space.

At its most basic, LeWitt's work can be compared to the traditional assignment for beginning photography classes to photograph an egg under all possible lighting conditions. Just as the beginning photography student learns from this exercise that a white egg can appear as all shades of gray, even black against a bright white background, viewers of LeWitt's spheres are made aware that the core subject of photography is light, and the play of light and shadow.

TS

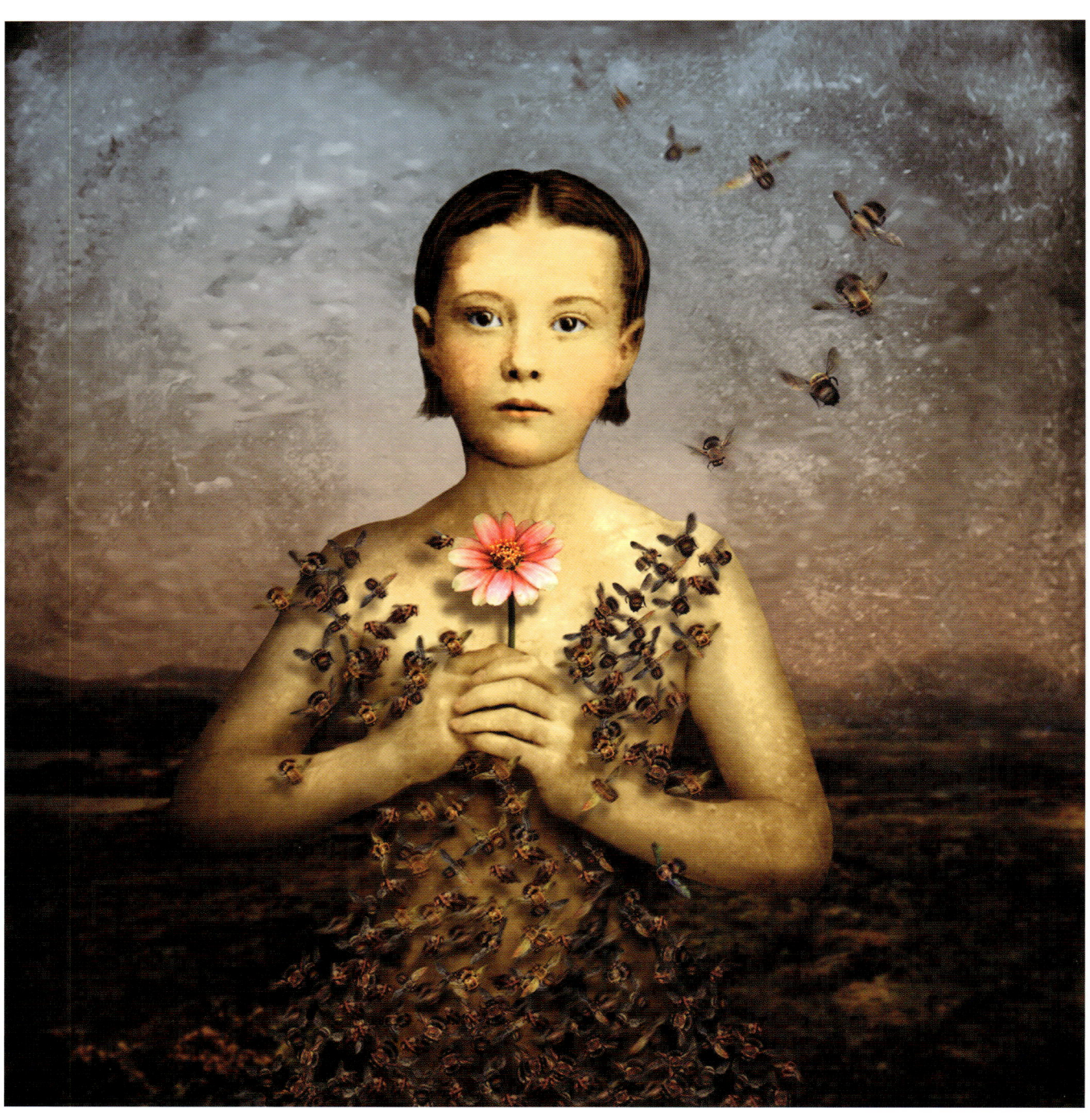

MAGGIE TAYLOR
American, born 1961

GIRL WITH A BEE DRESS
2004, pigment inkjet print [Epson]
image: 58 x 58 in. (147.3 x 147.3 cm)
sheet: 62 ¾ x 60 ¼ in. (159.4 x 153 cm)
Gift of Jerry N. Uelsmann and Maggie Taylor
2007.24.3

Maggie Taylor is a master of contemporary digital media but with imagery and an expressive imagination firmly rooted in Surrealism and even 19th-century sources. She first studied photography at Yale University, but her interest in staged tableaux and constructed images was out of sync with the tradition of Walker Evans-style documentary that still dominated that school's teaching at the time. At the University of Florida in her graduate studies, she found great encouragement working with Evon Streetman and Jerry Uelsmann, resulting in increasingly complex and bizarre color photographs of still-life arrangements of disparate elements such as children's toys, dead animals or decaying vegetation. She truly developed her distinctive vision, however, when she began working with Photoshop and shifted to using a scanner rather than a conventional camera and film to produce images.

Like much of Maggie Taylor's work, *Girl with a bee dress* both charms and disarms the viewer. It is easy to be drawn into the sweetness of the girl's calm expression, a flower held against her chest, but the swarm of bees hovering over her is truly not of this world and challenges any conventional sense of comfortable clothing. Taylor's masterful combination of photo-graphic realism and digital manipulation adds to this image's unsettling power. The girl's face was taken from a 19th-century portrait, while Taylor herself posed for the body. The bees are all from digital scans of real bees— all meticulously positioned by Taylor into convincing positions in the Photoshop image. Although the background, color, and all elements of the picture are freely manipulated by Taylor, the image retains a disturbing veracity. The fantasy is transparent enough that we don't fear for the girl being stung, but we might still cringe as we imagine ourselves in her place.

TS

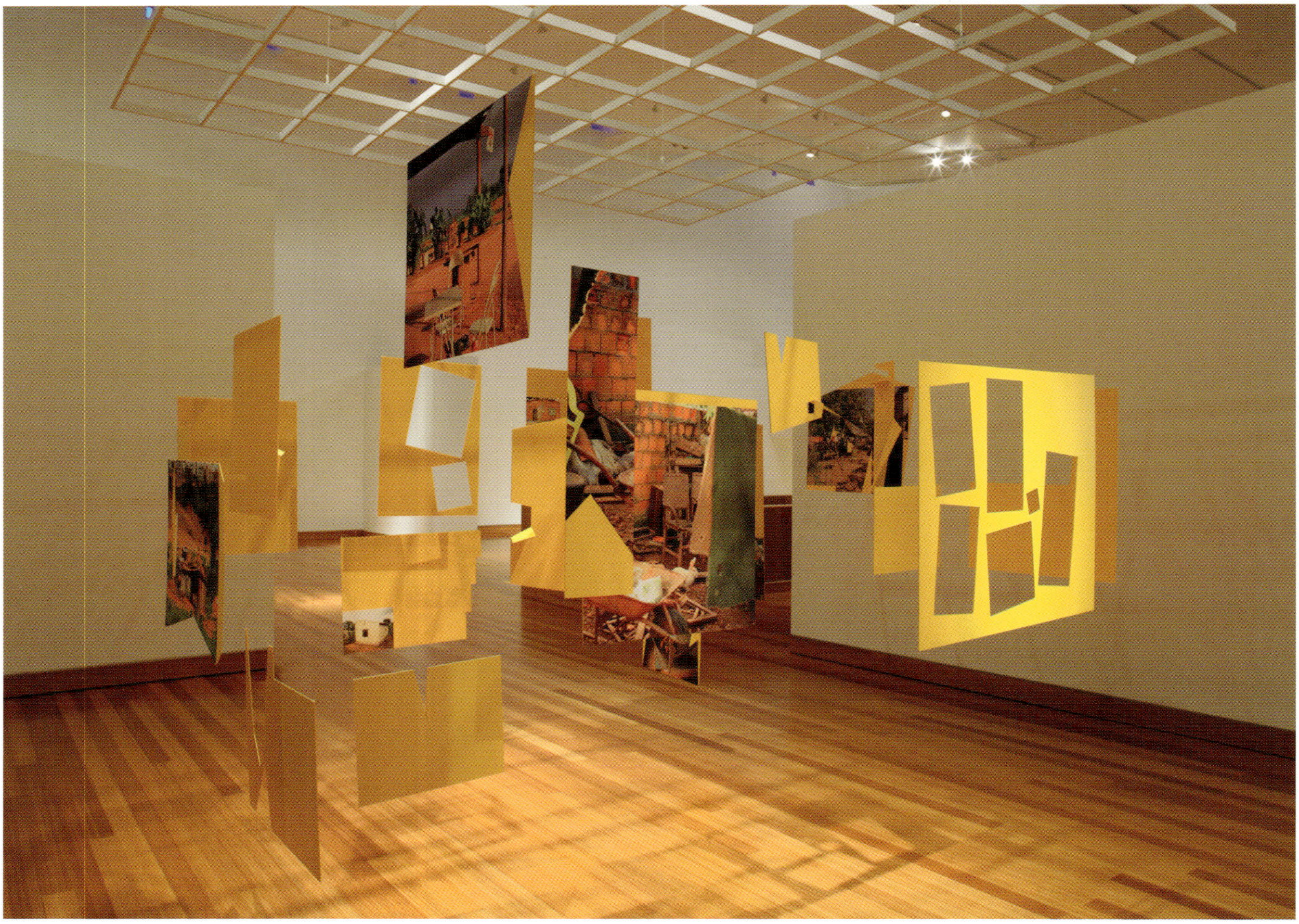

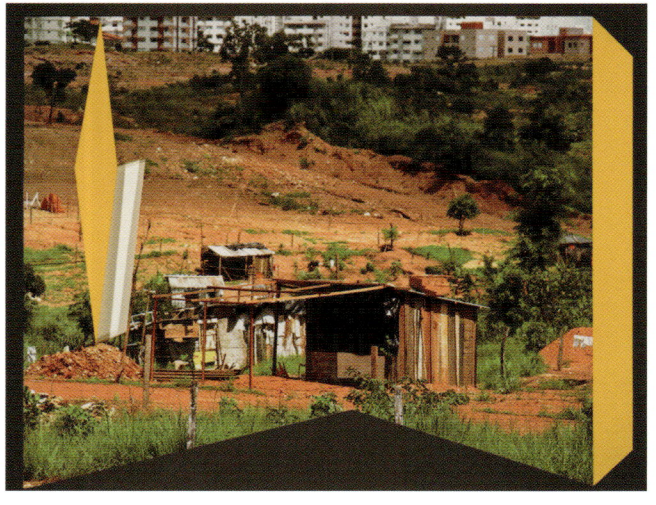

Sergio Vega
American, born Argentina, 1959

Shanty Nucleus after Derrida
2006, wood grid, filament, photographs
on board
144 x 144 in. (365.8 x 365.8 cm)
Museum purchase, gift of John Beck and
Municipal Bond Partners, Joseph Wittenstein,
Managing Partner, by exchange. Partial gift
of the artist.
2007.13

left, bottom: detail

Born in Argentina and based in Florida, Sergio Vega produces installations that bring together diverse elements of modernist architecture, Brazilian art, documentary photography and avant-garde strategies. His work provides an incisive critique of history, art and contemporary culture, examining the pressures of colonial legacies and globalization. With ironic humor he points to the disparity between utopian visions and the dystopian realities of everyday life.

Over the last decade, Sergio Vega has worked on a project *El Paraíso en el Nuevo Mundo* (Paradise in the New World), a title taken from the book of the same name by 17th-century Spanish scholar, Antonio de León Pinelo. Intrigued by Pinelo's claim that the Garden of Eden was located in South America, Vega traveled to Mato Grosso in the Brazilian Amazon to test his theories.

Shanty Nucleus after Derrida presents a collage of photographic images portraying typical shanty houses in Mato Grosso. Revealing social disparities, the shanties are set against a background of soaring forms of modernist architecture. The photographs are affixed to various geometric shapes that hang in fragments from a grid, allowing the viewer to interact with and walk through the work. Loosened from the frame and the wall, they function as sculpture. The form and the title of the work, *Shanty Nucleus*, is an homage to Brazilian artist Hélio Oiticica, an artist who, in the early 1960s, proposed launching painting into sculptural space.

Referring to the deconstructive theories of philosopher Jacques Derrida, Vega creates an ironically fantasized Eden of shanties, a paradoxically constructed and deconstructed collage in a pristine architectural display. Shanties are made of cardboard boxes, plastic sheeting and industrial debris. Pieced together from found detritus, they exist as a conglomeration of fragments, a distortion of collage where function subjugates form.

KO-S

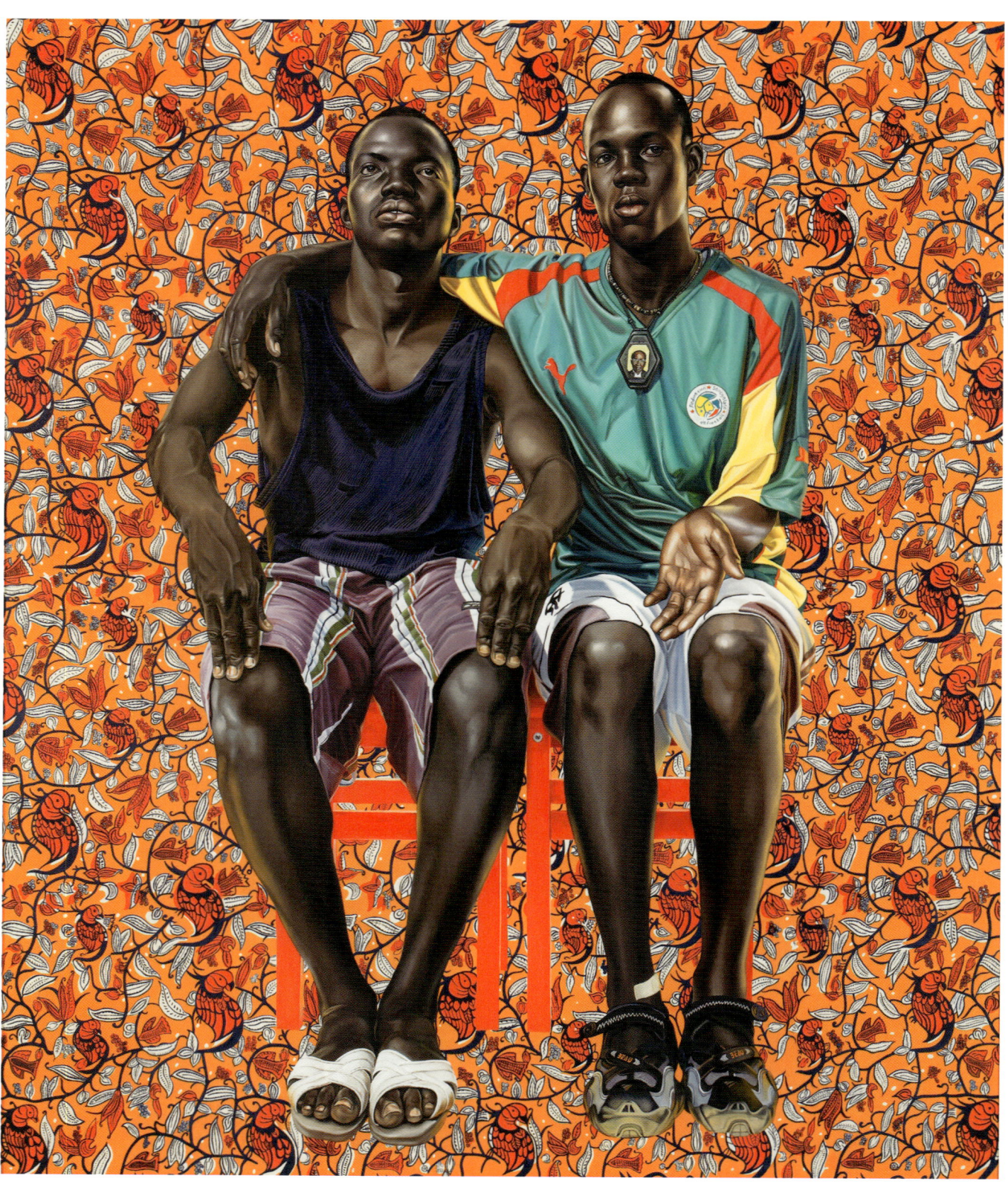

Kehinde Wiley

American, born 1977

Dogon Couple

2008, oil on canvas
96 x 84 in. (243.8 x 213.4 cm)
Museum purchase, funds provided by the
David A. Cofrin Acquisition Endowment
© Kehinde Wiley, Courtesy Deitch Projects.
2008.50

Kehinde Wiley has received wide recognition for his portraits of urban African American men. Wiley's work juxtaposes the hip-hop realities of Harlem and the South Central neighborhood of Los Angeles with the high art conventions of European portrait painting from the 17th to the 19th centuries. In paintings with heavy frames and ornate backgrounds, Wiley's models assume the poses of the privileged and historical elite. Through the devices of irony and parody, Wiley examines notions of power, portraiture and historical representation.

Wiley continued his research during recent trips to Asia, Africa and South America. The painting *Dogon Couple* is part of his project, *The World Stage: Africa, Lagos-Dakar*. In Dakar, Wiley became interested in post-colonial public sculptures as representations of history and heroism, works that celebrate independence, nationalism and ethnic diversity. *Dogon Couple* is modeled after a specific public monument in Dakar that is in turn based on a traditional archetypal West African sculpture from the Dogon people of Mali. The figures from Mali embody creation, productivity and the interdependence between man and woman. In the painting, the two young men assume the same poses portrayed in the sculpture; however, in this case the emphasis is on the partnership between the men.

Dressed in hip-hop modern clothing, Wiley's African subjects have a superficial affinity to their American counterparts. However, here their apparel does not indicate a local context but rather reveals the reach of global economy and culture. The design of the painting's ornate backdrop alludes to an even earlier stage of global economy when Dutch traders marketed the design of Southeast Asian textiles to West African countries. These textiles were ultimately adopted as emblems of national identity. One young man wears a pendant bearing the image of Leopold Sédar Senghor, former president of Senegal and one of Africa's most acclaimed poets. Senghor is known for coining the term "negritude," which identified and asserted the power of black people across borders.

Wiley uses the historical chronicle of public art and the chance encounters of immediate experience to effect a productive collision. The collision destabilizes conventional historical and contemporary representations of global power and disenfranchisement. Through the irony of his paintings, Wiley questions hierarchical authority that remains largely unchallenged.

KO-S

Dulce María Román *Curator of Modern Art*

Dulce Román joined the staff of the Harn Museum of Art in 1999 and was appointed to her current position in June 2001. She is responsible for the development and management of the Harn's modern collection of art including nearly 1,000 works from the United States, Latin America and Europe. In her role as Curator of Modern Art, Román has curated a number of original exhibitions for the Harn including *Uncommon Glazes: American Art Pottery, 1880-1950* (2009); *From Dürer to Renoir: European Prints from the Harn Collection* (2007-2008); *Picturing the Times: Prints and Photographs from the New Deal Era* (2006); *Ansel Adams: Visualizing the American Landscape* (2004); and *Santos: Contemporary Devotional Folk Art in Puerto Rico* (2003-2004). Prior to joining the staff of the Harn Museum, she served as a researcher of Spanish art at the Frick Collection in New York from 1992 to 1996 and the Department of European Paintings at the Metropolitan Museum of Art in New York from 1996 to 1997. Román holds a Bachelor of Arts in Psychology from Harvard University and Master of Arts and Master of Philosophy degrees in Art History from Columbia University in New York.

Kerry Oliver-Smith *Curator of Contemporary Art*

Kerry Oliver-Smith oversees the contemporary collection and exhibitions of international art at the Harn Museum of Art. Encompassing art in all media after 1945, the collection is featured in the Mary Ann Harn Cofrin Pavilion and adjacent Robert and Nancy Magoon Garden. Oliver-Smith has curated more than 27 exhibitions in addition to the museum's experimental *RISK* Cinema series. Select exhibitions include *Allan Sekula: TITANIC's wake* (2004-2005); *Cuba Avant-Garde: Contemporary Cuban Art from the Farber Collection* (2007); *German Legacies: The Photography of Max Becher and Andrea Robbins* (2002); *Sergio Vega: Modernismo Tropical* (2002); *Insistent Memory: The Architecture of Time in Video Installation* (2000); and *Modern Czech Photography* (2000). She is currently working on *Project Europa: Imagining the (Im)Possible*, an exhibition that has garnered major support from the Andy Warhol Foundation. She has lectured and published on many exhibitions and artists and has organized lectures and performance art events. Prior to her appointment as Curator of Contemporary Art in 1999, she served as the Curator of Education at the Harn Museum. She was a founder and artistic co-director of Florida's Hippodrome State Theatre, and has also worked extensively in film and theater including projects in the United States, England, Scotland and Spain. She holds a master's degree in Film and Media Studies from the University of Florida, where she is currently pursuing her PhD.

Thomas W. Southall *Curator of Photography*

Thomas W. Southall has been Curator of Photography at the Harn Museum of Art since fall 2004. He is a graduate of St. Lawrence University (BA 1973) and the University of New Mexico (MA 1977). He was a professor of Art History and Curator of Photography at the Spencer Museum of Art at the University of Kansas from 1977 to 1987. From 1988 to 1995 he was Curator of Photographs at the Amon Carter Museum, Fort Worth, Texas. In 1996 he was awarded a Joshua C. Taylor Fellowship at the National Museum of American Art, Smithsonian Institution, Washington, DC. He was Visiting Professor of Art History at the University of New Mexico in the fall of 1995 and at the College of Santa Fe from 1997 to 1998. From 1998 to 2004, he was Curator of Photography at the High Museum of Art, Atlanta, Georgia.

Southall has curated numerous exhibitions with publications including *Chorus of Light: Photographs from the Sir Elton John Collection* (2000); *Revealing Territory: Photographs of the Southwest by Mark Klett* (1992); *Walker Evans and William Christenberry: Of Time and Place* (1990); and *Diane Arbus: Magazine Work* (1984). Exhibitions he has organized since coming to the Harn include *Aura of the Photograph: The Image As Object* (2006); *Photographic Formalities: From Ansel Adams to Weegee* (2007); *Almost Alice: New Illustrations of Wonderland by Maggie Taylor* (2008); and a series of *Highlights from the Photography Collection*.

INDEX OF ARTISTS

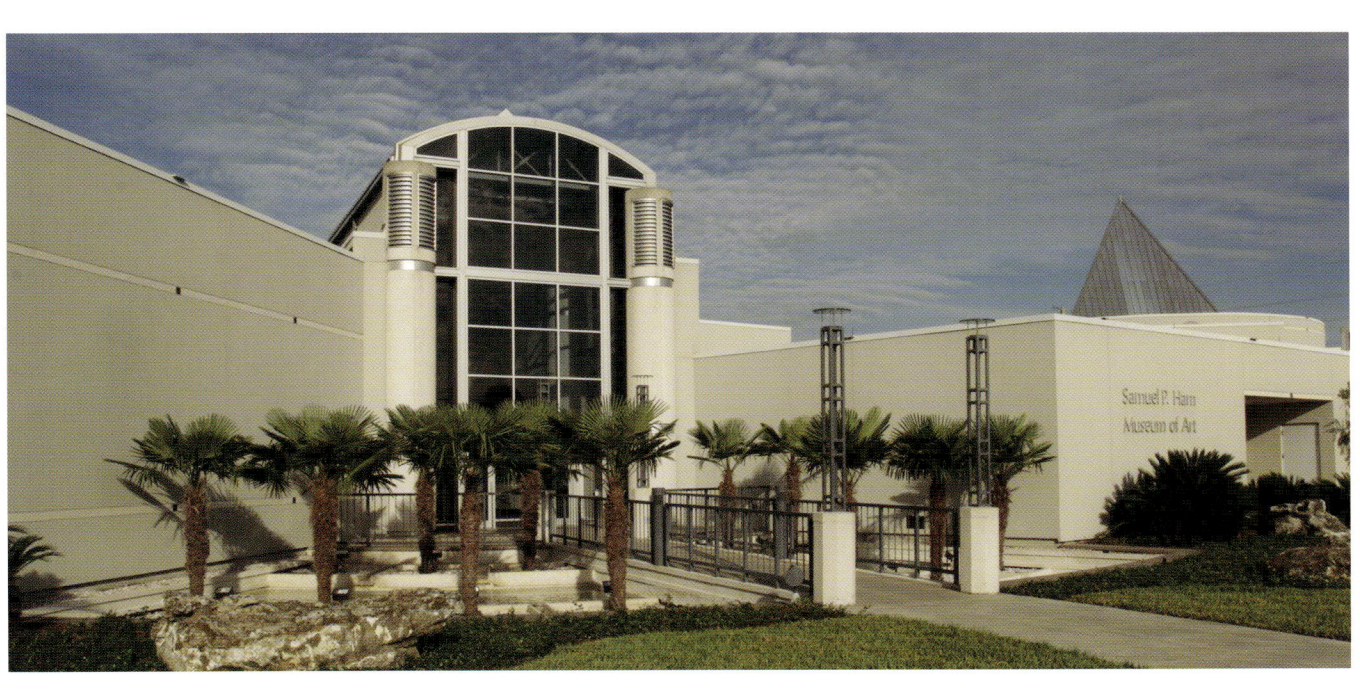